THE SCHOOL PORTFOLIO
T O O L K I T

A Planning, Implementation, and Evaluation Guide for Continuous School Improvement

VICTORIA L. BERNHARDT, Ph.D.
Executive Director
Education for the Future Initiative

Professor
Department of Professional Studies in Education
College of Communication and Education
California State University, Chico, CA

EYE ON EDUCATION
6 Depot Way West
Larchmont, NY 10538
(914) 833-0551
(914) 833-0761 Fax

Library of Congress Cataloging—in—Publication Data

Bernhardt, Victoria L., 1952-
      The school portfolio tool kit: a planning, implementation, and evaluation guide for continuous school improvement/ Victoria L. Bernhardt.
            p. cm.
      Includes bibliographical references and index.
      ISBN 1-930556-21-7
      1. School improvement programs-United States. 2. Portfolios in education-United States. 3. School management and organization-United States. 4. Educational evaluation-United State. I. Title.

LB2822.82.B48 2002
371.2'07–dc21

                                                                    2001040773

10 9 8 7 6 5 4 3 2 1

ALSO AVAILABLE FROM EYE ON EDUCATION

DATA ANALYSIS FOR COMPREHENSIVE SCHOOLWIDE IMPROVEMENT
By Victoria L. Bernhardt

THE SCHOOL PORTFOLIO: A COMPREHENSIVE FRAMEWORK FOR SCHOOL IMPROVEMENT 2/E
By Victoria L. Bernhardt

DESIGNING AND USING DATABASES FOR SCHOOL IMPROVEMENT
By Victoria L. Bernhardt

THE EXAMPLE SCHOOL PORTFOLIO: A COMPANION TO THE SCHOOL PORTFOLIO
By Victoria L. Bernhardt, et al.

MEASUREMENT AND EVALUATION: STRATEGIES FOR SCHOOL IMPROVEMENT
By McNamara, Erlandson, and McNamara

COACHING AND MENTORING FIRST-YEAR AND STUDENT TEACHERS
By India J. Podsen and Vicki M. Denmark

**MOTIVATING AND INSPIRING TEACHERS:
THE EDUCATIONAL LEADERS' GUIDE FOR BUILDING STAFF MORALE**
By Todd Whitaker, Beth Whitaker, and Dale Lumpa

CREATING CONNECTIONS FOR BETTER SCHOOLS: HOW LEADERS ENHANCE SCHOOL CULTURE
By Douglas J. Fiore

DEVELOPING PARENT AND COMMUNITY UNDERSTANDING OF PERFORMANCE-BASED ASSESSMENT
By Kathryn Anderson Alvestad

BUDDIES: READING, WRITING, AND MATH LESSONS
By Pia Hansen Powell

RESEARCH ON EDUCATIONAL INNOVATIONS 3/E
By Arthur K. Ellis

TEACHING, LEARNING AND ASSESSMENT TOGETHER: THE REFLECTIVE CLASSROOM
By Arthur K. Ellis

CONSTRUCTIVIST STRATEGIES: MEETING STANDARDS AND ENGAGING ADOLESCENT MINDS
By Chandra Foote, et al.

STRATEGIES TO HELP SOLVE OUR SCHOOL DROPOUT PROBLEM
By Franklin P. Schargel and Jay Smink

TECHNOLOGY TOOLS FOR YOUNG LEARNERS
By Leni Von Blanckensee

ACKNOWLEDGEMENTS

Dedicated to my four "Js" — Judy, Joy, Jody, and Jamie

Since the first draft of *The School Portfolio* back in 1993, teachers and administrators in the schools, districts, and states with which I have worked have graciously volunteered their time to review drafts of my books. It is because of their understanding of, and commitment to, continuous improvement that these books have become products for which I am proud and for which many school personnel praise their readability.

For the creation of this book I gathered together a group of very special reviewers—those who have been through School Portfolio and Data Analysis Train the Trainers workshops, who have presented one or both of the workshops to schools or districts, and who have begun to work with schools on building school portfolios. These are seasoned professionals whose insights continue to excite and impress me. I am in deep appreciation for their generosity of time and energy to review drafts of *The School Portfolio Toolkit*. My extreme gratitude is extended to the following individuals from California, Indiana, Iowa, Kansas, Michigan, Missouri, Nevada, New York, Ohio, Pennsylvania, South Carolina, Texas, Vermont, and Washington: Jonelle Adams, Sandy Austin, Peggy Christie, Sue Clayton, Cheryl Cozette, Bill Deeb, Marilyn Dishman-Horst, Lin Everett, Elaine Hassemer, Rhonda Hays, Mike Kirby, Anita Kishel, Sara Laughlin, Mary Leslie, Gary Manford, Andy Mark, Terri Martin, Mark Maynard, Doug Miller, Sheryl O'Connor, Paul Preuss, Virginia Propp, Sherry Reed, Donna Rinckel, Gail Robbins, Joy Rose, Tony Rose, Julie Schmick, Penny Swenson, Marlene Trapp, Zana Vincent, Glenda Vinson, Judith Weaver, Judy Weber, Debbie Weingarth, and Jody Wood. Joy Rose and Andy Mark gave additional time and energy by reviewing more than one draft, which did not go unnoticed. Joy was always available and ready to help with any part of the task. She would even drive for hours to meet with me to support the work. Her editing skills are sharp and appreciated. A special thank you to reviewer "extraordinaire," Judy English, from the Leadership Academy, Missouri Department of Elementary and Secondary Education. Judy added her wonderful, inspired touches throughout *The Toolkit*, but especially to the Professional Development chapter. Judy wrote a version of most of the professional development activities. She and Jody Wood added their facilitator knowledge and experiences to the activities that appear throughout the CD.

Additionally, since the first draft of *The School Portfolio*, Education for the Future staff has willingly worked on these books. I tried to keep the writing of these books separate from our office work because I didn't want staff to have *one more thing* to do. But yet, each one wanted to have some part in this special production. These are the people who help make extraordinary things happen in amazing periods of time. I continue to be awed by and grateful for the talent, skills, and dedication of Lynn Varicelli. Lynn has loved to produce the layout of these books and she did another masterful job with this one. Not only did she provide the final layout, she hung in there through multiple drafts and conflicting reviews. Brad Geise did a stellar job in developing the *School IQ* found on the CD. He also managed the work on the CD in my traveling absence. Deborah Furgason added her talents with the cross-reference matrices and helped whenever and wherever she was needed, while keeping the office running at its usual high level of quality. Alicia Hamilton diligently oversaw the reference and resource lists and helped where she was needed. Lynn, Brad, Deborah, and Alicia, along with Sally Withuhn, Mary Foard, and Melissa Escalera worked hard on gathering documents, pictures, references, and tools for *The Toolkit*. Leni von Blanckensee and Marcy Lauck provided advice and comprehensive reviews. These two individuals helped create some of these tools for our former Train the Facilitators workshops that are now being folded into *The Toolkit*.

I am so grateful for the wonderful connection Education for the Future has with Marcy and Tom Lauck who gave so much of themselves to make this product look professional and appealing to the readers. Thank you for the beautiful layout design. We could not have done it without you. Thank you again and again. I am also grateful to have connected with MC² Design Group consultants, Brian Curtis and Christian Burke, for the CD design work and cover—I would recommend them to anyone! As I would Tom Devol (that's *loved* spelled backwards), our outstanding professional photographer.

I thank my husband, Jim Richmond, for again providing his brand of support for this work. He does a lot of what I should be doing around the house so I can pursue these publications and the work I love, with very little grumbling.

A huge thank you is required for my publisher, affectionately known as *Cousin Bob,* Mr. Robert Sickles. Cousin Bob is considered a part of the Education for the Future family. He is always pleasant to be with, responsive, helpful, courteous, and he gets our books out faster than humanly possible. I am grateful for all you do for us. Thank you.

Thank you to SBC for continuing to believe in this work. SBC has shown that if you can stick with a winning formula long enough, the rewards will be greater than ever expected. No one could ever imagine that this work, which started in the early 1990's, could evolve into something from which the whole country could benefit.

This acknowledgement section could not be complete without thanking you, the reader, and you, the school personnel working with continuous school improvement, who have believed in and tried *The School Portfolio*. I love *The School Portfolio,* maybe more than ever. After watching innovations come and go over time I am feeling very good that *The School Portfolio* is a powerful tool and very much a comprehensive framework for school improvement that can withstand the sands of time. As I say in all my acknowledgement sections, I do hope this book exceeds your expectations and if it does, it is because of the continuous improvement that has resulted from your insights, direction, assistance, and support all along the way. Thank you.

In Appreciation,
Vickie Bernhardt
August 2001

ABOUT THE AUTHOR

Victoria L. Bernhardt, Ph.D., is Executive Director of the Education for the Future Initiative, a not-for-profit organization whose mission is to build the capacity of all schools at all levels to continuously improve. Dr. Bernhardt is also Professor on leave from the Department of Professional Studies in Education, College of Communications and Education, at California State University, Chico. She received her Bachelor of Science and Master of Science degrees from Iowa State University in the fields of Statistics and Psychology and her Ph.D. in Educational Psychology Research and Measurement, with a minor in Mathematics, from the University of Oregon.

Under Dr. Bernhardt's leadership, the Education for the Future Initiative has received dozens of awards, including being named one of the top business-education partnerships in the world when it received the NOVA Corporation Global Best Award for Educational Renewal and Economic Development in 1996.

The author's first book, *The School Portfolio: A Comprehensive Framework for School Improvement* (Second Edition, 1999) assists schools with clarifying the purpose and vision of their learning organizations as they develop their school portfolios. *Data Analysis for Comprehensive Schoolwide Improvement* (1998) helps learning organizations use data analysis to determine where they are, where they want to be, and how to get there—sensibly, painlessly, and effectively. *The Example School Portfolio* (2000) shows what a completed school portfolio looks like and further supports schools in developing their own school portfolios. *Designing and Using Databases for School Improvement* (2000) helps schools and districts think through the issues surrounding the creation and uses of databases established to achieve improved student learning.

Dr. Bernhardt is passionate about her mission of helping all educators continuously improve their classrooms, their schools, their districts, and states by gathering and analyzing actual data—and not using hunches and "gut-level" feelings. She has made numerous presentations at professional meetings and has conducted hundreds of workshops on the school portfolio, data analysis processes, and school improvement at local, state, regional, national, and international levels.

Dr. Bernhardt can be reached at:

Victoria L. Bernhardt
Executive Director
Education for the Future
400 West First Street
Chico, CA 95929-0230
Tel: 530-898-4482
Fax: 530-898-4484
vbernhardt@csuchico.edu
http://eff.csuchico.edu

TABLE OF CONTENTS

5   STUDENT ACHIEVEMENT

6   QUALITY PLANNING

7   PROFESSIONAL DEVELOPMENT

12 IMPLEMENTING THE SCHOOL PORTFOLIO

Case Studies from Around the Country

FOREWORD

Funding education programs is the SBC Foundation's main priority. As the philanthropic arm of SBC Communications, the Foundation is committed to supporting initiatives that foster improved student achievement, teacher preparedness, minority student success, and increased use of technologies in the classroom.

We believe that the future success and growth of our communities depend upon the success of our educational system. Each year, nearly forty percent of the Foundation's grants support educational improvement in our nation's schools. Since 1996, the Foundation has awarded almost ninety million dollars in grants for education and technology programs.

Our commitment to improving education is why the Foundation has continued its support of Dr. Victoria Bernhardt's exemplary work for more than a decade. A pioneer for education reform, Dr. Bernhardt's work and the Education for the Future Initiative have set the standard for successful school reform. The Education for the Future Initiative works with schools, districts, counties, regions, and states to continuously improve their organizations for student achievement increases. And, most important, they are achieving measurable success.

In Dr. Bernhardt's first book, *The School Portfolio: A Comprehensive Framework for School Improvement* (Second Edition, 1999), she illustrates how educators can create a "school portfolio," a systemic framework for planning, monitoring, and evaluating school improvement. In this latest book, *The School Portfolio Toolkit,* she provides schools with the necessary tools for creating, implementing, and maintaining a school portfolio, as well as strategies to bring about continuous school improvement that will lead to increased student learning. She reviews how to build a learning organization that makes sense for students, and how to help that organization continuously improve itself. Her results-oriented approach to school reform will help school personnel organize a school portfolio, as well as offer processes and strategies to move school staff into and through continuous improvement.

Dr. Bernhardt's leadership has helped many students achieve academic success while motivating educators to broaden educational opportunities for students. The valuable information found in this latest book can help school administrators and teachers increase a child's potential to succeed; we can't think of a more important endeavor.

SBC is pleased to support Dr. Bernhardt and the Education for the Future Initiative because through their efforts, we can make a difference in the lives of children in our communities by preparing them for the exciting challenges and opportunities that lay ahead.

Nancy Gerval
President, SBC Foundation
175 Houston Street, Suite 200
San Antonio, TX 78205
http://www.sbc.com/community/sbc_foundation

PREFACE

Since the publication of *The School Portfolio: A Comprehensive Framework for School Improvement* (Second Edition, 1999), teachers and administrators have been asking me to put together a "how to" book for building a school portfolio. I kept this idea on the back burner because I thought schools had to create every part of the portfolio for it to make a difference.

As I watched school staffs struggle with the mechanics of putting together the school portfolio product, I realized that I could make the product and the process easier by sharing a variety of "tools." This realization led to the writing of *The School Portfolio Toolkit: A Planning, Implementation, and Evaluation Guide for Continuous School Improvement.* This book was written not only to make putting together the school portfolio product and process easier, but also to clarify how to "do" the elements that make a difference with continuous school improvement. *The Toolkit* is a compilation of ideas, examples, suggestions, activities, tools, strategies, and templates for producing school portfolios that will lead to continuous school improvement. This *Toolkit*—

▼ assists in creating a vision for where the learning organization wants to be in the future

▼ guides the comprehensive data analysis work to understand the results the learning organization is getting

▼ helps build a plan to eliminate the gap between where the learning organization is now and where it wants to be

▼ provides strategies for implementing and evaluating the plan

▼ supports the continuous improvement of all aspects of the learning organization with the ultimate goal of improving achievement for all students

With the emphasis being placed on high stakes testing and state accountability, it is imperative that all schools use a comprehensive approach to data analysis and school improvement. We can no longer be guided by our guts or hunches, no matter how well intentioned. *The School Portfolio* allows schools to tell and illustrate their own stories by using their own data to support and demonstrate improvements that are made in schools at every level every day.

Intended Audience

This *Toolkit* is intended for teachers and school and district administrators who want and need to use data to continuously improve what they do for children. The hope is that anyone, regardless of her/his training in data analysis or school improvement, can pick up this book, understand every part of it, and use the tools to begin and then continue on the continuous school improvement journey with enthusiasm and confidence.

Other groups targeted are professors who teach school administration and graduate level education courses since all professional educators must learn how to gather and use data in this time of high-stakes accountability.

I hope you find *The School Portfolio Toolkit: A Planning, Implementation, and Evaluation Guide for Continuous School Improvement* to be helpful as you work through the processes of using data to continuously improve student learning and the teaching that makes such learning possible.

Victoria L. Bernhardt
Executive Director
Education for the Future
400 West First Street
Chico, CA 95929-0230
Tel: 530-898-4482
Fax: 530-898-4484
vbernhardt@csuchico.edu
http://eff.csuchico.edu

CHAPTER 1

INTRODUCTION: Why a Toolkit?

Chapter Objective: LAY OUT THE STRUCTURE OF THE BOOK AND CD AND DESCRIBE HOW TO USE THEM

THE SCHOOL PORTFOLIO POEM

garden

A school portfolio is like a garden—
It takes planning and hard work,
requires the weeding out
of unnecessary elements,
and promotes positive
feelings. You're proud
to show it off!

photograph album

A school portfolio
is like a photograph album—
It brings back memories for
the people involved, shows
changes over time, and
introduces people to
thinking in ways they
have never thought before.

master's painting

A school portfolio
is like an old master's painting—
It captures the school's essence,
and yet, a closer look
reveals interesting
details. The more you
study it, the more you see.

wise friend

A school portfolio
is like a wise friend—
It listens, clarifies your ideas,
and is something you don't
want to lose. Most of all,
it provides insight to help
you create your future.

Many people of Education for the Future, 1994

Note. From *The School Portfolio: A Comprehensive Framework for School Improvement*, Second Edition (p.8), by Victoria L. Bernhardt, 1999, Larchmont, NY: Eye on Education. Copyright © 1999 Eye on Education, Inc.

THE SCHOOL PORTFOLIO REVIEW

The school portfolio is a purposeful, ongoing, dynamic, and fluid collection of work that tells the story of a school and its systemic continuous improvement efforts to better serve its clients—the students. The school portfolio clearly spells out the purpose and vision of a school. It measures and ensures congruence of all parts of the organization to enable the attainment of the vision. It is a framework and a tool for continuous school improvement.

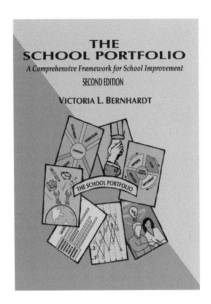

Purposes and uses of a school portfolio are to:

▼ establish one living document that describes an overall school plan and the school's vision, mission, beliefs, and rationale for improvement

▼ document efforts on a number of elements important to school improvement and align them with the vision

▼ understand the complexities of the schoolwide organization

▼ provide readily accessible and necessary information for data-driven decision making

▼ reflect on progress and purpose

▼ troubleshoot the continuous improvement efforts of the school

▼ assess and guide the school's unique approach to continuous schoolwide improvement

▼ demonstrate accountability

▼ communicate to all stakeholders

▼ enhance and/or replace a local, state, or regional accreditation process

▼ support any application for recognition, resources, etc.

The elements of a school portfolio include the following:

▼ *Information and Analysis* establishes systematic and rigorous reliance on data for decision making in all parts of the organization.

▼ *Student Achievement* supports schools in moving teachers from providers of information to researchers who understand and can predict the impact of their actions on student achievement.

▼ *Quality Planning* assists schools in developing the elements of a strategic plan including a vision, mission, goals, action plan, outcome measures, and strategies for continuous improvement and evaluation.

▼ *Professional Development* helps staff members, teachers, and administrators change the manner in which they work, i.e., how they make decisions; gather, analyze, and utilize data; plan, teach, and monitor achievement; evaluate personnel; and, assess the impact of new approaches to instruction and assessment on students.

▼ *Leadership* assists schools in building shared decision making and leadership structures to implement the vision to impact their specific population, culture, and climate.

▼ *Partnership Development* assists schools in understanding the purposes of, approaches to, and planning for educational partnerships with business and community groups, parents, other educational professionals to increase student learning.

▼ *Continuous Improvement and Evaluation* assists schools in further understanding the interrelationships of the components of continuous improvement and in improving their processes and products on an ongoing basis.

Each of these elements has a rubric known as a *Continuous Improvement Continuum* that shows what it might look like if a school took a specific *approach* to that element, and *implemented* the element using that approach, with a resulting *outcome*. The *Continuous Improvement Continuums* (CICs) were developed from the literature on school improvement and quality business management and represent how schools typically move from being "reactive" to "proactive" schools. A complete set of the newly updated *Continuous Improvement Continuums* and the above overview are downloadable on the accompanying compact disc.

WHY A TOOLKIT?

The world of education has been talking about school improvement for decades. Programs and strategies have been adopted by schools and districts; some have even been thoroughly implemented. Some school improvement processes have led to improving schools. Most school improvement processes are dropped when the next round of reform breezes onto the scene, or when the work gets hard. One process that continues to survive the fads blowing in and blowing out is the school portfolio. As one Ohio school administrator put it:

> *The school portfolio is too logical and too effective to be considered a fad. When a school begins to put its story together in a school portfolio, they want to know how the story will end...you know what I mean?*

The staff of Education for the Future definitely understand what this administrator means. We know that when schools document their school improvement efforts, clarify their visions, align everything they do in their schools to the vision, they get results. We know that when school personnel can see results and progress being made, they will continue on that journey. We also know that if they cannot see that they are making progress, staffs are likely to stop the process and the progress.

The School Portfolio: A Comprehensive Framework for School Improvement (Bernhardt, 1999) and *The School Portfolio Toolkit* are about building a learning organization that makes sense for student learning and about helping that learning organization to continuously improve everything it does for its learners. The school portfolio is the organizer, communicator, and tool to this end. This book, *The School Portfolio Toolkit*, was written to support school personnel with the mechanics of putting together a school portfolio as well as offer processes and strategies to move whole school staffs into and through continuous school improvement. The intent is to make this hard work easier for entire school (and district) staffs.

Anyone using this *Toolkit* to begin work on school portfolios will find it helpful to be familiar with *The School Portfolio: A Comprehensive Framework for School Improvement* (Bernhardt, 1999); *Data Analysis for Comprehensive Schoolwide Improvement* (Bernhardt, 1998); *The Example School Portfolio, A Companion to the School Portfolio: A Comprehensive Framework for School Improvement* (Bernhardt et al.,

The School Portfolio Toolkit was written to support school personnel with the mechanics of putting together a school portfolio as well as offer processes and strategies to move whole school staffs into and through continuous school improvement.

2000); and *Designing and Using Databases for School Improvement* (Bernhardt, 2000). *The School Portfolio Toolkit* has many references to the concepts that are discussed at length in these books. The main purpose of *The Toolkit* is to provide tools for creating, implementing, evaluating, and maintaining continuous school improvement efforts that will lead to increased student learning—via the school portfolio.

ORGANIZATION OF THE TOOLKIT

The School Portfolio Toolkit is organized to direct the development of a continuous improvement school effort—via the school portfolio—and the organizational work behind the scenes. *The Toolkit* includes this book and a compact disc (CD) which is found inside the back cover of the book. The book describes how to start and maintain the process and product. The accompanying CD provides:

▼ documents for downloading and use in continuous school improvement, in building a school portfolio, and activities to use in working with staff

▼ presentation files for presenting the concepts to others

The CD contents are described in the Appendix with references to where each file can be found in the book and on the CD. The CD files related to each chapter are also listed at the end of each chapter. Documents and tools on the CD are noted in the text with an icon. The chapters that follow suggest approaches for engaging entire staffs in the work of continuous school improvement via the school portfolio. Each chapter deals with one topic related to the school portfolio and continuous school improvement.

Even though the structure of this book might suggest that the process of continuous school improvement via the school portfolio is sequential or linear, it is not. One must begin wherever the learning organization is and build from there, so start where it makes sense to you. Assessments using tools such as the *Continuous Improvement Continuums* will help schools see what they need to do next and whether or not the pieces fit together. For schools that are "stuck," using the continuums will get them moving or at least motivate staffs about how to move forward.

TOOLKIT CONTENTS

The contents of this book are summarized below.

Chapter 1   Introduction: *Why a Toolkit?*

The Introduction provides a review of the school portfolio and an overview of *The School Portfolio Toolkit*, written to support the creation of a school portfolio product, and implementation of the school portfolio process.

Chapter 2   Continuous School Improvement: *Understanding the Big Picture*

This chapter provides an overview of continuous school improvement and specifically the framework for school improvement used in *The School Portfolio* (Bernhardt, 1999) and *The School Portfolio Toolkit*. The object of the chapter is to review the big picture of continuous school improvement.

Chapter 3   The School Portfolio: *Getting Started*

Chapter 3 offers suggestions about how to get groups started in this never-ending commitment to school improvement and the building of a school portfolio. This chapter includes references to documents that can be downloaded from the CD and used to get a jump-start on the process. The object of this chapter is to help schools find a way to begin the school portfolio process and product.

Chapter 4   Information and Analysis: *The Data*

The gathering, analysis, and use of comprehensive data set the school portfolio apart from many school improvement efforts. This chapter and the files related to it on the CD provide suggestions, activities, and tools for surveying students, parents, and teachers; analyzing student achievement data; getting to the root causes of problems; mapping school processes; and charting, synthesizing, and using the data. The object in Chapter 4 is to provide tools and strategies for getting staffs engaged in using data effectively to support continuous improvement that leads to increased student learning.

Chapter 5 Student Achievement: *Creating a Vision*

With every part of the school portfolio focused on the vision, it is evident that the vision has to be clear, shared by every member of the organization, and be a guiding force for the organization and its continuous improvement work. Chapter 5 provides a process for supporting the creation of a vision that will be shared by all members of the staff.

Chapter 6 Quality Planning: *Planning to Accomplish the Vision*

Quality schools have one vision and, therefore, should have one plan to reach that vision. This chapter provides guidance and strategies in the development of the one plan to accomplish the vision.

Chapter 7 Professional Development: *Implementing the Vision*

The majority of the work with respect to implementing the vision will be done under the dictum of professional development. Leaders must make sure that the school is "recultured" for change, and that everyone in the organization understands her/his role in accomplishing that vision. Professional development, when embedded effectively in a learning organization, will lead to the implementation of the vision faster than ever imagined and will save money in the long run. This chapter focuses on effectively planning, implementing, and evaluating professional development in a continuously improving learning organization.

Chapter 8 Leadership: *Building a Leadership Structure to Implement the Vision*

The leadership infrastructure of the learning organization is crucial in implementing the vision and bringing every member along in the process. How to build and implement a leadership infrastructure that will assist the learning organization in implementing its vision is the object of this chapter.

Chapter 9 Partnership Development: *Involving Partners to Implement the Vision*

Partnerships with parents, business, the community, the district, and higher education can make the vision for the learning organization exciting, relevant, and conducive to developing students into capable working members of society. Partnerships do not just happen; they need to be sought out, planned, and nurtured. This chapter provides tips and examples on planning and implementing effective partnerships.

Chapter 10 Continuous Improvement and Evaluation: *Evaluating the Implementation of the Vision*

The Continuous Improvement and Evaluation chapter illustrates how assessments on the *Continuous Improvement Continuums* can help staffs understand where they are and what they need to do to move forward in the big picture of continuous improvement. Other ways to evaluate progress and processes are covered in this chapter.

Chapter 11 Updating the School Portfolio: *Maintaining the Momentum*

Now that the product and the processes are in place, how does a school keep continuous schoolwide improvement going? The object of this chapter is to provide ideas about keeping the process and product alive and healthy.

Chapter 12 Implementing the School Portfolio: *Case Studies from Around the Country*

Chapter 12 summarizes different approaches taken by real schools, school districts, a county, and a state to establish and maintain school portfolios in their learning organizations.

At the end of each of chapters 3 through 12 is a list of files that appear on the CD and questions to help organize subsequent steps in the process.

Appendix Overview of the School Portfolio Toolkit CD Contents

The Appendix provides a list of the files that appear on the accompanying CD. These files are presented in order of mention, along with a description of the file's content, file type, and where each can be found on the CD.

Glossary of Terms

The Glossary defines terms used throughout the book and on the accompanying CD.

The School Portfolio Toolkit Compact Disc

The accompanying CD contains documents to assist staffs in creating a school portfolio, and in helping them take staffs through the process of the school portfolio and continuous school improvement. Documents include:

▼ *Adobe® Acrobat®* read-only files for downloading and printing

▼ *Microsoft® Word* files for customizing, printing, and placement in your school portfolio

▼ *Microsoft® Excel* template files for creating graphs and charts to print or to place in descriptive texts

▼ A *Microsoft® Powerpoint* presentation of the school portfolio to assist in presenting an overview to others

▼ Compressed files for fast downloading

▼ *School IQ*
   ◆ *FileMaker Pro©* runtime application for processing questionnaire data
   ◆ A collection of HTML and *FileMaker Pro* databases for collecting questionnaire data via a web server

The CD has been maximized to run on Windows 98, Windows 2000, Windows NT 4.0, Windows ME, and Macintosh OS 8.1 and above.

SUMMARY

The School Portfolio Toolkit is a book and a compact disc that contains suggestions, activities, strategies, templates, and examples to direct the development of a continuous school improvement process—via a school portfolio. Chapter 1 provides a quick overview of the contents of *The Toolkit* and how to use it.

CHAPTER 2

CONTINUOUS SCHOOL IMPROVEMENT:
Understanding the Big Picture

Chapter Objective:

To understand the big picture of continuous school improvement is like...

Understanding the circle of life.

Knowing the target and all that it will take to hit it.

Reaching for your goals/stars (keeping the goal in view).

Knowing there is no end (improvement is a lifelong journey).

Knowing where you are while seeing the steps you want to take.

Building a frame of reference so you don't lose track of where you are and where you are going.

Knowing the destination of a journey and the major highlights along the way.

Knowing the real purpose that suddenly gives meaning to everything you've been doing.

The School Portfolio Toolkit Reviewers

The school portfolio is both a process and a product of continuous school improvement that leads to reculturing the school for change; getting community ownership and support; building a mission and vision based on the values and beliefs of the school community and the purpose of the school; identifying what we expect students to know and be able to do; engaging in professional development activities that will lead to the vision; and improving learning for all students and staff.

Without building a map in stone, this chapter reviews the major pieces in the big picture of continuous school improvement which is directly aligned with the school portfolio process. The school portfolio is an approach to achieving the big picture of continuous school improvement complete with a measurement device to gauge and communicate progress. Completing a school portfolio should lead to continuous school improvement. Figure 2.1 on pages 14-15, show how the journey could evolve, the parts of which are described beginning on page 16.

THE BIG PICTURE OF CONTINUOUS SCHOOL IMPROVEMENT

School improvement processes begin for many different reasons. It might be that the school community determines that its students should be getting better student achievement results. It might be that the staff determines they want their students to get better student achievement results. Perhaps the state is mandating better results and threatening a take-over if student achievement is not improved. Maybe the school just decides it likes the idea of a school portfolio and wants everyone to get involved in the development of one. The outcome results in school improvement. For whatever reason, the school improvement process begins. The fact that a school improvement process begins around a crisis is not all bad. Most school improvement experts encourage *creating a sense of urgency* as an essential ingredient for change to occur. One way or another, we must get staff's commitment to change. (Chapter 3 focuses on different ways to get a staff started in the process of continuous school improvement by building and using the school portfolio.)

FIGURE 2.1

The Big Picture
of Continuous School Improvement

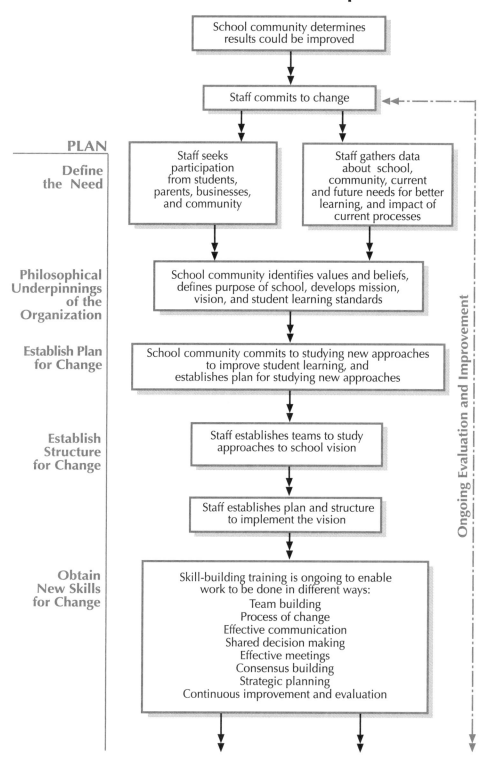

School community determines
results could be improved

Staff commits to change

PLAN

**Define
the Need**

Staff seeks
participation
from students,
parents, businesses,
and community

Staff gathers data
about school,
community, current
and future needs for better
learning, and impact of
current processes

**Philosophical
Underpinnings
of the
Organization**

School community identifies values and beliefs,
defines purpose of school, develops mission,
vision, and student learning standards

**Establish Plan
for Change**

School community commits to studying new approaches
to improve student learning, and
establishes plan for studying new approaches

**Establish
Structure
for Change**

Staff establishes teams to study
approaches to school vision

Staff establishes plan and structure
to implement the vision

**Obtain
New Skills
for Change**

Skill-building training is ongoing to enable
work to be done in different ways:
Team building
Process of change
Effective communication
Shared decision making
Effective meetings
Consensus building
Strategic planning
Continuous improvement and evaluation

Ongoing Evaluation and Improvement

FIGURE 2.1 (Continued)

The Big Picture
of Continuous School Improvement

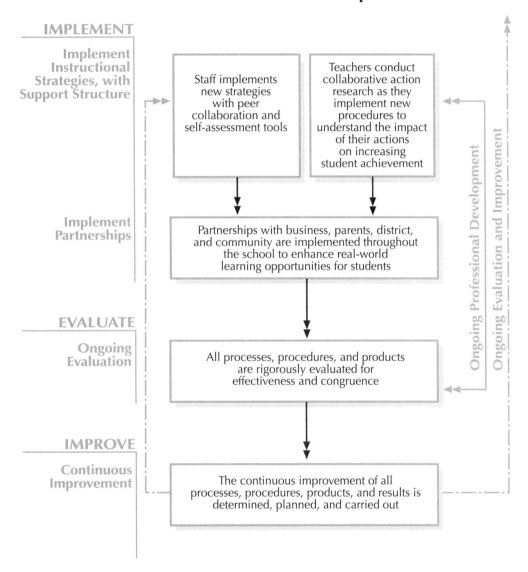

Plan

Define the Need

An understanding of the results achieved by the learning organization is very important in beginning a continuous school improvement process. With this understanding, a school can create solutions for solving the real problems by getting to the *root causes* of the problems. Perceptions, demographics, student achievement, and process data are critical for this understanding. It is in this area schools require help. (See Chapter 4, Information and Analysis: *The Data*.)

Philosophical Underpinnings of the Organization

The learning organization needs to define its philosophical underpinnings or guiding principles. In addition to self-discovery, this process will inform the organization of what is possible. Since it is known that humans can act only in congruence with what they value and believe about situations, schools must understand the values and beliefs of the individuals within the organization in order to create a shared direction or a shared vision. When values and beliefs of the members of the organization have been identified, a purpose for the organization will be clear and agreement will follow. From that purpose, a mission can be developed or redefined. With the purpose and mission, a vision can be developed that is based on what the members of the organization expect students to know and be able to do. What these philosophical underpinnings or the guiding principles of the school represent, then, is the target of everything that happens in the school. They also represent new actions with the intent of getting different results. (Chapter 5 focuses on creating that vision.)

Establish Plan for Change

Once the vision or a shared direction is identified, the staff must create action to study approaches and strategies to achieve that shared direction. After agreeing upon approaches and strategies, a plan to implement the shared direction must be developed. This plan includes actions, timelines for the actions, person or persons responsible, how the vision will be implemented, how the implementation of the vision will be evaluated, and resources required for the actions. (Chapter 6 focuses on creating a plan to implement the vision.)

Establish Structure for Change

The leadership structure or the way in which decisions are to be made on a day-to-day basis needs to flow with the vision. It needs to look like the vision, feel like the vision, and help with the implementation of the vision. If the vision is not clear, or if there is a need to study different approaches, then perhaps study teams will need to be identified within the leadership structure to investigate different aspects of the vision. Teams can recommend approaches for implementing the vision to the leadership team and full staff. (Chapter 8 studies leadership with respect to implementing the shared vision.)

Obtain New Skills for Change

Once the vision or shared direction is clarified, all other parts of the organization will need to be calibrated into alignment with that vision, in order to ensure the implementation of the vision and to help everyone in the organization understand her/his role in implementing the vision. Professional development will assist individuals in implementing the vision. Furthermore, professional development should be about implementing the vision. Professional development must be ongoing, include everyone on staff, and be focused on implementing the vision through a systematic plan of action. Individuals believe that certain approaches to teaching students could lead to increased student achievement, but they may not have the skills to implement their beliefs. Therefore, staff must be very honest about where they are with respect to their abilities to carry out the vision and make sure they get the support they need to carry their loads. Support structures such as peer coaching with feedback, and professional development with follow-up for skill building must be included in the plan to make sure everyone can and will implement the vision. Decisions about professional development design will naturally be driven by the vision and mission. (Chapter 7 is about professional development.)

Implement

Implement Instructional Strategies with Support Structures

The continuous school improvement plan or strategic action plan will spell out the steps involved in implementing the vision along with the persons responsible, their responsibilities, and the timeline. The timeline, leadership structure, and professional development will motivate each individual within the organization to understand her/his role in implementing the vision and will ensure that each has the skills to implement the vision. The action plan itself should include structures for supporting the implementation of the vision such as teacher planning time, classroom observation time, mentoring, and peer coaching. The plan should also include self-assessment tools so that teachers are clear about what the vision would look like if they were implementing it as compared to where they are right now. This tool can provide feedback to the whole staff about improving the implementation of the vision. Other implementation support strategies could include teacher action research. (The implementation of the vision is covered in Chapters 7-10.)

Implement Partnerships

Parents, the community, the district (including colleges and universities), and businesses are very important to schools because they can help ensure that students achieve the standards. Schools need to think about how partners can help them implement the standards. Working with partners includes understanding their ideas about how they can support the implementation of the standards and the vision. Identifying mutual partner benefits is key. (Partnerships are discussed in Chapter 9.)

Evaluate

Ongoing Evaluation

A continuously improving learning organization uses evaluation to understand the impact and effectiveness of its actions in an ongoing fashion as opposed to waiting until the end of the year or the end of the plan to determine that it did not work. Continuous improvement requires reflecting on the parts of the system and how the parts work together to form a whole organization. (Chapter 10 provides examples and discussion to this end.)

Improve

Continuously Improve

A continuously improving learning organization understands the impact each process, procedure, and product has upon the other. In conjunction with evaluation data, the learning organization determines what to improve and makes those improvements on an ongoing basis. Continuous improvement is a never-ending process. (Chapter 11 focuses on maintaining the implementation momentum.)

SUMMARY

The Big Picture of Continuous School Improvement reviews the major pieces of continuous school improvement that leads to schoolwide change for increased student learning. These elements are:

▼ Plan
- ◆ Define the need
- ◆ Philosophical underpinnings of the organization
- ◆ Establish plan for change
- ◆ Establish structure for change
- ◆ Obtain new skills for change

▼ Implement
- ◆ Implement instruction strategies, with support structures
- ◆ Implement partnerships

▼ Evaluate
- ◆ Ongoing evaluation

▼ Improve
- ◆ Continuous Improvement

ON THE CD RELATED TO CONTINUOUS SCHOOL IMPROVEMENT

▼ The Big Picture of Continuous School Improvement

CHAPTER 3

THE SCHOOL PORTFOLIO: Getting Started

Chapter Objective: TO HELP SCHOOLS FIND A WAY TO BEGIN THE SCHOOL PORTFOLIO PROCESS

The intent of the work of the school portfolio is not to have schools start over with their school improvement efforts. The intent is to pull together elements of work that the school has completed, and is in the process of completing, into one efficient document that lives on. We want schools to start wherever they are and with whatever they have. We also want schools to continue on their journeys for a long time, measure their progress along the way, and make the progress they desire.

One of the unique features of the school portfolio is that it is a product and a process. This means that no matter where your staffs are with respect to continuous school improvement, no matter what has been done, there is an entering point that will fit your situation. Some staffs respond best to starting a product—which leads to conversations about school improvement—followed by the process. Others respond to process first and then to documenting the processes in the product. The *ABCs of The School Portfolio,* as well as the *Overview, Purposes and Uses,* the *School Portfolio Summary Chart,* and activities for familiarizing workshop participants with the school portfolio, provide a big picture for understanding the creation of a school portfolio from beginning to end and are downloadable from the CD.

Below are some ways to start the physical product and to enter the process of the school portfolio with your school or with a network of schools. Documents and templates available for use and downloading on the accompanying CD are described throughout the chapter, are listed at the end of the chapter, and are briefly described in the Appendix. When a document appears on the CD, the CD icon will appear in the text.

START BY BUILDING THE PHYSICAL PRODUCT

Building a school portfolio is a beneficial activity for starting a continuous school improvement process. Not only will you be proud to show the story of your school and your progress, you will also see that some elements of your school are in alignment with one another and some are not. For instance, in documenting your school's professional development, you may find that what you have been doing will not lead to the implementation of the vision. Perhaps your current professional development is what the staff want, but is not what the staff need for moving closer to making the school's vision a reality.

> *We want schools to start wherever they are and with whatever they have.*
>
> *One of the unique features of the school portfolio is that it is a product and a process.*

Enrolling staff in the process of school improvement right where they are is important. A few individuals might begin this process, but ultimately the entire staff must become a part of it. Self-discovery is key in moving the process along. There will be hurdles and challenges, but each step of the process will be necessary. As the process becomes meaningful to staff, the resulting portfolio is owned by everyone on staff. The school portfolio, then, can be a useful tool for all.

Basic steps in starting the school portfolio product  CD-ROM are described below.

Step 1: Determine Who Will Take Charge

Someone needs to be responsible for creating, maintaining, and updating the school portfolio.

Step 2: Get the Technology

To build a school portfolio, one needs minimally a good wordprocessing and charting program. We use *Microsoft® Word* and *Microsoft® Excel.* We also use these two programs or a planning program, such as *Microsoft® Project*, *Microsoft® Visio* (also includes flowcharting tools and organization charts), *MacSchedule*, and *FastTrack Schedule for Macintosh* to develop action plans. For more sophisticated technology uses, such as page layout, we use *QuarkXPress™* or *Adobe® PageMaker®*, and for flowcharting we use *Inspiration®*. Web authoring programs are also nice to have and use. There are many, many options for web authoring; too many to mention here.

Step 3: Organize the Material

Most of the schools with which we have worked like to put their portfolios in three-ring binders with cover slots, otherwise known as view binders. Schools find binders, with sheet protectors, or laminated pages, useful for their hard copy documentation. The binders allow for the back-and-forth movement between sections and categories. Teachers can pull out and add items fairly effortlessly. The view pockets allow them to show a "picture" of the school or to express the vision of the school with the path to the vision spelled out inside the portfolio.

A three-ring binder with a view pocket nicely displays the portfolio cover.

Step 4: Print Out Index Dividers

Labels  for dividers are already set up for you. You will need to purchase index dividers and labels. We use 8th-cut index dividers and clear labels. You will notice that we also show year 2002, 2003, and 2004 labels as placeholders. Type in the actual years with which you are working so that you are setting up your school portfolio for displaying over time. Organize your materials with that longitudinal collection in mind.

Index dividers and labels for the school portfolio.

Step 5: Print Beginning Pages

On the CD, locate two sets of *Beginning Pages* files.  One set has the school portfolio header and footer; the other set has no header and footer, so you can print these pages onto your school's header paper. Choose a set and print them, preferably in color, to place behind the indices. The beginning pages give a clear statement of intent for each section. Your readers and staff will see what you are trying to do with each section, and will stay focused on the intent. With these pieces in place you will have a good strong beginning. *The School Portfolio Poem* shown at the beginning of Chapter 1 introduces your portfolio.

Choose a set of beginning pages to place in the school portfolio.

Step 6: Create a Layout

The School Portfolio Toolkit CD includes color templates for headers and footers in three different formats.  Find the format with which you are most familiar. You may choose left or right headers which will require you to pay attention as you print, or you may choose a more centered header so you do not have to be concerned about keeping the left pages on the left side and the right pages on the right side. You may want to replace the graphic placeholder with a graphic of your own mascot or logo. Open the file of your choice, type in your school name, and add your logo or mascot. If you want to print using a black-only laser printer and still have color headers and footers, print out the header/footer pages and use them like stationery. Margins are set up for you to start typing.

School portfolio headers and footers.

Step 7: Design the Cover

The three-ring view binders with the clear front pockets allow you to insert a beautiful custom cover to describe the school. Covers can show mascots, a collage of pictures, student artwork, enlarged pictures, or the story of the school vision (see photo on page 22). (Examples of covers, spines, and their dimensions appear on the CD.)

Pictures tell the story of the school and are a wonderful addition to the school portfolio.

Step 8: Add Pictures

Pictures are a wonderful addition to a school portfolio. The school portfolio tells the story of the school. Pictures go a long way in helping to tell this story. If you do not have a way to add digital pictures (i.e., access to a digital camera or to a scanner) you can always leave space in the text and paste in the pictures. We often use this approach and take the pages to a professional copy center to produce extra copies.

Step 9: Make Multiple Copies

Think about the number of copies of the school portfolio that you will need and how you are going to get the copies. You might want to make several copies as you go along, or make one original and have copies made at a professional copy center. Schools often find that they need four copies of their portfolio.

▼ One copy is for the principal's office: in case potential partners come in and want to know more about how they can support the school's vision.

▼ One copy is for the teachers' lounge or a location for teacher committees to access the plan and the data.

▼ One copy is for the front counter, lobby coffee table, or the library for general access. Parents love to look through the school portfolio. Students like to look through it as well. Real estate agents have used school portfolios to show potential home buyers about the school in a particular neighborhood.

▼ One copy is for the district office. Just think. They will never have to call you again to ask for specific information about your school.

Of course, a system must be put into place to update all copies periodically. This will be discussed further in Chapter 11.

Step 10: Fill the Binder

Start with existing reports. Start to fill the binder with documentation you already have. Every school has some sort of file or grant application that describes the school. Most schools have program review reports, accreditation reports, or self-assessments. Start with these files and build from there to produce the message you want to use for your school portfolio and for all other reports in the future. Determine how you would like to describe your school and update it for your school portfolio to become the school's official description. Begin to match other parts of these reports to the categories of the school portfolio. You will find that many of these reports include the same content desired in your portfolio. The indices as described above in Step 4 will assist you in pulling the pieces of these reports into meaningful categories.

Step 11: Process the Alignment

As the parts of the portfolio are being gathered and placed in the binder, you can begin to see if the pieces are in alignment with the vision, and to each other. Ask yourselves questions like:

▼ Does the vision make sense for who we are—students, staff, community and partners?

▼ Will currently planned professional development help us implement the vision?

▼ What evidence do we have that align beliefs and behaviors?

Make notes while putting the pieces together. The assessments on the *Continuous Improvement Continuums* (described in the process section below) will also help you determine alignment, as well as clarify next steps to secure that alignment.

Step 12: Follow the Next Steps

The next steps that come out of your review of the portfolio pieces or the assessment on the *Continuous Improvement Continuums* will inform staff of how and where they must enter the school improvement process. Follow those next steps while the information is new.

START WITH THE PROCESS

A Word About the Leader of the School Improvement Effort

Literature on school improvement over the past fifteen years has proven that a strong leader is necessary in the school improvement arena. While the literature is, in part, referring to the role of principal and staff as shared-decision makers, there is another leader whose role is very important—the leader who is guiding the school improvement process—who may or may not be the principal. Sometimes that leader will be a teacher volunteer, a teacher on special assignment, an assistant principal, a district staff member, or even a parent.

The term "facilitator" will purposefully not be used here because we believe that the individual who leads this work will realistically be a member of the learning organization, or a close organizational colleague. This person or these persons who will lead the progress toward the vision will be called upon to guide the content.

By definition, a facilitator is a person who guides a process and not the content—staying removed from the group. There are times when a facilitator is necessary in the process of building a school portfolio, but we also know that it is not always possible to engage someone without a vested interest in the process and content. It is more important to us that a leader, regardless of position, be responsible to lead the process and maintain the momentum. This "leader" should be someone who can prioritize the process, as well as the content. Even though the focus here is on lead persons close to the change process taking place at the school level, the concepts covered in this toolkit are also appropriate for a person leading or even facilitating a district effort or efforts of a group of schools within a district or region.

As a leader, there are several ways to start the school portfolio process in your school, or with a group of schools. It is most important to think about how you will get staff to feel the ownership. Many processes talk about "buy-in." We want more than "buy-in." We want everyone in the organization to feel ownership of the school portfolio product and process, and to help create both.

Below are tools and approaches to getting started with the process and in gaining that ownership.

Group Process Tools

On the CD are several group process tools and activities that will be referenced throughout this book. The tools are:

- ▼ Running Efficient Meetings
- ▼ Ground Rules
- ▼ Meeting Etiquette
- ▼ Norms of Behavior
- ▼ Coming to Consensus
- ▼ Guidelines for Brainstorming
- ▼ Issue Bin/Parking Lot
- ▼ Affinity Diagram Activity
- ▼ Cause and Effect Analysis Activity

- ▼ Fishbowl Activity
- ▼ Forcefield Analysis Activity
- ▼ Placemat Activity
- ▼ T-Chart Activity
- ▼ "X" Marks the Spot Activity
- ▼ Quadrant Diagram Activity

Use these tools to get group consensus, to run effective meetings, to develop a collaborative culture, and to review data.

Start the Process with Staff

Basic steps in getting started with the school portfolio process [CD-ROM] are described below.

▼ *Develop a Sense of Urgency for Improvement*

We believe that school personnel want every student to achieve at her or his highest level. We also believe that every school knows it can improve its services to children. The school portfolio is a framework that will assist schools in documenting their current practices for understanding the impact of their practices on students and for understanding how to improve systematically and systemically.

▼ *Help Staff Understand All the Purposes and Uses of the School Portfolio*

Help staff understand how they can work smarter, not harder, by understanding the processes that make a difference with their students. Help them understand that they can build a portfolio once for many purposes and uses, and how they can use it to measure progress and show growth over time. The school portfolio helps to refine processes and eliminate programs or activities that may be time-intensive and do not lead to desired results. The school portfolio is a comprehensive and reflective document. It is designed to be the one living document that describes the entire organization so that the complexities of the school (the needs, processes, and results) are well-understood to get to the root causes of problems and to understand what to change, in order to increase student achievement.

▼ *Present an Overview of the School Portfolio*

The School Portfolio Toolkit includes files entitled *School Portfolio Overview*, *School Portfolio Purposes and Uses*, and the *School Portfolio Summary Chart* to use as handouts, and a *Microsoft PowerPoint School Portfolio Presentation*. The presentation can be used to print transparencies; view with a projector; view as note pages to print prepared notes with slides for presentation preparation; and print as handouts with three slides per page.

▼ *Use the Continuous Improvement Continuums*

Use the *Continuous Improvement Continuums* (CICs) to understand each category of the school portfolio and to measure where the school is on the seven continuums. The results might provide that sense of urgency needed to spark enthusiasm for your school improvement efforts.

The most beneficial approach to assessing on the Continuums is to gather the entire staff together for the assessment. When using the first time, plan for three hours to complete the assessments on all seven categories.

Start the assessment by stating or creating the ground rules, setting the tone for a safe and confidential assessment, and explain why you are doing this. Provide a brief overview of *The School Portfolio* and then, taking each section one at a time, have each staff member read the related Continuum and make independent assessments of where she/he believe the *school* is with respect to *Approach*, *Implementation*, and *Outcome*. We recommend using individual 8 1/2 x 11 copies of the Continuums for individual assessments. Then, have each staff member note where she/he believes the school is with a colorful sticker or marker on a large poster of the Continuum. The markers allow all staff to see how much they are in agreement with one another. If only one color is used for the first assessment, another color can be used for the next assessment, and so forth, to help gauge growth over time.

When all dots have been placed on the enlarged continuum, look at the agreement or disagreement of the ratings. Starting with *Approach*, have staff discuss why they believe the school is where they rated it. Keep discussing until the larger group comes to

Have staff members make their independent assessments of where they believe the *school* is on the *Continuous Improvement Continuums*.

Check to see if the discussion has led staff to consensus.

consensus on one number that reflects where the school staff is right now. You might need to make a quick check on where staff is with respect to coming to consensus, using a thumbs up, thumbs down "vote." Keep discussing the facts until consensus is reached. *Do not average the results—it does not produce a sense of urgency for improvement.* We cannot emphasize this enough! Keep discussing until agreement can be reached by everyone on a number that represents where "we" are right now. When that consensus is reached, record the number and move to *Implementation* and then *Outcome.* Determine *Next Steps.* Proceed in the same way to the next six categories. Directions for facilitating the assessment and coming to consensus are on the CD, as well as camera-ready copies of the *Continuous Improvement Continuums,* example reports, and reporting and graphing templates.

Staff gather together to make their group assessment on the *Continuous Improvement Continuums.*

During the assessments, make sure someone records the discussions of the Continuum assessments for the narrative sections of the portfolio. The discussion will encompass what the school has for each section and other things needed to be gathered or done. One could also ask more directly during the assessments what the school has for each section and what they need to gather or document. The *School Portfolio Summary Chart* can help you record what evidence you have for each section and additional data, artifacts, or evidence you need. Schools might want to exchange facilitators with a neighboring school or district to have someone external to the school conduct the assessments. This will enable everyone in the school to participate and provide an unbiased, but competent person, to lead the consensus-building piece. Assessing over time will help staff see that they are making progress. The decision of how often to assess on the *Continuous Improvement Continuums* is certainly up to the school. We recommend no less than twice a year—about mid-fall and mid-spring—when there is time (or has been time) to implement next steps.

Staff independent assessments and consensus discussions will ultimately lead to a number that represents where the *school* is right now, with respect to *Approach, Implementation,* and *Outcome.*

▼ *Appeal to Staff to Improve Through the Use of Data*

Good data that show student achievement results and the impact of school processes become very contagious. Informational data, graphed and charted, create demands for more good data. Graphed questionnaire results are a beginning to understanding the current practices and changes that must be made to get different results. Effectively and meaningfully graphed schoolwide student achievement results almost always call for classroom-level student achievement results. Ideally, teachers would start the school year with the historical student achievement results of their current rosters of students. Processes built into the learning organization to use data regularly will surely result in student learning increases. (Chapter 4 focuses entirely on this data piece.)

▼ *Begin with a Mission for the School Portfolio*

One teacher was told his job was to develop a school portfolio for his high school's regional accreditation self-review. He attended a school portfolio workshop and thought he could just whip the product together in no time. He pulled apart old reports and started placing them in their appropriate locations in his portfolio binder. It was not long before he realized there were many areas that needed to be aligned. He found discrepancies in the reports. He also found major pieces missing such as a shared vision. He soon had to solicit the assistance of the rest of the staff. Since they had not owned the process or the product, he had a hard time getting their attention.

The teacher thought about how they accomplished work at other times. By reflecting, he realized that they needed to identify a mission for the school portfolio. That mission needed to clearly lay out, in their terms, the purposes and uses of the school portfolio. With that mission, staff agreed to help with the administration of questionnaires and to work on a shared vision. The school portfolio mission started them on their continuous improvement journey.

▼ *Motivate Staff through External Incentives*

Many of our school portfolio schools use the school portfolio process to apply for, and receive, state and national distinguished or achieving school awards, or to apply for grant programs. They have found that the school portfolio provides a solid framework for knowing what they need to do to improve, to document what they did, and then to describe their improvement results. Most award programs want to know more about the school portfolio when reviewers see the product, as well as the results of the process. Additionally, business corporations call the school portfolio "an easy sell." External incentives could result in short-term compliance if these incentives are not channeled into long-term continuous school improvement. One way to show staff that they are engaging in a continuous school improvement process by initially building the story of their school once, and using it for many requirements, would be to set up a cross-reference matrix, showing commonly requested requirements. On the CD are some cross-reference matrices that show how the school portfolio requirements align with the following:

- Baldrige Education Criteria for Performance Excellence
- Bay Area School Reform Collaborative (BASRC) Criteria
- California Program Quality Review (PQR)
- Immediate Interventions/California Underperforming Schools Program (II/USP)
- Coordinated Compliance Review (CCR)
- Improving America's Schools Act (IASA)
- Indiana Strategic and Continuous School Improvement and Achievement Plan (ISCSIAP)
- Interstate School Leaders Licensure Consortium Standards (ISLLC)
- Kansas State Board of Education's Quality Performance Accreditation System
- Michigan School Improvement Plan
- Missouri School Improvement Program (MSIP)
- National Staff Development Council (NSDC) Standards
- New York Comprehensive District Education Planning
- North Central Association Commission on Accreditation and School Improvement (NCA-CASI)
- North Dakota Education Improvement Process Standards
- Ohio Continuous Improvement Plan (CIP)
- Southern Association of Colleges and Schools (SACS)
- U.S. Department of Education Blue Ribbon Schools Program
- Western Association of Schools and Colleges (WASC)

> *The school portfolio has become a framework that quickly, but gently, moves schools into understanding how they got the results they are getting now and what they need to do to get different results.*

Also on the CD are matrix templates for you to cross-reference your specific requirements with school portfolio sections, two of which have NCA and WASC requirements already in the matrix.

▼ Help Them Get Past a Challenge

With the accountability issues on many state's agendas, the school portfolio has become a framework that quickly, but gently, moves schools into understanding how they got the results they are getting now and what they need to do to get different results. These schools become exceptionally proud of their portfolios after they have succeeded in something that was initially threatening, very stressful, and potentially harmful to their organization.

▼ Reculture the School for Change

For any of these approaches to work, a culture for change must be established. Staff must understand that the main purpose for engaging in continuous school improvement is to improve student learning and achievement. Roles must be defined and norms for effective dialogue prevail. The group process tools mentioned earlier in this chapter can assist you with leading a group into dialogue.

Working with a Group of Schools on Developing School Portfolios

If working with leadership teams from a few or several schools, you may find each school at a different starting place. Honor where each is and from where each came. Work on making the end product real and the process to get to the end product exciting and doable.

Plan to start with a school portfolio overview workshop. Schools come to the overview workshops in various states of readiness. It is legitimate that one person would be sent to a workshop from a school to "investigate" the concept of the school portfolio. It is entirely possible that representatives of schools could attend and never want to begin a school portfolio. Ideally, we want committed leadership teams to attend so they can begin outlining their portfolios during the workshops.

After an overview, an individual might go back to her/his school and tell staff that they need to be interested in the school portfolio, and then send a leadership team to another workshop; or they might ask a presenter to come to the school to do an overview for the entire staff. Inviting a presenter or trainer to come to the school to present the overview to the entire staff will ensure that everyone is hearing the same thing at the same time and the presenter/trainer can incorporate the assessment on the *Continuous Improvement Continuums* while doing the overview. This kind of support could definitely take a day; although an overview can be done in three to four hours.

Let's say a committed leadership team comes to an overview. They take good notes and leave with a comprehensive list of next steps. They go back to the school and try to present what they learned to the whole staff. At some point, that school might contact you or another expert for additional support. Items for which assistance is most often requested include one or more of the following:

▼ Questionnaire construction, administration, and/or analysis and interpretation

▼ Student achievement analyses and interpretation

▼ Writing sections of the portfolio

▼ Organizing sections of the portfolio

▼ Creating a vision and mission

▼ Planning to implement the vision

▼ Creating one school plan

▼ Helping to get all requirements met with one document

▼ Facilitating staff assessment on the *Continuous Improvement Continuums*

▼ Assisting them in determining the root causes of problems

▼ Reculturing their school for change

▼ Learning how to keep the momentum going

▼ Planning for professional development

▼ Planning for partnership development

▼ Seeing example school portfolios

▼ Creating a leadership structure

▼ Getting all aspects of the organization in congruence with the vision

▼ Analyzing and recommending to them appropriate instructional and assessment strategies

School staffs participating in a School Portfolio Overview Workshop.

We strongly recommend that a network of schools be established from an interested group of schools. That way you can have a set time every other month (or so) when the leadership teams get together to talk about progress. Each meeting's theme can be focused on professional development related to one or more of the categories, and the schools can support each other when the leader is unavailable.

When working with a network of schools, you might want to use the following steps at your first meeting:

▼ Provide an overview of the school portfolio process to make sure everyone understands (*School Portfolio Overview, Purposes and Uses,* and *The School Portfolio Presentation,* presentation outline and script will assist you to this end, as will *The School Portfolio: A Comprehensive Framework for School Improvement* [Bernhardt, 1999]).

▼ Lay out timelines (example agendas, scope and sequence, and timeline files that you may customize also appear on the CD).

▼ Show examples. *The Example School Portfolio* (Bernhardt et al., 2000) is a tool published for this purpose. If you have a school willing to go out front when the others are lagging behind, use the opportunity to work quickly with that first school, so its experience can become an example for the others.

▼ Teach them how to go back to their schools and assess on the *Continuous Improvement Continuums* and how to report the results. Please note that when facilitating the assessment, if you can leave a school with the report of its assessment on that day or get the report to them the next day, the staff will stay more engaged in the process than when they receive the report many days later. Build the reports as you go through the assessment, using the instructions and templates provided.

▼ As a closing activity, have them list both the benefits and their concerns about creating a school portfolio (see *School Portfolio Concerns Activity*).

For the second meeting, you might have the groups:

▼ Report on their *Continuous Improvement Continuums* assessments.

▼ Share the questions that emerged from the CIC assessment. (Note that each Toolkit chapter has *Frequently Asked Questions* 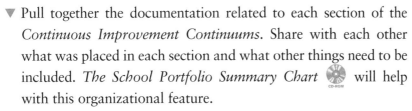 related to that chapter.)

▼ Pull together the documentation related to each section of the *Continuous Improvement Continuums*. Share with each other what was placed in each section and what other things need to be included. *The School Portfolio Summary Chart* will help with this organizational feature.

▼ Encourage the schools to begin writing the school portfolio sections using the section templates found on the Toolkit CD.

For the third meeting:

▼ Check progress and support technology pieces, such as data graphing, scanning, and wordprocessing.

▼ Provide time to put the pieces together.

Subsequent meetings:

Provide support for—
▼ Data analysis interpretation (Chapter 4 and the CD)
▼ The visioning process (Chapter 5 and the CD)
▼ Planning (Chapter 6 and the CD)
▼ Professional development planning (Chapter 7 and the CD)
▼ Leadership development (Chapter 8 and the CD)
▼ Partnership development planning (Chapter 9 and the CD)
▼ Continuous school improvement and evaluation (Chapter 10 and the CD)

Effective use of group work time in the workshop
What participants do during the group work time allotted in the workshop depends somewhat upon whether they are attending with a leadership team or alone.

School teams usually choose to complete one of the following activities:

▼ Use the *Continuous Improvement Continuums* to do a preliminary assessment of the school, and think about next steps.

▼ Think about what data and documentation the school already has that can be used to develop the school portfolio. Next, think about what else is needed using the *School Portfolio Summary Chart.*

**Group work time
in an Overview Workshop.**

District office staff might work with a school team, if appropriate, or work with support providers to determine how they can provide support to schools.

Solo attendees from individual schools can be grouped. The role of this group will be to become more knowledgeable about the school portfolio process by reviewing and discussing the chapters in the book in order to plan for presenting the information to their respective sites after the workshop.

SUMMARY

The School Portfolio is a process and a product. There are many ways to begin the school portfolio process and/or product. Each school must find its own way to start either or both. Sometimes the building of the product leads to the process. Other times the process requires documentation for improvement, which is why the product becomes so valuable.

FREQUENTLY ASKED QUESTIONS ABOUT GETTING STARTED 💿
CD-ROM

▼ **Why would I want to put together a school portfolio?**

The intent of a school portfolio is to create one document that describes your school, lays out your vision, and documents your growth toward that vision over time. The top three reasons for putting the pieces together would be to:

 ◆ Improve your learning organization on a continuous basis to ensure student learning

 ◆ Understand the impact of current processes on student achievement and the organization

 ◆ Understand how to improve current processes

After your portfolio is developed, you will never need to recreate it; it is a living document.

▼ **How long does it take to put a school portfolio together?**

Starting with an official document that you have right now such as a state evaluation, regional accreditation, school report card, or grant application that describes the context of the school and your current vision, you can put together a skeleton portfolio essentially in one day.

Adding questionnaire, demographic, student achievement and process data, especially if it has not been done before, will take longer and might require outside help. Doing all the hard work from scratch without extra time or support will take about one school year. (This would include gathering the data, conducting a self-assessment, getting a shared vision, creating one comprehensive plan, and documenting all the elements.) However, with data analysis support, and some solid staff development days, the work can be done in a matter of weeks. After the first draft is finished, updating is much easier and quicker.

▼ Around what categories should we organize the school portfolio?

We are proposing that you begin by using the categories that are described in the book, *The School Portfolio* (Bernhardt, 1999). The following seven categories: *Information and Analysis, Student Achievement, Quality Planning, Professional Development, Leadership, Partnership Development,* and *Continuous Improvement and Evaluation* contain common elements that are often asked in requests for proposals, and in your state and regional reviews. They are very good starting points for specific requirements or reports. You might want to add sub-headings to each category. However, if your state has specific criteria, or if you have been working with a funding agency or requirement that has other categories the school is already using, you can use those categories as long as all the major elements of data, vision, planning, professional development, leadership, partnership development, and continuous improvement and evaluation are embedded within.

▼ How do you add to your portfolio over time?

Adding to your portfolio can be done in a variety of ways. That process is something you and your staff need to think through at the very beginning so that you can set up your indices to add to the sections easily and quickly. Some schools make annual tabs for the current and next five years. Others tend to rewrite the sections in order to keep all elements of the binder current. You will want subcategories so you can find your information quickly and easily. (Also see Chapter 11.)

The first thing you can do is to be very clear on its purpose. The school portfolio that we are talking about here is a comprehensive and reflective document. It is designed to be the one living document that describes the school. The school portfolio describes the entire organization so that the complexities of the school (the needs, processes, and results) are well understood to get to the root causes of problems, in order to increase student achievement. We have found that having the entire staff conduct a self-assessment on the *Continuous Improvement Continuums* entices them into the work. Leadership is also a vital component for the success of a school portfolio.

▼ What one thing do schools say they wish they had known when they started their school portfolios?

Schools that did not start with the *Continuous Improvement Continuums* have said that they wish they had known how powerful and helpful they would have been. The assessments practically write the portfolio for them, and they serve as a unifying force for staffs.

▼ Where did the *Continuous Improvement Continuums* come from?

In 1991, participating Education for the Future Initiative schools worked with Education for the Future staff to develop an "authentic" measurement tool that would provide useful information to the schools about where they are in the school improvement process and clarify where they are going. A set of rubrics known as the Continuous Improvement Continuums (CICs) resulted from the work. The Continuums are based on what we were learning with the schools and the literature on school improvement. The CICs provide criteria for implementing systemic school change. Schools across the country have found these tools to be invaluable in maintaining a shared school vision, keeping the parts of their complex learning systems congruent, understanding the interrelationships of the parts, assessing progress, and providing overall direction.

▼ How often do you assess on the Continuums?

It is certainly up to the school when to assess on the Continuous Improvement Continuums. We recommend no less than twice a year—at the beginning of the school year and at the end. For the first time, early fall is good. For ongoing years, we recommend assessing in mid-fall and mid-spring, when there is still time to implement "next steps." In the beginning, schools with low initial ratings may want to assess three times that first year to show and know progress is being made.

▼ What do we do with these ratings?

It is important to document where you are each time you conduct an assessment on the Continuous Improvement Continuums. The Continuous Improvement and Evaluation chapter is a good place to store the results and a summary of the discussion. The discussion around the ratings is a beginning for the text that can go in each section of the school portfolio.

▼ What about student work? Where does it go in the portfolio?

Certainly there is a logical place for student work within the Student Achievement section of the school portfolio. We find that schools do put examples of student work in the Student Achievement section; however, the portfolio often becomes so cumbersome that the student work more often than not ends up in another binder. Many schools with school portfolios find the reflective document to be so helpful to the school that teachers want the same support to establish teacher portfolios which house student work. Schoolwide student achievement analyses will definitely go into the portfolio.

▼ Have any schools set up an electronic portfolio?

Yes. With word processors and computers so available, the school portfolio exists in an electronic format in many schools. We have schools that have put their portfolios on a web page. Because most of our schools refer to charts, graphs, data, and plans for decision making, most have found it most valuable to have the hard copy handy to use on an ongoing basis at the school. There is no reason not to have both, but the hard copy is valuable in that one can quickly move back and forth between sections, pull things out, and compare papers to other documents for continuous improvement.

▼ **Is there a problem with the public seeing all our information?**

This is a very good question and one that the school portfolio developers will need to consider. It might be that as you build your school portfolio copies, there will be variations in each copy. For the public portfolio, you will not want to show sensitive data analysis work. The copy for teachers should be most inclusive; however, individual student scores belong in a locked filing cabinet.

YOUR QUESTIONS

▼ What questions do you have about getting started?

▼ How will you start your school portfolio?

ON THE CD RELATED TO GETTING STARTED

▼ FAQs—Frequently Asked Questions About Getting Started

▼ Getting Started
- ◆ ABCs of The School Portfolio
- ◆ School Portfolio Overview
- ◆ School Portfolio Purposes and Uses
- ◆ The School Portfolio Summary Chart
- ◆ The School Portfolio Overview Activity
- ◆ ABCs Activity

▼ Getting Started with the School Portfolio Product
- ◆ Index files
- ◆ Beginning Pages with *The School Portfolio* Header
- ◆ Beginning Pages without a Header
- ◆ Headers and Footers
- ◆ The Cover

▼ Getting Started with the School Portfolio Process
- ◆ Group Process Tools and Activities
  - • Running Efficient Meetings
  - • Ground Rules
  - • Meeting Etiquette
  - • Norms of Behavior

- Coming to Consensus
- Guidelines for Brainstorming
- Issue Bin/Parking Lot
- Affinity Diagram Activity
- Cause and Effect Analysis Activity
- Fishbowl Activity
- Forcefield Analysis Activity
- Placemat Activity
- T-Chart Activity
- "X" Marks the Spot Activity
- Quadrant Diagram Activity
- ◆ School Portfolio Presentation
  - School Portfolio Slideshow Presentation (includes outline and script)

▼ Continuous Improvement Continuums
- ◆ Continuous Improvement Continuums (CICs)
- ◆ CICs Self-Assessment Activity
- ◆ CICs Baseline Report Example
- ◆ CICs Follow-up Years Report °Example
- ◆ CICs Baseline Report Template
- ◆ CICs Graphing Templates

▼ Cross-Reference Matrices of the School Portfolio
- ◆ Baldrige Education Criteria for Performance Excellence
- ◆ Bay Area School Reform Collaborative (BASRC) Criteria
- ◆ California Program Quality Review (PQR)
- ◆ California Immediate Interventions/Underperforming Schools Program (II/USP)
- ◆ Coordinated Compliance Review (CCR)
- ◆ Improving America's Schools Act (IASA)
- ◆ Indiana Strategic and Continuous School Improvement and Achievement Plan (ISCSIAP)
- ◆ Interstate School Leaders Licensure Consortium Standards (ISLLC)
- ◆ Kansas State Board of Education's Quality Performance Accreditation System
- ◆ Michigan School Improvement Plan
- ◆ Missouri School Improvement Program (MSIP)
- ◆ National Staff Development Council (NSDC) Standards
- ◆ New York Comprehensive District Education Planning

- North Central Association Commission on Accreditation and School Improvement (NCA-CASI)
- North Dakota Education Improvement Process Standards
- Ohio Continuous Improvement Plan (CIP)
- Southern Association of Colleges and Schools (SACS)
- U.S. Department of Education Blue Ribbon Schools Program
- Western Association of Schools and Colleges (WASC)
- Matrix Templates:
  - School Portfolio and Blank Column Template (for *Your School*)
  - School Portfolio, NCA, and Blank Column Template (for *Your School*)
  - School Portfolio, WASC, and Blank Column Template (for *Your School*)

▼ Working with a Group of Schools on the School Portfolio
- Example Agendas:
  - Recommendations for a School Portfolio Overview Workshop Agenda
  - School Portfolio Overview Example Agenda
- Example Timelines:
  - School Portfolio Scope and Sequence
  - Timelines for Working with a Group of Schools
  - School Portfolio Implementation Timeline Template
  - School Portfolio Concerns Activity

▼ Writing Templates
- Introduction to the School Portfolio Section Template Files
- Introduction Section Template
- Overview Section Template
- Information and Analysis Section Template:
  - Questionnaire Results Template
  - Student Achievement Results Template
- Student Achievement Section Template
- Quality Planning Section Template
- Professional Development Section Template
- Leadership Section Template
- Partnership Development Section Template
- Continuous Improvement and Evaluation Section Template

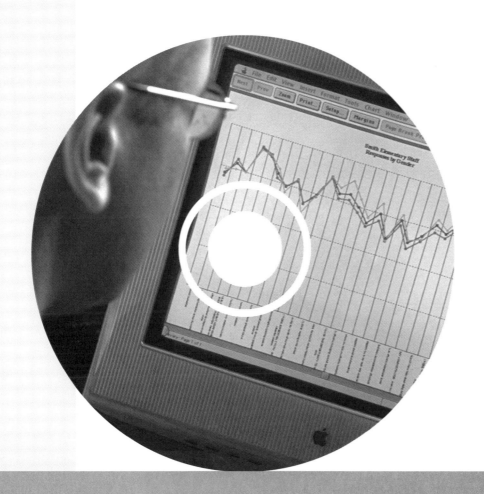

INFORMATION AND ANALYSIS:
The Data

Chapter Objective: TO LEARN EFFECTIVE TOOLS AND STRATEGIES FOR USING DATA THAT LEAD TO INCREASES IN STUDENT LEARNING

> *Data is like...*
>
> The ocean. At first it seems too vast and changeable to master. But as one delves into it, it begins to reveal the secrets of its organic interconnections.
>
> The stars in the night sky – myriad and seemingly random that can be shaped by the mind into constellations of meaning.
>
> A stained glass window. It has many pieces. Individually each piece is unique, but together the pieces display a beautiful message.
>
> Data is like a jar full of buttons, until you sort them and look for specifics, you can't appreciate their value or purpose.
>
> A jigsaw puzzle. The separate pieces may show interesting detail, but together you can see the whole picture. It represents going from the unknown to the known.
>
> Data Analysis Workshop, August 2000
> Greensburg, Pennsylvania

Gathering, analyzing, and utilizing data about the school is a feature of *The School Portfolio* that sets it apart from many school improvement frameworks. Education for the Future staff members understand that schools that gather and use data in their school improvement efforts make the desired changes and get increased student learning. Schools that do not use data often end up leaving their school improvement processes behind long before they know if what they are doing is making a difference.

The Information and Analysis section of the school portfolio houses most of a school's data. A template for an Information and Analysis school portfolio section, as well as the items to include in the Information and Analysis section, and *Frequently Asked Questions About Information and Analysis* appear on the CD.

Since starting a continuous school improvement effort with our schools is always a challenge, we begin with data. We appeal to school staffs to commit to the school improvement process by looking at the data to help guide the process and inform them if what they are doing is making a difference with student learning. So, what are these data, how can they become so powerful, and how does one engage staff into gathering and using appropriate data?

WHAT DATA?

Within the context of the school portfolio, schools need to gather and analyze multiple measures of data. Following are the most obvious data that need to be gathered and the reasons for doing so:

▼ *Demographic data* are needed to describe the school context. These data provide the over-arching context for everything that the school does with respect to school improvement. These contextual data show who the students, staff, and community are, and how they have changed over time.

▼ *Perceptual data* can tell schools about student, parent, and staff satisfaction with the work of the school. Perceptual data can also help the school understand what is *possible* in the big picture of school improvement and what has been done internally to meet school improvement goals.

▼ *Student learning data* help schools see the results they are getting now. These data tell schools which students are succeeding academically and which are not. They also guide planning, leadership, partnership, and professional development efforts.

▼ *School process data* provide staff with information about their current approaches to teaching and learning, programs, and the learning organization. It is these processes that will need to change to achieve different results.

Collectively and interactively, these data begin to inform schools of the impact of current programs and processes on their students—so they can decide what to change to get different results. These data can also assist schools in understanding the root causes of problems as opposed to just focusing on symptoms. Figure 4.1 shows these different categories of data and the information one can extract when intersecting the different categories. An article entitled *Multiple Measures* summarizes this graphic.

FIGURE 4.1

Multiple Measures of Data

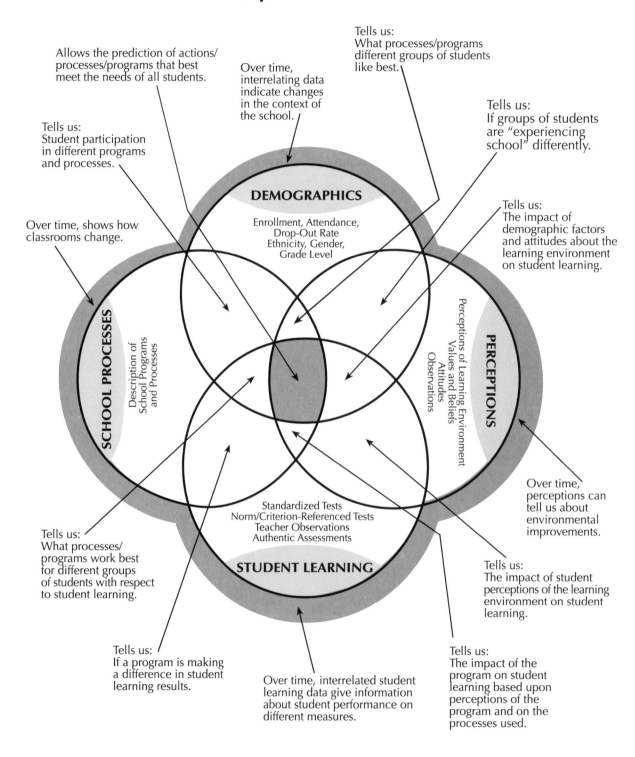

Allows the prediction of actions/processes/programs that best meet the needs of all students.

Tells us: Student participation in different programs and processes.

Over time, shows how classrooms change.

Over time, interrelating data indicate changes in the context of the school.

Tells us: What processes/programs different groups of students like best.

Tells us: If groups of students are "experiencing school" differently.

Tells us: The impact of demographic factors and attitudes about the learning environment on student learning.

Over time, perceptions can tell us about environmental improvements.

Tells us: The impact of student perceptions of the learning environment on student learning.

Tells us: The impact of the program on student learning based upon perceptions of the program and on the processes used.

DEMOGRAPHICS

Enrollment, Attendance, Drop-Out Rate Ethnicity, Gender, Grade Level

SCHOOL PROCESSES

Description of School Programs and Processes

PERCEPTIONS

Perceptions of Learning Environment Values and Beliefs Attitudes Observations

STUDENT LEARNING

Standardized Tests Norm/Criterion-Referenced Tests Teacher Observations Authentic Assessments

Tells us: What processes/programs work best for different groups of students with respect to student learning.

Tells us: If a program is making a difference in student learning results.

Over time, interrelated student learning data give information about student performance on different measures.

Note. From *Data Analysis for Comprehensive Schoolwide Improvement* (p.15), by Victoria L. Bernhardt, 1998, Larchmont, NY: Eye on Education. Copyright © 1998 Eye on Education, Inc. Reprinted with permission.

The School Portfolio: A Comprehensive Framework for School Improvement, Second Edition (Bernhardt, 1999) and *Data Analysis for Comprehensive Schoolwide Improvement* (Bernhardt, 1998) are resources that describe in depth how to go about gathering the data mentioned above and how to conduct appropriate analyses. *Designing and Using Databases for School Improvement* (Bernhardt, 2000) describes how to set up databases to do this work comprehensively and cohesively. This information will not be repeated here, but it will be referenced. Instead the focus will be on creating the incentives for change with data and providing strategies for getting all staff involved in using the data.

CREATE THE INCENTIVE FOR SCHOOL IMPROVEMENT WITH DEMOGRAPHIC DATA

Information and Analysis is a very special and important section of the school portfolio. Information and Analysis is where schools describe who they are and the context of the school. It is the place in which staffs get to know themselves and their school, again, and where others get to know them and the school. Most of these data fall into the category of demographic data. School, community, administrator, and teacher profiles appear on the CD to help gather some of this information, if there is not a database already doing that in the school. The profiles consist of suggested items. There are many more possibilities.

Templates for making demographic graphs quickly and easily, and to help those who need extra assistance in moving from numbers to graphs, are also provided.

The important thing about this section of the school portfolio, as it relates to continuous school improvement planning, is to clearly answer the questions:

▼ Who are our students?
▼ Who are our staff members?
▼ Who is our community?

Looking at demographics gives a clear indication with whom we are working currently, and with whom we have been working over time. It also allows us to see trends that could help us predict with whom we will be working in the future. This information, combined with student achievement results, will tell us how well we have been doing with different groups of students over time. Using historical data, we can actually anticipate our population changes in the future. This information can help us think about needed changes in instructional strategies and our physical capacity to meet the needs of the students who will come to us in the future. Our ultimate goal is to prevent failure by being able to predict the impact of our actions on different groups of students. When planning for new school buildings or shifts in class sizes over time, for instance, every piece of demographic information is crucial. *Questions to Guide the Analysis of Demographic Data* 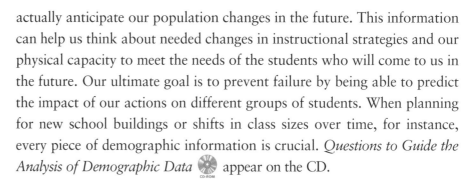 appear on the CD.

History Gram

When building a school portfolio and beginning this school improvement process, no doubt one will hear cries of "been there, done that" and "*another* school improvement process!" It is important to appreciate where each staff member has been with respect to school improvement in the history of the school (and perhaps in other schools in which they have worked) and to understand this history.

A Washington state school staff gathering by the year on the timeline that they arrived at the school.

One way to pay homage to each and every staff member and the history of the school is to build a history gram—a timeline and a review of events in the history of the school. Stretch out poster paper or a roll of newsprint and draw a timeline starting when the school was built or when the first current staff member arrived. Under the timeline write key words that you want the staff to consider, such as *era*, *culture*, and *values*. Post the timeline on the wall. When staff are gathered, have each staff member stand by the year she/he entered the school. Then have staff think about what was happening at the time they came to the school. Have them "name" the era and write the name on the timeline under the year. Also have them write what they thought the "culture" of the school was and the prominent "values" of that era. As staff describe the feel of the school at the time they arrived, the history of the school and its transformations are recorded, and can be placed in the school portfolio. After describing the changes over time, debrief what everyone saw and heard. Most often, staff will notice that they started many school improvement efforts over the years that were stopped when the work got hard. The final analysis is the key—*This time we need to stick with it.* This is an activity for which you will want to have a camera handy. The photograph and the story that unravels will need to be documented in the Information and Analysis section of the school portfolio to begin the story of the school; hopefully this history gram can entice all staff to commit to the process long term, perhaps in ways they never have before. The *History Gram* has been written as an activity.

The Washington state school staff building a human bar graph depicting when she/he arrived at the school.

CREATE THE INCENTIVE FOR SCHOOL IMPROVEMENT WITH PERCEPTIONS DATA

Questionnaires can help schools measure student perceptions of the learning environment, parent satisfaction with the school, and staff perceptions of the learning organization. It is important to remember that a person's perception is also her/his reality. Therefore, collecting this type of data is extremely important.

A staff taking an online questionnaire.

The CD provides examples of student, staff, and parent questionnaires for paper or electronic administration. The staff questionnaire focuses on items related to having a vision that is truly shared and aligning all parts of the learning organization to the vision. The staff questionnaire results will inform staff if there is a vision, if it is shared, if staff believe there is one plan to achieve the vision, if staff believe the professional development is appropriate for implementing the vision, and what they believe will increase student learning. The student and parent questionnaires will help staff understand the learning organization from the perspective of the students and their parents. Please read *Administering the Questionnaires* to maximize your administration of these questionnaires to get a 100 percent return rate from staff and students, and a very high return rate from parents.

We know that it is crucial to gather these data mentioned above. We also know that it is equally important to graph the data to form pictures of what the data are saying. Good data and good graphs of the data are natural attractions for getting many individuals to look at the data. Good graphed questionnaire data will get staff talking about the relationship of the high scores to each other, the relationship of the low scores to each other, and the relationship of student, parent, and staff results with each other. Graphed questionnaire data can become the catalyst to begin dialogue about what to do differently to change the results.

Brad Geise, the author of *School IQ* (*School Improvement Questionnaire Solutions*), with perception questionnaire graphs.

On the CD is the *School IQ* (*School Improvement Questionnaire Solutions*) which includes a custom-designed questionnaire database application that will calculate the averages, standard deviation, and the number and percentage of responses for each item option for each questionnaire. The start and help databases included with *School IQ* describe the *IQ's* function and uses and how to copy and paste averages into the graphing templates. One can literally administer the staff questionnaire, for instance, and look at the graphed results in the same hour—provided the instructions are followed.

Guiding the Discussion of Questionnaire Results

A school improvement leader may choose to guide the discussion of questionnaire results with staff. One approach would be to give copies of the graphed questionnaire results to all staff members and ask subgroups of staff to focus on one set of questionnaires (i.e., student, parent, staff). One staff member per subgroup records the information as the members of the subgroup systematically indicate what they are seeing in their set of graphs. The leader of this activity must ensure that staff members are not attempting to come to conclusions until all analyses are made. The subgroups report their findings. Members of other subgroups would be able to add what they see in the results. Finally, all subgroups work together to understand the relationship of the student, staff, and parent questionnaire results collectively and to make next steps for improvement. The *Fishbowl Activity* might be used to debrief the questionnaire results (located within Group Processes). *Questions to Guide the Analysis of Perceptions Data* are found on the CD. These questions ask staff to look at the relationship of the most positive items and the most negative items and then to understand the differences in responses received from the different subgroups. The *Analysis of Questionnaire Data Table* helps staff look across staff, student, and parent questionnaire results.

Interpreting Questionnaire Results in Narrative

A brief narrative excerpt of the results of a student questionnaire and an example line graph (Figure 4.2) follow. A discussion of methods of communicating data analysis results are presented in depth in Chapter 10, beginning on page 179 of *Data Analysis for Comprehensive Schoolwide Improvement* (Bernhardt, 1998). Basically, the narrative needs to describe the facts.

Example Narrative Excerpt
of Student Questionnaire Responses

In Spring 2001, Forest Lane Elementary School students were asked to complete a questionnaire designed to measure how they felt about their learning environment. The 342 responses were averaged and graphed, disaggregated by gender, and also disaggregated by ethnicity and grade level.

The black dots on the line graph in Figure 4.2, show the overall averages to each of the items to be in agreement—above 3.0 on a five-point scale, with 5 representing "strongly agree," 4 representing "agree," 3 representing "neutral," 2 representing "disagree," and 1 representing "strongly disagree." In other words, no item's average fell in the disagree category. Overall results are described below.

Students were in strongest agreement to:
- *My family wants me to do well in school*
- *My family believes I can do well in school*

The next most strongly agreed to items were:
- *My principal cares about me*
- *My teacher believes I can learn*
- *My teacher is a good teacher*

Although still in agreement, the items that received the lowest averages were as follows:
- *Students at my school treat me with respect*
- *Students at my school are friendly*
- *I have choices in what I learn*
- *I have freedom at school*

The lowest average was approximately 3.4, still in agreement.

Average responses by male and female students generally clustered around the average of total responses. In general, students that identified themselves as female responded in slightly stronger agreement than the males, although both groups were in agreement with all the items on the questionnaire. (Note: the number of females and males do not add up to the total number of respondents because some students did not identify themselves by gender.)

FIGURE 4.2

Forest Lane Student Questionnaire Responses by Gender
Spring 2001

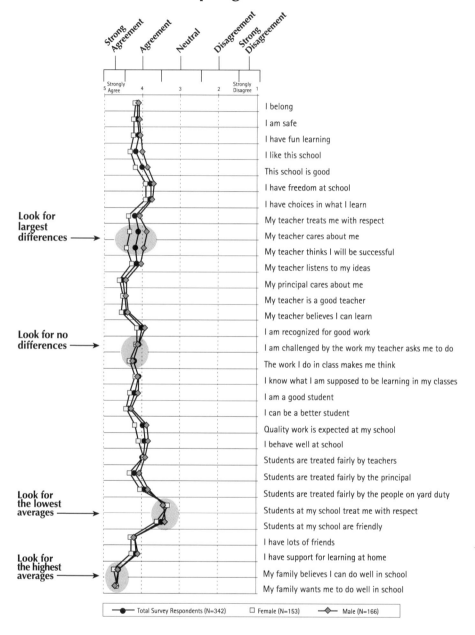

Things to look for:

- Items with the highest averages
- Items that show passion
  (i.e., strongly agree, strongly disagree)
- Items with the lowest averages
- Items in "strong agreement"
- Items in "agreement"

- Items with a "neutral" response
- Items in "disagreement"
- Items in "strong disagreement"
- Differences in responses, if
  different groups are shown
- Relationship of like-scoring items

There are also times when you want to show questionnaire data over time, to show positive change, or to compare responses. Again, a line graph is an excellent choice to present data as a whole, but distribution bar graphs (similar to the ones shown in Figure 4.3) can also be used to get a greater level of detail by graphing the number or percentage choosing each response option.

FIGURE 4.3

Questionnaire Item Distribution Analyses
Teacher Predictions of Student Perceptions
Spring 2001

**Bar distribution graphs are a way to present numbers
(or percentages) of individuals who chose each response option.**

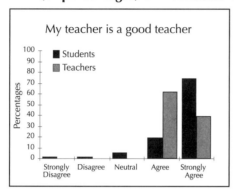

My teacher is a good teacher

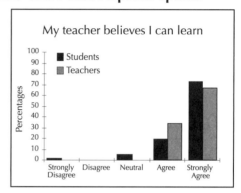

My teacher believes I can learn

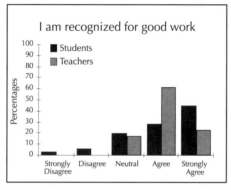

I am recognized for good work

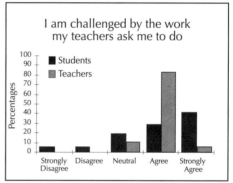

I am challenged by the work
my teachers ask me to do

Students (N=187)
Teachers (N=24)

Things to look for:

• Where the average came from—if an average came from a variety of responses, or if the majority of respondents marked the response option that equals the average.
• Items in which respondents are passionate (all responses strongly agree or all strongly disagree.)
• Discrepancies in responses by groups completing the questionnaire.
• The story unfolding by comparing two groups or two years on the same graph, provided the items are consistent.

One can also show one year's data from one group in bar graphs such as these to understand where the averages came from (e.g., a "3" can be an average of many "3" responses, or a combination of 2's and 4's or 1's and 5's.) The comparison of two groups can show how in tune the predicting group is to the predicted group. The comparison of two years can show how the attitudes changed or differences between two groups in different years. And when we compare two groups (or subgroups) of different sizes, percentages are a more accurate way to describe results.

An example of how the results of a comparison such as the graph displayed in Figure 4.3 might be described in a school portfolio as follows:

The student and teacher responses were graphed in distribution form from "strongly disagree" to "strongly agree" to look more closely at the patterns of the responses.

With this distribution we wanted to see in which areas either students felt strong passion about the items and/or teachers thought the students would feel passion. In other words, we wanted to see which responses were mostly strongly agree or strongly disagree responses, as opposed to spread out over all of the response options. We also wanted to see how "in tune" the teachers are to the students.

Teachers predicted that the students would respond positively to these items, but not as strongly as the students actually responded:

- *My teacher believes I can learn*
- *My teacher is a good teacher*
- *I am recognized for good work*
- *I am challenged*

Figure 4.4 on the following page shows a scatter graph comparing student responses to teacher predictions of student responses. In reporting these results, one needs to keep perspective. While there is a difference in responses to the item, *Students are treated fairly by the people on yard duty,* it is not the only information that can be gleaned from this graph. Note the difference, along with the other information, make recommendations, and move on.

Narrative templates to describe questionnaire results are provided on the CD.

FIGURE 4.4

Teacher Predictions of Student Responses
Spring 2001

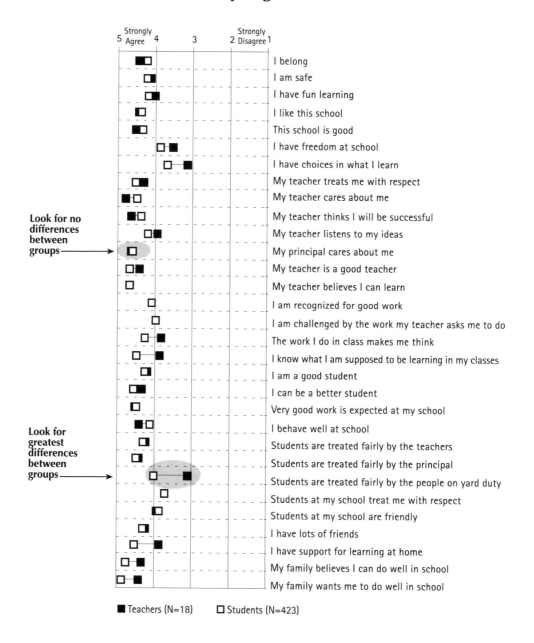

Things to look for:
- **Greatest differences**
- **No differences**
- **Relationships between (among) items with large (or no) differences**
- **Further analyses required to understand the differences**

Analyzing Open-Ended Questionnaire Results

Open-ended questions should not be overlooked when assessing perceptions of the learning environment. While open-ended responses to questions are very time-consuming to compile, one can get a complete sense of the learning environment by asking students, for instance, two questions—*What do you like about this school? What do you wish was different?*

Sample responses:

▼ What I like most about this school are the teachers. I like the way they have fun making us learn.

▼ What I wish was different is, I wish we didn't ever have to leave this school.

There is no fast or automated way to analyze open-ended responses. The best way to do it is to type the list of open-ended responses (if they were not typed via the online administration route). Review the responses and add up the number of times students said the same thing. Place the number, in parentheses, after the statement, eliminate the duplicates, and revise your list. You will need to make judgment calls about how to collapse the items when parts of the responses are different. Figure 4.5 shows the open-ended list in the left-hand column. The other two columns show how the list can be condensed. Use *one* of these approaches—not two or three. The middle column, labeled "Eliminate Duplicates," shows the number of times students wrote *teachers*—the main thought—and so forth. The right-hand column, labeled "Add Descriptors," shows the number of times teachers were mentioned and in parentheses indicates the descriptions and the number of times the descriptors were mentioned. For example:

▼ teachers (6)
▼ caring (3)
▼ learning (3)

Whichever approach you use is okay. It is important to capture the feelings of the respondents. The open-ended responses can paint the picture of your school.

FIGURE 4.5

Aggregating Open-Ended Responses

All Responses	Eliminate Duplicates	Add Descriptors
I like the caring teachers and the friendly school	The teachers (8)	The teachers (8) (e.g., nice, 2; respect/fair, 2; caring, 1; good, 1; way of learning, 1)
I like that our school is new and the teachers are nice	The principal (2)	The school (3) (e.g., friendly, 1; new, 1; nice, 1)
I really like our new principal and my friends	My friends (3)	The principal (2)
I have a good teacher and friends who treat me nice	The school (3)	My friends (3) (e.g., treat me nice, 1)
I like the way teachers make us learn things	My classes (2)	My classes (2)
I feel safe and treated with respect from teachers	Recess (2)	Recess (2) (e.g., playground equipment, 1)
I like my teacher and the principal	Social Studies (1)	I feel safe
My teacher treats me with respect	P.E. (1)	Social Studies
I like recess, social studies, P.E., and music	Playground equipment (1)	P.E.
I like my friends and my nice teacher	Music (2)	Math
I like recess and the slide and the swings	Reading (1)	Not too much homework
We have a nice school	Math (1)	Music (2)
I like reading and music and math	I feel safe (1)	Reading
Not too much homework	Not too much homework (1)	

CREATE THE INCENTIVE FOR SCHOOL IMPROVEMENT WITH STUDENT LEARNING DATA

To use data effectively in a school requires getting people involved in looking at and using student achievement data. When staff see the comprehensive view of the results they are getting now, they will easily engage in ongoing dialogue of what needs to change to get different results.

The ideal approach would be to have the student achievement data analyzed for the staff so they could spend their time understanding and using it. Unfortunately, this is not always possible. Most schools in our country receive standard reports only—from the test publishers and, if they are lucky, more in-depth reports from their district offices. If they want analyses beyond the standard reports, schools must make a request, sit back and hope their request gets fulfilled. This truly is unfortunate, as we know that school personnel can use data very effectively and usually want to dig deep into the data. Analyzing data leads to teachers' new understandings and renewed commitments to their learning organization and to teaching their students.

Some schools hire outside consultants to help them set up their own systems for data analysis when the district is not willing to make data accessible to teachers and school administrators. Ideally, we would like to see districts set up data warehouses with historical data for the entire district, and then provide online access for school administrators and teachers. (*Designing and Using Databases for School Improvement* [Bernhardt, 2000] will help personnel think through the establishment of a database to assist with the analyses.)

The important point is to analyze measures of data thoroughly, independently, and inter-dependently. As teachers study the results, they will want more and deeper analyses.

Guiding the Discussion of Student Learning Results

Using small groups again, staff could divide up the different student achievement data and graphs, and record what they are seeing, using guiding questions (*Questions to Guide the Analysis of Student Achievement Data*). The questions focus on looking for highest and lowest achieving subtests and subgroups, and their relationships. Other activities for looking at data are included on the CD with Group Processes.

Many school and district representatives want to know how to analyze their student achievement data. While this is addressed in detail in the other Bernhardt books already mentioned, we want schools to use a score that has equal intervals in order to follow cohorts over time, disaggregated by the different demographics of the school. Normal Curve Equivalent (NCE) averages can be used, as shown in Figure 4.6. This graph follows the same groups of female and male students on three different math subtests from grade two to grade four. With NCE averages, we would want to see the subgroups improving over time. If the subgroup scores are not improving over time, one needs to dig deeper to find out why. There are reasons for looking at the same grade level over time for perspective. However, the cohort analyses are much more informative for looking at student progress and school processes.

FIGURE 4.6

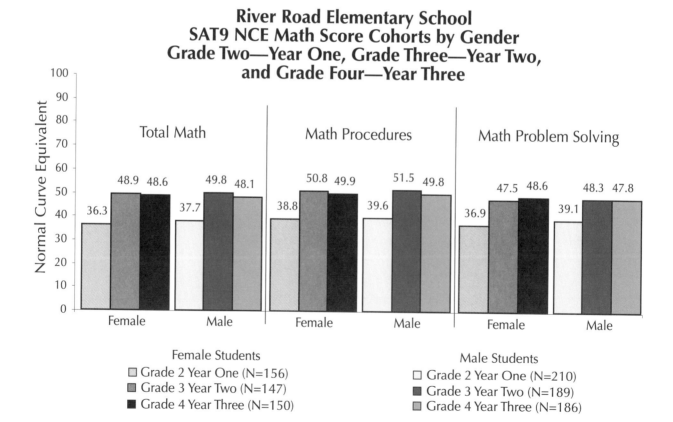

**River Road Elementary School
SAT9 NCE Math Score Cohorts by Gender
Grade Two—Year One, Grade Three—Year Two,
and Grade Four—Year Three**

Female Students
☐ Grade 2 Year One (N=156)
◼ Grade 3 Year Two (N=147)
◼ Grade 4 Year Three (N=150)

Male Students
☐ Grade 2 Year One (N=210)
◼ Grade 3 Year Two (N=189)
◼ Grade 4 Year Three (N=186)

Some other powerful schoolwide analyses involve the distribution of results. Distributions can be created to look at the whole school for one subtest (Figure 4.7), cohorts from grade to grade and year to year (Figure 4.8), and then subgroups of student responses from grade to grade and year to year. One can see the normal curves that form each year in looking at the deciles of student scores. One can also see the normal curve moving to the right in time, indicating that the school is moving most of its distribution of students to the right or "up"; hopefully implying that all students are improving. In the latter analyses, staff would be able to ask themselves questions such as:

▼ Where are our special education students across our distribution?

▼ Are our special education students improving at the same rate as our other students?

▼ Where are our English Language Learner students across our distribution?

▼ Are English Language Learners improving as rapidly as our English Language Speakers?

These questions should lead to the all important question: *What are we doing to teach these special populations?*

FIGURE 4.7

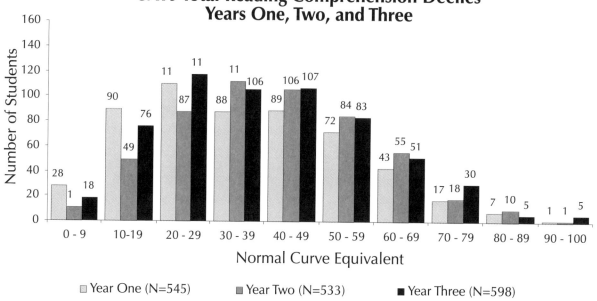

**River Road Elementary School
SAT9 Total Reading Comprehension Deciles
Years One, Two, and Three**

FIGURE 4.8

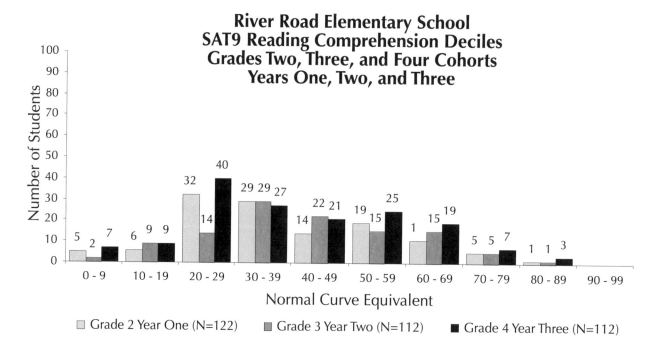

**River Road Elementary School
SAT9 Reading Comprehension Deciles
Grades Two, Three, and Four Cohorts
Years One, Two, and Three**

Frequency tables can also provide powerful information about deciles and quartile performance. A quartile table is shown below (Figure 4.9) for grade three reading comprehension for four years of data. These data are from a state that gives state tests in grades three, six, and ten. Students are in different schools at each of these grade levels. The next step would be to follow these third graders as sixth graders, three years later, in the middle school.

FIGURE 4.9

River Road Elementary School
Grade Three Students
Reading Comprehensive Quartiles from 1998-2001

Quartiles	1998		1999		2000		2001	
	Number	Percent	Number	Percent	Number	Percent	Number	Percent
76 - 99	20	47.6	20	40.0	14	32.6	15	39.5
51 - 75	9	21.4	20	40.0	17	39.5	12	31.6
26 - 50	9	21.4	5	20.0	11	25.6	8	21.1
1 - 25	4	9.5	0	0	1	2.3	3	7.9

This table can be graphed also, such as two versions on the following page. Figure 4.10 shows the number of students scoring at each quartile during this time frame, while Figure 4.11 shows the percentage of students scoring at each quartile, over time.

FIGURE 4.10

Number of Normal Elementary School
Grade Three Students in each
Reading Comprehension Quartile from 1998-2001

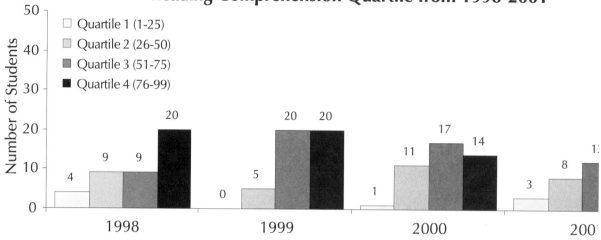

FIGURE 4.11

Percent of River Road Elementary School
Grade Three Students in each
Reading Comprehension Quartile from 1998-2001

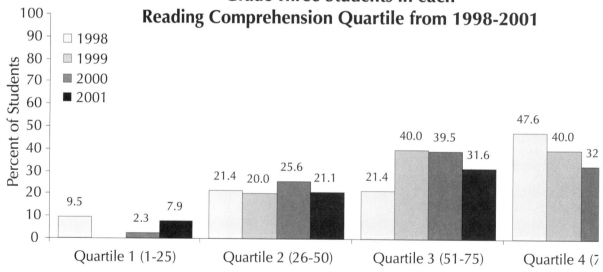

A series of Student Achievement Graphing Templates to guide analyses similar to these shown in Figures 4.6, 4.7, 4.8, 4.9, 4.10, and 4.11, have been provided on the accompanying CD, along with example narratives.

Student Achievement Analyses Related to Multiple Measures

Many schools that qualify for specific federal and/or state funding are required to report student achievement progress in terms of at least three proficiency or achievement levels, over time, and disaggregated by demographics such as gender, ethnicity, and free and reduced lunches. These proficiency levels are often referred to as multiple measures of student achievement, or the triangulation of student achievement data. The main purpose for using multiple measures is to accurately assess student performance related to standards and then to use the data to improve instruction.

The multiple measures assessments provide students with fair, multiple, and varied opportunities to demonstrate what they know and can do. Using multiple measures compensates for the imperfections in every assessment tool.

Examples of multiple measures include:

▼ Student grades
▼ Running records
▼ Norm-referenced test results
▼ Criterion-referenced test results
▼ Writing samples
▼ Oral language samples
▼ Classroom assessments

When using multiple measures, schools and/or school districts must determine cut scores for each measure, gather the results, and determine if each student is proficient with respect to the standard. An example (Figure 4.12 and narrative) ⊛ follows:

FIGURE 4.12

Our Elementary School Reading Proficiency

Norm-Referenced Test — Normal Curve Equivalent

Grades	Reading Scores	1–29	30–39	40–49	50–59	60+
A	6			Meets Grade-level Standard		
	5			Meets Grade-level Standard		
	4			Meets Grade-level Standard		
	3				Meets Grade-level Standard	
	2					
	1					
Grades	Reading Scores	1–29	30–39	40–49	50–59	60+
B	6			Meets Grade-level Standard		
	5			Meets Grade-level Standard		
	4			Meets Grade-level Standard		
	3				Meets Grade-level Standard	
	2					
	1					
Grades	Reading Scores	1–29	30–39	40–49	50–59	60+
C	6			Meets Grade-level Standard		
	5				Meets Grade-level Standard	
	4				Meets Grade-level Standard	
	3					Meets Grade-
	2					
	1					
Grades	Reading Scores	1–29	30–39	40–49	50–59	60+
D/F	6					
	5					
	4					
	3					
	2					
	1					

Our Elementary School's
Multiple Measures Chart

Our Elementary School uses reading grades, a reading assessment rubric, and normal curve equivalent (NCE) scores from their norm-referenced reading assessment as the three multiple measures to determine if students are "proficient in reading." Teachers determined that to be considered proficient with respect to grades, students must receive a C or higher; with respect to the norm-referenced test, they would have to score at or above 50 NCE; and to be proficient with respect to the reading assessment, they would have to score a four or higher on the six-point rubric. Meeting two of the three proficiency levels would declare a student to be proficient. There were some shades of gray involved as well. Teachers did not want to declare a student proficient if she/he scored a D or F, or 1 or 2 on the rubric, or 1-29 on the norm-referenced test, even if she/he exceeded the proficiency levels on the other measures. The teachers designed a table (Figure 4.12) to determine quickly and easily if a student is proficient or not, as measured through their multiple measures.

Analyzing these results, schoolwide, Our Elementary School could calculate the number and percentage of students meeting the reading proficiency at grade three for the past three years as shown in Figure 4.13 below. If the measurements were consistent across grade levels, one could follow the same students in their next grades, over time.

FIGURE 4.13

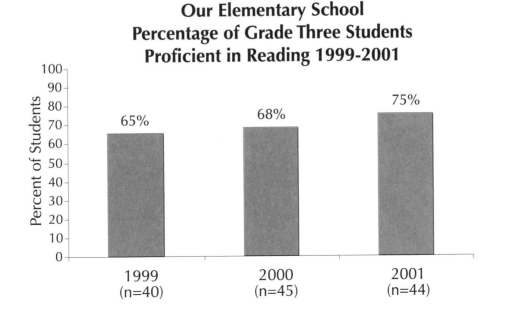

**Our Elementary School
Percentage of Grade Three Students
Proficient in Reading 1999-2001**

Analyses Related to Standards

One way we can make the general analyses just described more powerful would be to link them to curriculum standards. For example—suppose teachers want to know more about implementation of a third grade reading standard. Ultimately, they want to be able to answer the following questions:

▼ What processes are leading students toward meeting the standard by the end of grade three?

▼ Who and why are some students not meeting the standard by the end of grade three?

▼ How do student demographics impact these results?

▼ How does the way students are taught impact the results?

▼ What do we need to do differently to make sure all students meet the standard by the end of grade three?

School personnel might begin their analysis of the standard with a database of all students at the elementary school. From that database, teachers could look at how the third grade students scored overall. They might then separate the students into two clusters: those who met or exceeded the standard, and those who did not meet the standard. Figure 4.14 illustrates the example for the students who do not meet the third grade reading standard. As you work through the flowchart and dig deeper into the data, you can see how demographics, school processes, and perceptions get included in the conversation to improve the results. A similar figure could be made for the students who meet the standard.

FIGURE 4.14

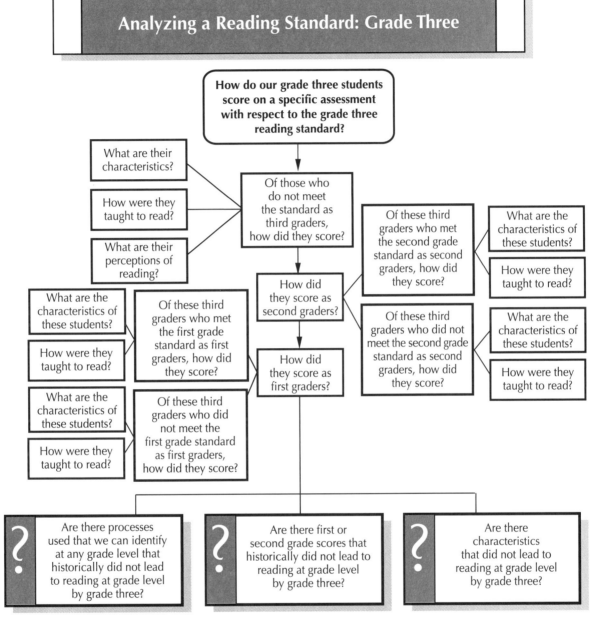

Analyzing a Reading Standard: Grade Three

How do our grade three students score on a specific assessment with respect to the grade three reading standard?

What are their characteristics?

How were they taught to read?

What are their perceptions of reading?

Of those who do not meet the standard as third graders, how did they score?

Of these third graders who met the second grade standard as second graders, how did they score?

What are the characteristics of these students?

How were they taught to read?

How did they score as second graders?

Of these third graders who did not meet the second grade standard as second graders, how did they score?

What are the characteristics of these students?

How were they taught to read?

What are the characteristics of these students?

How were they taught to read?

Of these third graders who met the first grade standard as first graders, how did they score?

How did they score as first graders?

What are the characteristics of these students?

How were they taught to read?

Of these third graders who did not meet the first grade standard as first graders, how did they score?

? Are there processes used that we can identify at any grade level that historically did not lead to reading at grade level by grade three?

? Are there first or second grade scores that historically did not lead to reading at grade level by grade three?

? Are there characteristics that did not lead to reading at grade level by grade three?

To find out who these students are and how their learning experiences add up to current results, one of the first things educators would want to know is the demographics of the students falling into this category as defined by gender, ethnicity, mobility, home language, socioeconomic status, etc. To learn more about how previous scores relate to third grade scores, each student's second grade scores, as well as first grade scores, could be reviewed. This breakdown could reveal more about the standard (i.e., Must students meet the first grade standard at a certain level in order to meet the third grade standard? Must students meet the second grade standard at a certain level in order to meet the third grade standard?). In fact, from these breakdowns, one can see whether there are students who met the standard one year and not the next two years, or whether there are students who met the standard for two years and not one year—and determine which year might be the most important for reaching the third-grade standard. Then, by looking at the characteristics of the students by previous scores, one could see if standards attainment is related to language fluency, to one particular element of demographics, or perhaps to the way students are taught. We really cannot know until we dig deeper.

By clustering students in different ways and thinking about how they were taught to read at each grade level (school processes), teachers could become clearer about the results they are getting. Clarifying how results are achieved will also clarify how processes need to be altered to get results that would ensure the success of all students and prevent student failures.

In fact, our ultimate goal in digging deeper is to "predict" and "prevent" student failures. In other words, historical student achievement data can be used to identify factors that can help teachers know when to intervene to prevent potential failure later on. For example, teachers would want to know the answer to the following question: For any subtest or test, are there first or second grade scores that never lead to reading at grade level by grade three?

We might find that any first grader scoring a 12 NCE (Normal Curve Equivalent) on a particular subtest historically never read at grade level by grade three. This would be extremely important information to have. In the following years, if a first grade student scores at 12 or below, teachers would want to intervene to do whatever is necessary to ensure that student's success. (Article by Victoria Bernhardt: *Databases Can Help Teachers with Standards Implementation* [CASCD, 1999].)

Standards Implementation

Implementing standards has two important parts. First, curriculum alignment to national and state standards is critical for success in achieving on state tests. Also, monitoring the curriculum is much easier if the curriculum is aligned. The second part is deciding and setting a local performance standard. At what level do we want students to perform? Setting a standard helps us to diagnose achievement of individual students and our programs in order to understand strengths and weaknesses in our school.

A good tool for understanding how to set a local standard is the frequency table. For schools considering multiple measures of student achievement, the frequency table (Figure 4.15) helps teachers to see how different types of assessments measure achievement.

For example, if students do well on one type of assessment, but not on another, what does that mean for instruction?

FIGURE 4.15

Quartile/ Performance Level Disaggregations

Norm Referenced Test	99 - 76 4th Quartile	75 - 51 3rd Quartile	50 - 26 2nd Quartile		25 - 1 1st Quartile
State Assessment	**Advanced** Reading (100-93) Math 4/7 (100-75) Math 10 (100-70) Writing (5.0-4.40)	**Proficient** Reading (92-87) Math 4/7 (74-60) Math 10 (69-60) Writing (4.39-3.75)	**Satisfactory** Reading (86-80) Math (59-48) Math 10 (59-48) Writing (3.74-3.0)	**Basic** Reading (79-68) Math (47-35) Math 10 (47-35) Writing (2.99-2.3)	**Unsatisfactory** Reading (67-0) Math (34-0) Math 10 (34-0) Writing (2.29-0)
Local Rubric 1 - 4 Scale	**4** Exceeds the Standard	**3** Meets the Standard	**2** Not Yet At Standard		**1** Needs Improvement

Above example of a frequency table
contributed by Sherry Reed & the QPA Crew,
Southeast Kansas Education Service Center — Greenbush, KS

Analyzing Student Achievement at the Classroom Level

Classroom teachers would benefit from having a database that would allow them to track student progress toward standards attainment throughout the year. Such a database would need to be supported by the teachers' attention to the processes used to help students achieve the standard. The teachers' ability to recognize processes that need to change would be supported by the information received from the data.

Figure 4.16 is an illustration of questions that can be answered through the use of a classroom database supporting standards implementation. At the beginning of the year, the teacher would identify the standard for the end of the year, and at the end of each quarter, including what it will look like when students meet the standard. Additionally, the teacher would start the year with historical assessment information on each student in her/his classroom. At multiple times during the year (e.g., quarterly), student progress related to the standard would be assessed. At each assessment, the teacher would see who is not making progress toward meeting the standard, to understand if the students not meeting the standard are having difficulty with similar or different concepts, and to intervene with different methods of instruction for those students. The data can also assist with the recommendation of different methods of instruction by looking at what has worked with other students of similar needs and issues.

Analyzing student achievement is discussed in depth in *Designing and Using Databases for School Improvement*, (Bernhardt, 2000), pages 74-81.

FIGURE 4.16

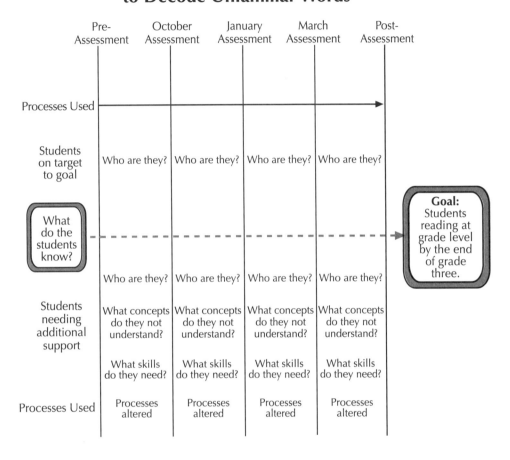

A Third-Grade Reading Standard:
Use Knowledge of Complex Word Families
to Decode Unfamiliar Words

	Pre-Assessment	October Assessment	January Assessment	March Assessment	Post-Assessment
Processes Used					→
Students on target to goal	Who are they?	Who are they?	Who are they?	Who are they?	
What do the students know?					**Goal:** Students reading at grade level by the end of grade three.
	Who are they?	Who are they?	Who are they?	Who are they?	
Students needing additional support	What concepts do they not understand?	What concepts do they not understand?	What concepts do they not understand?	What concepts do they not understand?	
	What skills do they need?	What skills do they need?	What skills do they need?	What skills do they need?	
Processes Used	Processes altered	Processes altered	Processes altered	Processes altered	

Digging Deeper into the Data

After a strong overview of schoolwide data disaggregated in many ways, teachers generally ask for help with data analyses at the classroom levels and/or ways to improve all students' results. Good data analyses lead to requests for more and deeper analyses.

Teachers love the distribution graphs, such as the ones in Figures 4.7 and 4.8 on page 64, and they usually want to dig deeper into what the analyses are telling them. The activity described on the following pages will help teachers understand *how* to move the distribution upward, or to the right. The activity could also be used to understand *who* in the distribution moved to the right, or into the next decile.

Digging Deeper: Teacher Analysis of Test Scores Activity

The *Teacher Analysis of Test Scores Activity* and templates 💿 will help teachers understand which students scored in the bottom deciles in the grade-level distribution and why, and can be adapted for grades, rubrics, or other assessments. The analysis can also be adapted to disaggregate the data by gender, ethnicity, or socioeconomic levels. Digging deeper consists of four steps:

▼ Identify students falling in the bottom 50th percentile deciles.

▼ Reflect on the topics (objectives) or content clusters that are lowest.

▼ Identify who, or where, the concepts are taught and how.

▼ Discuss how the concepts are being taught, how they should be taught, and changes that can be made within and across grade levels (or subject areas).

Step 1: Identify students falling in the bottom deciles.

Figure 4.17 identifies students who fall into the bottom 50th percentile deciles of the SAT9 Reading Comprehension subtest. The left-hand column of Figure 4.17 shows the bottom five deciles. Content clusters for Reading Comprehension are written across the first row. This grid is set-up for teachers to list the names of the students who fell into each of these bottom deciles for each content cluster. When this table is complete, you will be able to see the concepts with which students are having the most difficulty, and perhaps why the individual students are receiving low overall scores. Teachers will also be able to understand if it is one concept or five concepts that need to be taught differently.

With this table, teachers can focus on the lowest students, as well as the students who are scoring just barely below the 50th percentile or NCE (Normal Curve Equivalent). Those scoring close to the 50th percentile or NCE can be tutored and/or re-taught by a different teacher to get them over the 50th percentile by the next testing period.

FIGURE 4.17

Digging Deeper: Who is Scoring on the Bottom?
Reading Comprehension

Content Cluster (NCE)	Recreational	Textual	Functional	Initial Understanding	Interpretation
40 — 49	Carlos, Jon, Maria, Gina	Maria	Karen, Gina	Karen, Gina	
30 — 39	Peter, Karen, Billy	Susie, Billy, Peter, Karen, Gina	Carlos, Jon, Billy	Jon	Karen, Gina, Carlos, Jon, Billy
20 — 29	Susie	Carlos, Jon	Peter, Susie	Carlos, Bill, Maria	Peter
10 — 19			Maria	Peter, Susie	Susie, Maria
0 — 9			Carlos		

Step 2: Reflect on the content clusters that are lowest.

After the student table is completed, have staff reflect on the topics (objectives) or content clusters that are lowest, and the content clusters that are closest to reaching the 50th percentile. Most of the time there will be a trend, or one or several content clusters will stand out as being the most troublesome to the lowest scoring students.

Step 3: Identify which teachers are teaching the concepts and clarify how the concepts are taught.

Build a table, as shown in Figure 4.18, to identify who, or where, the concepts are taught and how. At the elementary level, teachers might want to adjust this grid to show in which subjects the concepts are taught. The resulting discussion could lead to meaningful process changes, needs for professional development, or even new programs, which is the goal of Step 4 of this activity. Perhaps by using process flowcharts, teachers can clarify how they teach specific concepts. (Discussed later in this chapter.)

FIGURE 4.18

Digging Deeper: Who is Teaching the Concepts?
Reading Comprehension

Objectives	Ms. Campbell	Mr. Green	Mrs. Kelley	Mr. Mason	Mr. Newton	Mr. Dodd	Mrs. Taylor
Recreational	✓	✓	✓			✓	
Textual	✓	✓	✓			✓	
Functional	✓	✓	✓			✓	✓
Initial Understanding	✓	✓				✓	✓
Interpretation	✓	✓	✓		✓	✓	
Critical Analysis	✓	✓	✓	✓	✓	✓	
Process Analysis	✓	✓	✓	✓		✓	

Step 4: Discuss how the concepts need to be taught and changes that can be made within and across grade levels (or subject areas) to ensure student attainment of the concepts.

Discuss how the concepts are being taught, how they should be taught, and changes that can be made within and across grade levels (or subject areas) to ensure student attainment of the content. As a variation, place cross grade-level teachers together to follow students across grade levels, over time, to understand individual student growth.

Any of these steps can be adjusted to focus on grade level, cross-grade level, or subject-specific content.

CREATE THE INCENTIVE FOR SCHOOL IMPROVEMENT WITH PROCESS DATA

Often we hear, "We have tried everything. There is no way to get these scores to improve." And then the excuses begin . . . sometimes schools at this point have not disaggregated their student achievement data or followed their cohorts of students over time. Other times they have done this and need some new information to move them to another place.

Flowcharting tools are visual pathways for taking staff to that next level. Ask staff to draw a picture of their processes using these tools. You might ask, "What are you doing to move students through your system with respect to reading?" or "What are you doing to teach reading in your classroom?"

Flowcharting tools are described in *Data Analysis for Comprehensive Schoolwide Improvement* (Bernhardt, 1998), starting on page 97. A summary is provided below and as an activity on the CD.

Charting School Processes

A flowchart can help describe and visualize a process. A flowchart allows everyone to see the major steps in a process, in sequence, and then evaluate the difference between the theoretical and actual, or actual and desired—by describing what teachers would like to be doing, and then by describing what teachers are really doing, or vice versa.

Typical symbols used in flowcharting follow:

A flowchart is a visualization of a process—a process everyone can see and understand in the same way.

Steps in establishing flowcharts follow:

▼ Define the beginning and the end of the process being charted.

▼ Decide on the level of detail to be used.

▼ Determine the major steps in the process and their sequence.

▼ Label each step in the process.

▼ Verify the flowchart. Is it clear?

▼ Evaluate. Compare the charted version of the process to the "desired" flow.

Understanding processes (e.g., instruction and assessment strategies, programs) is important because if we want different results, we must change the processes that bring about those results. *We cannot continue to do the same things over and over and expect different results.*

With respect to reading processes, we often find that schools will assess their students informally (or formally) and then place the bottom 20 percent in individualized instruction (no matter the grade level—elementary, middle, or high school). (See Figure 4.19 below.) When teachers review their processes in comparison with the results they are getting, they get their insights about what needs to change.

Using the standard and data, instead of 20 percent, teachers can see that the number of students not meeting the standard might not be 20 percent, it might be more, or less. The process identified in Figure 4.19 would then be incongruent with the needs of the students.

FIGURE 4.19

Typical Process Flowchart

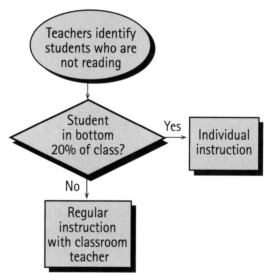

While the beginning flow of Figure 4.20 does not look that much different from Figure 4.19, making decisions using the standard and data would enable teachers to know exactly how many students need additional work. Instead of thinking in terms of a specific percentage of students to place in individualized instruction, perhaps a new approach to teaching reading must be considered for the classroom and the school.

FIGURE 4.20

Process Flowchart with Standard

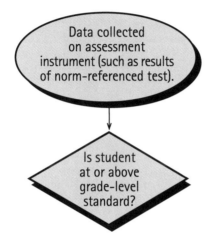

With the use of a database and data analysis, teachers and administrators can understand the congruence of their processes to the needs of the students. With the use of a database and data analysis, teachers and administrators would easily see who is not meeting the standard and what concepts or skills are not being achieved. (*Designing and Using Databases for School Improvement* [Bernhardt, 2000].)

Another type of flowchart is called the top-down flowchart as shown in Figure 4.21. This is probably the easiest and fastest way to chart processes. In a top-down flowchart one simply follows the primary steps of the process being analyzed and under each primary step writes in the secondary steps, and so on. A template for top-down flowcharting appears on the CD, along with an activity related to flowcharting. 🔘

FIGURE 4.21

Top-Down Flowchart

1a	Instructional Strategies	2a	Assessment Strategies	3a	Groupings
1b	If reading at or above grade level—regular instruction with classroom teacher using Reading Recovery strategies.	2b	All students assessed at the beginning of first grade level using Clay's Observational Survey. All students assessed using the Text Level and Dictation subtests mid-year and at the end of the year.	3b	Regular students are grouped in the classroom by ability and by Family Learning Teams.
1c	If below grade level and in the bottom 20% of the class—individual instruction with resource staff as part of the formal Reading Recovery program.	2c	Same as above.	3c	Reading Recovery students are grouped in the classroom by ability and by Family Learning Teams.
1d	If below grade level and not in bottom 20% of the class—Literacy Group instruction using Reading Recovery strategies with resource staff.	2d	Same as above.	3d	Literacy Group students are grouped in the classroom by ability and by Family Learning Teams.
1e	If not able to graduate from Reading Recovery program into Literacy Group or regular classroom—referred to the resource or special education program staff for additional assessment, or to receive additional ESL instruction.	2e	Same as above.	3e	Students grouped by program.

Continuous Improvement Continuum assessments are another way to analyze school processes. This approach 🔘 has already been described in Chapter 3.

CREATE THE INCENTIVE FOR SCHOOL IMPROVEMENT WITH ALL DATA

Most of the time different data elements will appear in bits and pieces, as would be implied from the previous descriptions. Fortunate schools with good data support systems might get the data all at once. The challenge becomes—how do we comprehend all these data independently and interdependently?

The Gallery Walk

One approach might be to set up a gallery walk to display all the data gathered by the school. The gallery would consist of enlarged graphs posted on the walls, including student achievement graphs, questionnaire graphs, demographic graphs, the results of the *Continuous Improvement Continuums* assessments, and process flowcharts. If the school has gone this far, a list of the school's values and beliefs, purpose, mission, and shared vision are also worth posting in the Gallery Walk. Next to each group of graphs should be a blank piece of chart paper with guiding questions across the top. These questions might be: *What do these data tell us about our strengths?* and *What do these data tell us about what needs to be improved?* Staff would then divide into small groups, walk around and look at the graphs, discussing the results, and documenting what they are seeing, not seeing, and listing other things they need to know.

**Set-up of a gallery walk:
Data graphs with chart paper for staff
members to write their observations.**

The results of the gallery walk would then be reviewed and staff, as a whole, in conjunction with what the school expects students to know and be able to do, would discuss, *What are the implications for school improvement?* and *What objectives do we need to set and how will we measure them?* This is a great activity to do around gap analysis, goal setting, and planning times (discussed in Chapters 5 and 6).

**Staff members viewing graphs
and writing their impressions**

Other activities that can be used to process all data with staff include: the *Fishbowl Activity*, the *Data Discovery Activity*, and the *Intersections Activities.*

Focusing the Data Around a Challenge:
The Problem-Solving Cycle

When the overall data points to a "challenge" or "problem" area, or when solutions are being considered, it is best to look at all the data before jumping onto solutions. The problem-solving cycle is a process to get everyone involved in looking at and using comprehensive school data, as well as a way to follow-up and dig deeper into problem areas. This process gives everyone on staff a chance to get her or his voice in the room before any data are considered, which makes it more probable that everyone will get involved in the solution when the data are analyzed.

The problem-solving cycle is described in depth in *Data Analysis for Comprehensive Schoolwide Improvement*, (Bernhardt, 1998), beginning on page 144, and is shown below in Figure 4.22. A description of the activity and worksheets to use with staffs are provided on the CD.

The first step requires an objective statement of the "problem." Step two asks staff to brainstorm why this "problem" exists. In step three, staff lists the questions they want to answer about the problem and the data required to answer the questions.

What will result within the first three steps is a comprehensive data analysis that will provide information about the problem, and put old "hunches and hypotheses" to rest. (As one can see, the entire nine-step process can be used later on to implement and improve processes.)

FIGURE 4.22

Problem-Solving Cycle

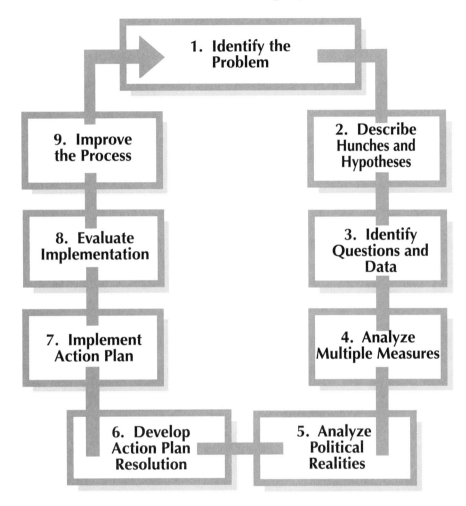

Note. From *Data Analysis for Comprehensive Schoolwide Improvement* (p.144), by Victoria L. Bernhardt, 1998, Larchmont, NY: Eye on Education. Copyright © 1998 Eye on Education, Inc. Reprinted with permission.

INTERSECTING THE DATA

As Figure 4.1 (Multiple Measures of Data, page 48) and the text of this chapter implies, each type of data, (e.g., demographic, student learning, perceptions, school processes), analyzed independently, provides important information. Intersecting the different types of data allows us to answer even broader questions. On the CD are two different activities for creating questions from intersecting data, *Intersections Activity* and *Creating Intersections Activity*. 🔾 Also on the CD is an article published in the Journal of Staff Development (2000, Winter), entitled *Intersections: New Routes Open when One Type of Data Crosses Another*. 🔾

GETTING TO ROOT CAUSES

Root causes are the real problems within our schools. We need to find out what these root causes are so we can eliminate the true problem and not just the symptom. The problem-solving cycle can uncover root causes. With the problem-solving cycle, it is easy to brainstorm why we think the problem exists. These reasons will hopefully surface the root or contributing cause of the "problem." The real knowing comes from looking at the data and answering a series of questions, including:

▼ Would the problem have occurred if the cause had not been present?

▼ Will the problem reoccur if the cause is corrected?

If the answers to these questions are "no," you are surfacing a root cause. If the answer is "yes," you may be looking at a contributing cause. For further study on root causes, see *A School Leader's Guide to Root Cause Analysis*, (Paul Preuss, 2000).

Another way to get to root causes is to have staff teams review, analyze the data, and ask probing questions to uncover the root causes:

▼ What data are indicating there is a problem or problems?

▼ What other indicators are there that might be related, using another piece of data?

Most problems within schools are caused by systems rather than people. Improvement of the system will result in reduction or removal of the problem. Teams that include processes in their analyses tend to not jump to solutions or conclusions as quickly as those who do not. At some point, when searching for the root cause, one must realize that the "problem" is really a result. What we are trying to do with these analyses is to uncover how we get our results. These very same processes can be used to uncover how we get our successes. Analyzing root causes has been written as an activity. ⊛ The *Cause and Effect* and *Affinity Diagram Activities* ⊛ can also be used to identify root causes.

SUMMARY

Most of the data gathered for continuous school improvement planning are placed in the Information and Analysis section of the school portfolio. These data should be comprehensive enough to answer the questions:

▼ Who are we?

▼ How do we do business?

▼ Where are we now?

These analyses are necessary for building the context of the school, understanding areas needing improvement, and identifying strengths.

FREQUENTLY ASKED QUESTIONS ABOUT INFORMATION AND ANALYSIS

▼ **Is it survey or questionnaire?**

Survey is a verb and is sometimes used as a noun. *Questionnaire* is a noun. To be correct, we survey students using a questionnaire. However, both are used interchangeably and are accepted in practice.

▼ **How do you determine the items to put into a questionnaire?**

Ideally, we would like the questions in our questionnaires to help a school know if it is getting to its vision, and if not—why not?

For example: The Education for the Future staff questionnaire asks questions that relate to staff's philosophies of the seven continuums (e.g., Do staff agree on the strategies that will increase student achievement? Is there a leadership structure in place that supports staff in implementing one shared vision?).

The Education for the Future student questionnaire asks students if they feel the way schools want them to feel when their vision is implemented (e.g., At school, I feel: safe; like I belong; I have choices in what I learn; adults think I can do the work).

Think about what you want to have happen at the school and avoid using questions that can be answered from another source or database. (e.g., For parents, often the tendency is to ask, *Did you attend Back to School Night?* You can gather this information from a guest register or you know which parents attended through other sources.) Resource: *Data Analysis for Comprehensive Schoolwide Improvement* (Bernhardt, 1998)—Appendix A is devoted to questionnaire construction; Appendix B shows sample questionnaires.

▼ **How do we disaggregate questionnaire data?**

First, you need to ask questions on the questionnaire that will allow you to disaggregate data, such as gender and ethnicity. We recommend asking these questions in a separate data box. Once you have the data from the questionnaires in a database or spreadsheet, it is a simple, technical issue of sorting the data by the responses to the items by which you want to disaggregate.

▼ **Can we code the questionnaires by student I.D. number so that we can compare question results to student records?**

Yes, you can. However, if you tell students that the questionnaires are anonymous, which tends to elicit the most honest responses, it would be inappropriate to code the questionnaires.

▼ **What is the best way to administer the questionnaires?**

The highly recommended best way to administer the questionnaires is electronically through a database program. We recommend setting up questionnaires on the computer so that they can be taken online and the results sent to a database that easily exports the calculated results to a graphing program. (Resource: *School IQ* on *The School Portfolio Toolkit* CD) Automate as much as possible.

Most schools or districts have scanning machines. If questionnaires can be set up on a scan-readable form for completion and scanning later, the results can be exported into spreadsheet form to eventually create graphs. It is ideal to design your own forms, if you can, so that the questions and response options are on the same page. Avoid having the questions on one page and the response options on another, which could lead to errors in completing the questionnaire. You must check the software that comes with the scanner to make sure this is possible. Most schools have computers that provide ways to complete questionnaires online making administration more fun and results accessible quickly.

▼ **How many response options should be made available per question?**

Statisticians vary as to the number of response options that should be made available per item. Some believe that you cannot discriminate between responses unless you have a 99-point scale. Others believe that seven points are necessary, while others feel that three to five points are fine for their purposes. We want enough response options so that we can distinguish between a *passionate* response and a *sort of* response. We have used seven, five, four, and three-point scales. We typically use a five-point scale, with *one* as strongly disagree; *two* as disagree; *three* as neutral or neither agree nor disagree; *four* as agree; and *five* as strongly agree. Our response options start on the left with one, and go to five, from the least to the most because it is brain-compatible. We are used to thinking from left to right and from the lowest to the highest number. If we interfere with this structure, we run the risk of respondents not completing the questionnaires. Many schools want the most positive response option to be first so those respondents will not see the negative option first. Actually, that is counter to the way the mind works, so you may be confusing your respondents. Help them out as much as possible.

▼ **When you provide neutral response options, don't averages turn out to be neutral?**

We have found that when what we are asking is very clear—and respondents know how to respond to the questions—neutral is a valid option. Scores do not typically average to be neutral, unless the question is unclear. Additionally, we want equal intervals in a scale to calculate averages. There is too much of a gap between agree and disagree, much greater than between agree and strongly agree, for instance. A middle point helps.

One of the reasons we encourage distribution graphs of the response options (e.g., bar graph of numbers or percentages responding one, two, three, four, and five) is that we are able to see if a three on a scale means that half of the people disagreed and half of them agreed, or if everyone responded with a three. If everybody felt neutral, that would give us a clue to look further into that question to see if the question was clear or if people did not have an obvious response for that item. If you are getting neutral responses to your questionnaire items, the first thing to look for are conjunctions in the questions (i.e., *and*, *or*).

▼ **At what grade are student responses to the questionnaires meaningful?**

We have had limited success using student questionnaires below the third grade. While students can often read the questions, they have difficulty completing the questionnaire if a teacher is not working with them as they complete the questionnaire. Some teachers use questionnaires for test practice with their students.

Students often need coaching on the word "neutral" and with identifying their ethnicity correctly. If giving questionnaires to third graders and below, consider using a three-point scale (1=Disagree, 2=Neutral, 3=Agree) or smiley faces. ☹ ☺ ☺

▼ How do you go from a questionnaire to a graph?

We want questionnaires designed for easy analysis and graph building. If we automate the administration of questionnaires, the graphing can be very easy, as long as the entire process has been thought through before beginning. We use the Chart Wizard in *Microsoft Excel* to make building graphs simple and fun. Questionnaire graphing templates are on the CD.

▼ What do demographic data have to do with student achievement?

Demographics are very important to use in conjunction with student achievement score analyses. The combination allows us to disaggregate data; that is, to pull out different student groups in order to see if each group is performing in a similar fashion or experiencing school in the same way. If we truly believe that all students can achieve, we really want to see every student and subgroups of students able to achieve. If we truly believe that all of our students should be experiencing school in the same way, we ought not to see differences when we split groups. Demographic information helps us get rid of hunches and hypotheses and replace them with facts.

▼ What standardized test do you recommend?

We cannot recommend a standardized test. What your school and/or district needs to do is to get descriptions and example test items from as many different sources as possible to see if they are congruent with what you are trying to do and with the state curriculum standards. Read about what other schools are doing and what they are finding. Ideally, consistent tests at every grade level will give you the most "predictive" power.

▼ Isn't it illegal to disaggregate student achievement data by ethnicity and socioeconomic status?

No, it is not illegal to disaggregate student achievement data by ethnicity or SES. It is a way of seeing if your school is meeting the

Consistent measures, over time, preferably at each grade level, are necessary to follow students over time and to show growth.

needs of all the students in your population. The *purpose* for the data is what is really important. It is not done to show differences or inequities or to build prejudices. Student achievement is disaggregated to ensure that all students are achieving, regardless of background. It is also a way of making sure that students do not fall through the cracks.

▼ How do you respond to someone who "only wants to raise test scores"?

One might suggest that we need to focus on processes that will help us know how to meet student-learning needs while raising test scores.

▼ How do you adjust to compare apples with apples and oranges with oranges if your school/district is using a different test at many different grade levels?

It might be time to rethink that assessment strategy. There is no good reason for changing tests at different grade levels. Consistent measures, over time, preferably at each grade level, are necessary to follow students over time and to show growth.

▼ What is significant impact? How do you know? What is real improvement?

Some people feel that we must look at significant differences or significant improvement to know if we really did improve. Others feel that any improvement is significant. For the most part, our bias is to focus on comprehensive analyses, understand impact, and not spend time focusing on significant differences. Technically, the term "significant difference" should only be used within the context of inferential statistics and probability theory.

▼ How do you use qualitative and quantitative data together to make sense?

When schools put their questionnaire results up next to their student achievement results, they are often surprised at the implied relationship—especially with disaggregated subgroup data. In other words, the students having difficulty getting high scores are likely to be the students having difficulty getting along with other students, or feeling as if they do not belong.

▼ **Where do you begin with a staff with limited experience with data collection and analysis and no experience in shared decision making?**

Start with data that are not so threatening, such as questionnaire data. Have staff determine highest and lowest responses and their relationships. One can also look at student achievement data analyzed at the school level. You might want to use a gallery walk approach as mentioned in this chapter and have a facilitator guide your discussions.

The best way to get staff over the fear of data is to put some quality data in front of them and help them see what the data are telling them. Good data lead to requests for more good data.

▼ **How do you convince teachers that data will help?**

You might not be able to convince them. But you can *show* them. It is best if they can see for themselves.

▼ **How do you help teachers understand the importance of data at the classroom levels?**

Our experience has shown that when teachers see and ultimately use quality data at the school level, they ultimately ask for data at the classroom level. Also giving teachers the data in a "picture" or graphic form has more impact than tables or numbers.

YOUR QUESTIONS

▼ What are your data telling you?

▼ What other data do you need to collect?

▼ What data analyses do you want to perform with your staff?

ON THE CD RELATED TO INFORMATION AND ANALYSIS AND THE DATA

▼ Items to Include in the Information and Analysis Section of the School Portfolio

▼ Information and Analysis Continuous Improvement Continuum

▼ Frequently Asked Questions About Information and Analysis

▼ Articles
  ◆ *Multiple Measures*
  ◆ *Databases Can Help Teachers with Standards Implementation*
  ◆ *Intersections: New Routes Open when One Type of Data Crosses Another*

▼ Demographics
  ◆ School Profile
  ◆ Community Profile
  ◆ Administrator Profile
  ◆ Teacher Profile
  ◆ Demographic Graphing Templates
  ◆ Questions to Guide the Analysis of Demographic Data
  ◆ History Gram Activity

▼ Perceptions
  ◆ Questionnaires:
    • Student Grade K-3
    • Student Grade 1-6
    • Student Grade 6-12
    • High School Student
    • Staff
    • Teachers Predicting Student Grade 1-6 Responses
    • Teachers Predicting Student Grade 6-8 Responses
    • Grade K-8 Parent
    • High School Parent
  ◆ Administering the Questionnaires
  ◆ *School IQ* (School Improvement Questionnaire Solutions):
    • Getting Started
    • Using Help

- Graphing Templates
- Online Templates
- Questions to Guide the Analysis of Perceptions Data
- Analysis of Questionnaire Data Table
- Example Narrative of Student Questionnaire Responses
- Example Graphs (ethnicity, gender, and grade questionnaire line graphs)
- Example Bar Graphs (for questionnaire items)

▼ Student Achievement Results
- Questions to Guide the Analysis of Student Achievement Data
- Student Achievement Graphing Templates:
  - NCE Scores Graphing Templates
  - NCE Decile Graphing Templates
  - Quartile Graphing Templates
  - Quartile Table Templates
- Example Narrative of Student Achievement Graphs
- Example School Multiple Measures Narrative
- Example School Multiple Measures Graphing Template
- Teacher Analysis of Test Scores Activity
- Teacher Analysis of Test Scores Tables 1 and 2 Templates

▼ School Processes
- Charting School Processes Activity
- Top-Down Flowcharting Template

▼ All Data
- Gallery Walk Activity and Questions
- Fishbowl Activity
- Data Discovery Activity
- Intersections Activity
- Creating Intersections Activity
- Problem-Solving Cycle Activity
- Root Causes Activity
- Cause and Effect Analysis Activity
- Affinity Diagram Activity

▼ Information and Analysis Section Templates
- Information and Analysis Template
- Questionnaire Results Template
- Student Achievement Results Template

CHAPTER 5

STUDENT ACHIEVEMENT:
Creating a Vision

Chapter Objective: TO SUPPORT THE BUILDING OF A VISION THAT IS TRULY SHARED BY ALL MEMBERS OF THE STAFF

Creating a vision is like...

Rowing a boat—you get to the destination a lot faster if the whole team rows in unison.

Playing in a band. Each person plays her or his instrument to the best of her or his ability—together the result is beautiful and rich.

A family deciding where to go for a vacation...

Professional Development Day, August 2000
Mabton School District, Washington

THE SCHOOL PORTFOLIO REFLECTS CONTINUOUS SCHOOL IMPROVEMENT PLANNING

The school portfolio is a comprehensive approach to Continuous School Improvement Planning for increasing student learning achievement. Continuous School Improvement Planning is the process of determining the long-term vision, purpose, and goals of the school and how to fulfill them. This process can be achieved through answering a series of questions.

Figure 5.1 shows how strategic questions can be answered to create a continuous school improvement plan and where you would place these answers in the school portfolio.

FIGURE 5.1

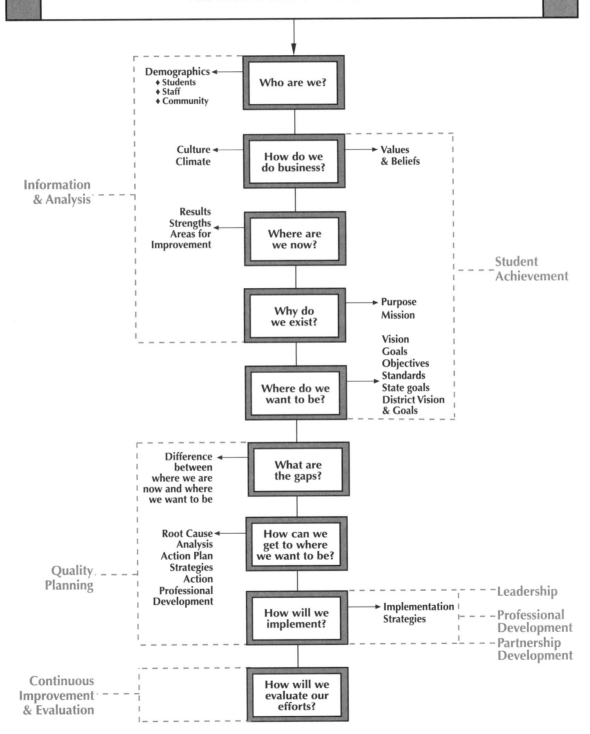

**Continuous School Improvement Planning
via The School Portfolio**

Demographics
♦ Students
♦ Staff
♦ Community

Who are we?

Culture
Climate

How do we
do business?

Values
& Beliefs

Information
& Analysis

Results
Strengths
Areas for
Improvement

Where are
we now?

Why do
we exist?

Purpose
Mission

Student
Achievement

Where do we
want to be?

Vision
Goals
Objectives
Standards
State goals
District Vision
& Goals

Difference
between
where we are
now and where
we want to be

What are
the gaps?

Root Cause
Analysis
Action Plan
Strategies
Action
Professional
Development

How can we
get to where
we want to be?

Quality
Planning

How will we
implement?

Implementation
Strategies

Leadership

Professional
Development

Partnership
Development

Continuous
Improvement
& Evaluation

How will we
evaluate our
efforts?

> **Continuous School Improvement Planning** is the process of determining the long-term vision, purpose, and goals of the school and how to fulfill them.

▼ *Question 1: Who are we?*

Continuous school improvement planning begins by asking the same question we answer with demographic data in Information and Analysis: *Who are we?* Specifically—

◆ Who are the students?

◆ Who are the staff?

◆ Who is the community?

The answers to question one are important in understanding the school's clients, the staff, the community, and to help determine future needs.

▼ *Question 2: How do we do business?*

The second question, *How do we do business?*, is answered through data related to the school's culture and climate, as measured with perceptive data, school processes, and values and beliefs. Most of these elements would be found in the Information and Analysis section of the school portfolio. Values and beliefs, addressed through questionnaires, are also a key component in building the vision, as described in the Student Achievement section of the school portfolio and in this chapter.

▼ *Question 3: Where are we now?*

The third data question, *Where are we now?*, requires a synthesis of student achievement, perceptions, demographic, and school process data to describe results and to uncover strengths, weaknesses, and needs.

▼ *Question 4: Why do we exist?*

The question, *Why do we exist?*, can be answered through determining the purpose/mission of the school, as described in this chapter and documented in the Student Achievement section of the school portfolio.

▼ *Question 5: Where do we want to be?*

This question is documented in the Student Achievement section of the school portfolio and is described in this chapter. *Where do we want to be?* is answered mostly through a schools vision, based on goals, objectives, and standards.

▼ *Question 6: What are the gaps?*

With the vision identified, we must understand the gaps between *Where we are now?* and *Where we want to be?* Gaps are determined by synthesizing the differences in the results the school is getting with its current process and the results the school wants to be getting for its students. This synthesis most often is found in Quality Planning; however, it could appear in Information and Analysis.

▼ *Question 7: How can we get to where we want to be?*

This question is found in the Quality Planning section of the school portfolio. *How can we get to where we want to be?* is key to unlocking how the vision will be implemented and how the gaps will be eliminated. The action plan, made up of strategies, actions, due date, timelines, responsibilities, and resources, needs to be created to achieve the vision and goals, and eliminate the gaps. This critical information is displayed in the Quality Planning section of the school portfolio and is described in detail in Chapter 6.

▼ *Question 8: How will we implement?*

This question is answered in the action plan. It includes how the vision will be implemented and monitored to ensure that it is implemented, including clarification of how decisions will be made, identification of professional development required to learn new skills and gain new knowledge, and the use of partners to achieve the vision. These parts are elaborated on in their own sections of the school portfolio, (i.e., Leadership, Professional Development, and Partnership Development), and are described in Chapters 7, 8, and 9, respectively.

▼ *Question 9: How will we evaluate our efforts?*

Continuous Improvement and Evaluation is the section that deals the most with continuously assessing the alignment of all parts of the system to the vision. This is the section that answers the question, *How will we evaluate our efforts?* (Chapter 10 focuses on Continuous Improvement and Evaluation.)

The rest of this chapter is focused on answering the questions, *Why do we exist?* and *Where do we want to be?*

> *Things are the way they are because they got that way. Unless things change, they are likely to remain the same. Change would be easy if it weren't for all the people. People don't resist change; they resist being changed.*
>
> **Laws of Organizational Change**
> **The Team Handbook**

CREATE A VISION AROUND A SHARED PURPOSE

> *Shared visions emerge from personal visions. This is how they derive their energy and how they foster commitment. If people don't have their own vision, all they can do is "sign up" for someone else's. The result is compliance, never commitment.*
>
> **Peter Senge**
> *The Fifth Discipline*

Peter Senge advises organizations wanting to establish shared visions to encourage individuals within their organizations to develop their own personal visions first. This is because the only vision that really motivates individuals is their own, and the best shared vision for a group must be representative of the group's individual visions.

We believe that the route to this shared vision begins with the analysis of strengths, weaknesses, and needs, as determined mostly through data analysis (covered in Chapter 4), and the values and beliefs of the individuals in the learning organization. These individual values and beliefs need to merge into core values and beliefs for the learning organization. Once the core values and beliefs are agreed upon, individuals can create the purpose for the learning organization. This purpose is important for creating a mission statement that everyone sees, knows, and uses.

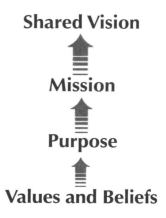

With the core values and beliefs, the purpose of the learning organization, and the mission statement in hand, individuals need time to describe their personal visions for the school. It is these individual visions that get combined to create that shared vision for all the individuals in the school.

We believe this process will create a vision that is shared, and one that everyone on staff will want to implement. We also believe that we must assist the learning organization in developing support structures to ensure the implementation of this shared vision in each classroom, across classrooms, and throughout the system.

The accompanying CD provides agendas, scripts, posters, and worksheets to download for use in creating a shared vision, an example of a shared vision, and support structures for implementing the visions. A discussion of steps in reaching a shared vision follows, starting with the values and beliefs, and ending with structures to support the implementation of a shared vision.

STEPS IN CREATING A SHARED VISION

▼ *Gather the Appropriate Participants*

Gather participants, including all staff members, parents, and appropriate community members, to create a shared vision. You will need a minimum of one day—preferably two days.

▼ *Ground Rules*

As with any group process, the facilitator needs to begin the session by laying out the *ground rules* that remind participants of the procedures to be used, to assure everyone that the conversation is about improvement, and that it is safe to speak openly and frankly in the room. An example list of ground rules follows:

FIGURE 5.2

GROUND RULES
This is a safe room There is no rank in this room All ideas are valid Each person gets a chance to speak Each person gets a chance to listen We are here to focus on the future Our purpose is improvement, not blame

Because many of these individuals have been through such processes before, the facilitator must appeal to the hearts of the staff members to enter this process one more time for the benefit of all the children. One could remind participants of why they became teachers in the first place. The majority of our most effective teachers would say that the reason they became teachers was "to make a difference in the lives of children." This process, then, is an opportunity to create a learning organization that will encourage staff members to make a positive difference in the lives of all the school's children. In fact, a warm-up activity could be designed around having staff recall why they became teachers and why they are still teaching.

This is a good time to refer to the *givens* (posted on the wall), or the issues that must be included in the vision. These givens would include such things as student learning standards and the district vision and goals.

▼ *Review the Data*

Graphs of questionnaire and student achievement results, summary of strengths, areas for improvement, and implications for school improvement, analyzed prior to the visioning day, can be posted on the wall for staff to refer to during the day.

▼ *Values and Beliefs*

Values and beliefs are an extremely important place to start the visioning process. Values and beliefs are at the core of who we are, what we do, and how we think and feel. Values and beliefs reflect what is important to us; they describe what we think about work and how we think it should operate. People cannot act differently from their values and beliefs. If we want our staff members to act in congruence with one another (which is why we want a shared vision), we must uncover values and beliefs about teaching and learning and then come to core understandings of values and beliefs for the school. These are the shaping force behind a truly shared vision or shared direction.

In the past few years, schools have been hard pressed for quality professional development time and dollars, so we have not had the luxury of weekend visioning retreats in relaxing locations. Therefore, we have had to focus our visioning efforts to create a shared vision during one professional development day with all staff and some community members. We have learned to become very focused. Our focused question (which is created by the leadership team of the school prior to the visioning day) to get to the values and beliefs of the individuals might be, *What do you believe about curriculum, instruction, assessment, and the environment related to the learning of students at this school? Or What are the curriculum, instruction, assessment, and environmental factors that support effective learning for our students?* These questions focus the staff on meeting the needs of

> **Values and beliefs** are at the core of who we are, what we do, and how we think and feel. *Values and beliefs* reflect what is important to us; they describe what we think about work and how we think it should operate.

their students while assessing basic values and beliefs. It takes about twelve minutes for individuals to write their values and beliefs.

Merging individual values and beliefs into group values and beliefs.

Individuals read their values and beliefs in their small group. Group members compare and merge ideas. Many agree to values and beliefs that they did not have on their original lists. This is fine. We want each group discussion to result in a core list of values and beliefs to which each member of that group can relate. This merging and posting on poster paper takes about 45 minutes. There should be no limit to the number of values and beliefs that emerge.

After posting and debriefing each group's values and beliefs, we move from the small group values and beliefs to the large group values and beliefs. Most of the time, the small groups discover that their values and beliefs are very similar. This makes it very easy to move to core values and beliefs for the learning organization. The facilitator could have group leaders stand by their group's posters, have one leader at a time read her/his group's values and beliefs, while the other group leaders mark the similar values and beliefs on their posters. The next leader reads what her/his group had on its list that is different while the others continue to mark off common values and beliefs. This process continues until what is left is a list that the large group determines represents its values and beliefs. These become the core values and beliefs of the learning organization.

Note: If it does not seem like a good idea to start with one list over any of the others, the facilitator could start a new list by asking the teams to identify the common values and beliefs across all group reports. Either approach will take about thirty minutes. A resulting list of core values and beliefs (Figure 5.3) would look something like the example on the next page.

FIGURE 5.3

What are the curriculum, instruction, assessment, and environmental factors that support effective learning for OUR HIGH SCHOOL students?

Our High School staff values and believes the following about the environment, curriculum, instruction, and assessment:
- students must feel safe
- teachers must be caring, knowledgeable, and in control of the learning environment
- curriculum, instruction, and assessment must all be interconnected
- communication between and among staff and students must be effective and respectful
- there needs to be strong collaboration within departments, between departments, and between staff and students
- staff believes that all students can learn
- diversity must be honored in learning and teaching
- students need success
- curriculum and instruction must be motivating
- teachers must promote and model lifelong learning

Curriculum must include:
- student choice
- high standards—clearly defined learning goals
- meaningful content
- research-based options
- alignment across grade levels and across curriculum
- active, inquiry-based discovery, learn-by-doing options
- integration of course work (team teaching)
- adequate textbooks and support materials
- modifications for special need students
- meta-cognition instruction

Instruction must be:
- student-centered (individualized instruction)
- research-based
- focused on the fact that all kids can learn
- clearly defined
- facilitated (teacher as facilitator as opposed to teacher as "all knowing")
- varied
- extensively organized
- assessed well (what gets assessed must be taught and what is taught must be assessed)

Assessment must be:
- purposeful — linked to learning goals
- performance-based
- used to guide classroom decisions
- used to improve instruction and curriculum
- communicated to students and parents
- ongoing and varied to meet the needs of the students

▼ Purpose

The *purpose* of the school is an important concept for staff members to consider. Purpose comes out of core values and beliefs—if this is what we value and believe about curriculum, instruction, assessment, and environment for our students' learning, *What is the purpose of this school? Why does our school exist?* The purpose must be compelling, flexible, broad, fundamental, inspirational, and enduring. The purpose should not describe what the organization does now. The purpose "must grab the soul" of each organizational member.

Again we begin with individual's creative thinking (about five minutes), move to small group agreement on a purpose (twenty minutes), and on to the large group consensus on purpose (thirty minutes). It is much easier to get group agreement on the purpose than on a mission statement, for instance. It is the purpose that is most important. Example:

> **The purpose of Our High School is to educate students to become lifelong learners, to become empowered and productive citizens.**

▼ Mission

After the purpose of the school has been agreed upon, a *mission* for the school will need to be "reapproved," revised, or written. The mission is a brief, clear, and compelling purpose statement that serves to unify an organization's efforts. An effective mission must stretch and challenge the organization, yet be achievable. It is tangible, value-driven, energizing, highly focused, and moves the organization forward. It is crisp, clear, and engaging—it reaches out and grabs people in the gut. People "get it" right away; it requires little or no explanation. A mission should walk the boundary between the possible and impossible.

The existing mission statement can be reviewed to see if it reflects the purpose of the school. If not, one of two approaches can be taken. If it looks as if the current mission statement will take only a little tweaking, perhaps the group can suggest new wording. If it looks as if the current mission statement will need much more work and time, have the group agree that a committee will craft the mission statement at a different time using the core values and beliefs and purpose, and return the drafts to the whole staff for approval. As long as the purpose is clear, the process can proceed

> **Purpose** is the aim of the organization: the reason for existence.

> The **mission** is a brief, clear, and compelling purpose statement that serves to unify an organization's efforts.

without the mission statement being completely written. Again, it is the purpose and its understanding that is most important. (Developing a mission could take anywhere from one minute to days! This is why we suggest delegating the task if it looks as if it will take some time.) A mission statement for Our High School follows. You will note that the mission is almost the same as the purpose in this case. This staff loved the clarity of the purpose statement and converted it to become their mission statement. This is the end target.

> **The mission of Our High School**
> **is to educate students to become life-long learners,**
> **who are empowered and productive citizens.**

▼ *Vision*

A *vision* represents what the school would look like, feel like, and sound like when the mission is implemented. A vision that is shared means that everyone in the organization understands it in the same way. Again, we want to start with personal visions and move to the large group vision. Individuals may want about sixty minutes to jot their thinking on paper. If the facilitator asks the individuals to think in terms of *Curriculum, Instruction, Assessment,* and the *Learning Environment,* the visions will be very much like the focused values and beliefs. Even if the questions about values and beliefs are not as specific as those used above, the values and beliefs ought to be 100 percent congruent with the personal visions that emerge. Personal visions can be merged into small group visions in about thirty to forty-five minutes. It will take forty-five to sixty minutes to merge small group visions into the larger group vision. An example shared vision (Figure 5.4) is shown on the opposite page, and another values and beliefs to vision example 🔘 appears on the CD.

The facilitator will want to ensure that all members of the staff understand the words in the same way. Because of the focused question used at the beginning, the vision quickly becomes very focused. If the values and beliefs were done well at the beginning, the vision will reflect these same ideas. Check often and ask for clarification and examples as you complete this work. Review the elements of the shared vision, and have staff summarize, as a recorder documents what the vision will look like, sound like, feel like, when the school implements it. Keep the discussion focused on the end, not the means.

> A *vision* is a specific description of what it will be like when the mission is achieved. A vision is a mental image. It must be written in practical, concrete terms that everyone can understand and see in the same way.

A group leader reading aloud her group's ideas of what school would like like, sound like, and feel like when the vision is implemented.

FIGURE 5.4

OUR HIGH SCHOOL
Shared Vision

Curriculum

Must be progressive, integrated into the larger school system, and be designed to help students meet standards. Curriculum must be:

- able to support what we are teaching and how we are doing — research-based curriculum
- deeper not wider (fewer classes at once)
- adaptive to student needs (individualized adaptive instruction)
- cross-curricular
- real-world relevant
- standards-based
- based on high standards, high expectations

Instruction

Must be specific, clear, and structured with varied strategies to have students buy into it and have ownership. Instruction must include:

- guided discovery / active inquiry
- performance orientation
- guest specialists / community / real world
- student-centered
- research-based options (support how we teach)
- engaging strategies (motivational, with student choice)
- flexibility, varied teaching

Assessment

Must be fair and just with varied forms, appropriate to the learning target and looks at the larger picture. Assessments must be:

- considerate of diverse learning styles
- used to drive classroom instruction as opposed to just tracking students
- ongoing
- appropriate to content
- easy to understand (teachers, students, parents, community)
- self-assessable by students, teachers, and administrators
- purposeful — related to and drive classroom instruction
- linked to targets / standards
- varied

Environment

The learning environment must be free from physical and emotional threats while giving students an equal opportunity to learn in an engaging, caring, and positive place of which they can be proud. The environment must include:

- mentoring relationships of all students with adults
- family-like, protective, and caring climate
- lower student-teacher ratio (daily)
- investigative options for fewer periods a day
- physical and emotional safeness
- challenging, engaging, relevant, not boring, and active features
- adequate resources for teachers and students
- collaboration among teachers, students, and administrators
- rewards / celebrations

The shared vision will need to be *documented* and shared with all individuals as soon as possible. Some facilitators insist on having staff write a narrative describing the scenario of what it would look like, sound like, and feel like when the vision is implemented. Other facilitators feel it must be narrowed to one or two sentences; still other facilitators feel that a list reflecting the vision (such as the one in the example on the CD) is ample for moving to the plan that will house the details. Facilitators must guide this discussion to focus the end target on students.

Our High School Vision Narrative

When the vision of Our High School is implemented, students will be happily and actively engaged in learning. The learning students will engage in will be real-world, relevant, active, and research-based, helping all students to meet or exceed the student learning standards. Students will graduate knowing they will have opportunities to become anything they want to be.

Teachers will work together to create an atmosphere of quality learning and connectiveness for the students' learning and futures. Teachers will use a variety of strategies and outside resources to ensure that student learning is relevant, challenging, and engaging. Assessments will be ongoing and related to instruction and the standards to ensure no student will "fall through the cracks." Excellence will be rewarded through celebrations that represent quality achievements on the parts of teachers and students.

▼ *Set School Goals*

After the vision is created, ask staff to agree on two to three school goals. School goals are the intended outcomes of the vision. Start again with individual, go to small group, and then compare across the groups to get two to three goals for the vision.

This is most often as far as a large group can get in one day. Before adjourning, it would be a good idea to have the individuals reflect on the shared vision with respect to its impact on them. It will help them make the vision theirs and to think about their next steps when they go back to their classrooms. Reflective questions might include:

- What do you need in order to transform your classroom into the shared vision?
- What support do you need to implement this vision in your classroom?

These questions can be given to staff to think about for a week or so, with a discussion to follow in the next staff meeting, or the facilitator may ask to collect the reflections so she/he can group the information to assess needs for the next discussion.

SUMMARY

A major component of the Student Achievement section of the school portfolio is the documentation of the answer to the question, *Where do we want to be?* Creating a shared vision begins with developing core values and beliefs and a purpose for the learning organization. From the purpose, a mission and shared vision can be developed. If the values and beliefs are established quite comprehensively, the vision that emerges will be 100 percent congruent to the values and beliefs. Under these circumstances, one can be fairly certain that the vision will be shared.

FREQUENTLY ASKED QUESTIONS ABOUT STUDENT ACHIEVEMENT 💿
CD-ROM

▼ **What is the difference between mission and vision?**

The *mission* is a brief, clear, and compelling purpose statement that serves to unify an organization's efforts. An effective mission must stretch and challenge the organization, yet be achievable. It is tangible, value-driven, energizing, highly focused, and moves the organization forward. It is a crisp, clear, and engaging statement that reaches out and grabs people in the gut. A mission has a finish line for its achievement and is proactive. A mission should walk the boundary between the possible and impossible. The mission should also reflect the purpose of the school. Some researchers would say the purpose and mission are the same.

A *vision* is a specific description of what it will be like when the mission is achieved. A vision is a mental image. It must be written in practical, concrete terms that everyone can understand and see in the same way.

▼ How will the vision play out differently at the elementary, middle, and high school levels?

The questions that get asked by the facilitator to get to the core values and beliefs, purpose, and vision can be the same at each school level. The higher the level (i.e., high school versus middle school versus elementary school), however, the harder it can be to come to agreement on working differently and together. This is because at the higher grades, staffs may be wrestling with traditional instructional strategies and content-specific classes. Some subject area teachers might believe that there is only one way to teach their subjects, while others believe it is time to integrate subjects.

▼ How can I tell if our vision is shared or not?

You might be able to tell if your vision is shared by watching teachers work congruently with one another—if each grade level builds on the previous and prepares students for the next level. Your staff and student questionnaires, and your student achievement results will also give you evidence. If there is a vision that is shared, staff anonymously will indicate there is via the staff questionnaire. The student questionnaire will also hint at a shared vision, particularly the open-ended results. Student achievement results will show steady progress for cohorts of students and individual students.

▼ How do you create that sense of urgency to create a vision and to do continuous school improvement planning?

The *Continuous Improvement Continuum* self-assessment can create a sense of urgency for continuous school improvement planning, as can the data analysis results. The facilitator of the visioning process can help create a sense of urgency also by appealing to the staff that this is an opportunity to build that school for which they went into teaching. The difference between where the school is and where the staff wants it to be creates the urgency.

▼ How do you change values and beliefs?

Values and beliefs are perceptions. Perceptions change after actions change. For example, if you want teachers to use technology, but they believe technology will not improve student learning, the only way you can change this perception is to have them try technology with students.

▼ **How do we create the time?**

Coming to consensus on a vision and creating a continuous school improvement plan does take time. Schools find that they can create time by thinking about what they can do more efficiently or not at all. Many schools have created time by moving announcements from faculty meetings to e-mail or to a note pad at the front office. Another way that schools create planning time is by banking minutes—adding five to fifteen instructional minutes to the school day, and then dismissing early, or starting late, one day a week.

YOUR QUESTIONS

Does a vision exist in your learning organization that is shared? (i.e., understood by everyone in the same way). How do you know?

How will you get a shared vision?

What are your goals for moving toward the vision?

▼ Short term:

▼ Long term:

ON THE CD RELATED TO CREATING A VISION AND THE STUDENT ACHIEVEMENT SECTION OF THE SCHOOL PORTFOLIO

▼ Items to Include in the Student Achievement Section of the School Portfolio

▼ Student Achievement Continuous Improvement Continuum

▼ Frequently Asked Questions about Student Achievement

▼ Creating a Vision
   ◆ Continuous School Improvement Planning via the School Portfolio
   ◆ Ground Rules
   ◆ Facilitator's Agenda for Creating a Shared Vision
   ◆ Agenda for Creating a Shared Vision
   ◆ Worksheets for Creating a Shared Vision
   ◆ Vision Notetaking Form
   ◆ Shared Vision Example: *Central City Elementary School*
   ◆ Vision Quote Posters

▼ Student Achievement Section Template

CHAPTER 6

QUALITY PLANNING:
Planning to Accomplish the Vision

Chapter Objective: TO DESCRIBE THE STEPS IN BUILDING A PLAN TO IMPLEMENT THE VISION

Quality planning is like...

A well orchestrated coaching session—it includes a big picture, the vision, skill learnings, practice, review, and improvement in a continuous cycle.

Electricity to a light bulb. Water to a plant. A cup of coffee in the morning. Fuel to a fire. A jumpstart to a dead battery!

Interpreting a musical score. There is a wide variety of needs and preferences of students; requires instruction and practice; requires collaboration with the entire orchestra to produce harmony (this is ongoing, job-embedded); leads to an assessment of the quality of performance and what patrons (students) take with them.

Taking a European vacation. You must have all the stakeholders involved in the process, a good map, and confidence in the travel agent that you select to ensure you get safely to your destination to reap the rewards of careful planning.

Missouri School Portfolio Awareness Session, February 2001
and *The School Portfolio Toolkit* Reviewers

A well-defined and well-executed school improvement effort has a continuous school improvement action plan that provides a logical framework for clarifying and achieving the vision. The school plan includes:

▼ an *assessment* of where the school is today and the factors that can be expected to influence it in the future

▼ a *mission statement* describing the school's purpose and function

▼ a *vision* that reflects the mission and the *values and beliefs* of the individuals who make up the organization

▼ *long-range goals* that capture the intentions of the mission and vision

▼ an identification of *objectives* that make each goal tangible

▼ an *action plan* that identifies the procedural steps needed to implement the goals and objectives, including strategies, timelines, responsibilities, and accountability

▼ an estimation of *resources needed*, based on the action plan

- ▼ a *leadership structure* to implement the vision, along with clarification of the roles and responsibilities of the members of the organization

- ▼ a description of *professional development* needed to equip all staff to implement the vision

- ▼ a plan for *evaluating* the implementation of the action plan and the continuous improvement of the entire learning organization

The plan to implement the vision is found in its own section of the school portfolio entitled "Quality Planning."

CHARACTERISTICS OF A QUALITY PLAN

Schools often get caught up in a myriad of plans or, worse yet, creating a plan for the district that never gets articulated or implemented. We have seen excellent plans that never get implemented because the school did not know how to use the plan. We also see gross injustices when schools are required to create one-year plans in isolation of a vision.

We know that a one-year plan, plus a one-year plan, plus a one-year plan, and so on, never leads to the implementation of a vision without the plan starting from a vision. Planning for compliance, meaning planning to fulfill an external request, often defeats the purpose of quality planning. Invariably, the plan becomes an assignment fulfilled rather than the result and reflection of a continuous process in which the whole school community participates. A compliance plan can become one person's plan and, often, staff in general do not have a *clue* about what's in the plan. They may know there is a plan, but that's as far as it goes. In the meantime, staff and students show up to do business as usual with no understanding about where their school is going and with little sense of purpose regarding their contributions toward implementing a plan for the purpose of moving toward a vision or a better tomorrow. For a plan to help a whole staff implement a vision, the planning committee must begin with the vision and work backwards to create the action steps to achieve the vision. A one-year action plan will emerge to begin the action to the vision.

STEPS IN CREATING AN ACTION PLAN

Figure 6.1 provides an overview of the steps in *Creating an Action Plan.* Discussion of these steps follow. An activity for taking staffs through the steps is on the CD.

FIGURE 6.1

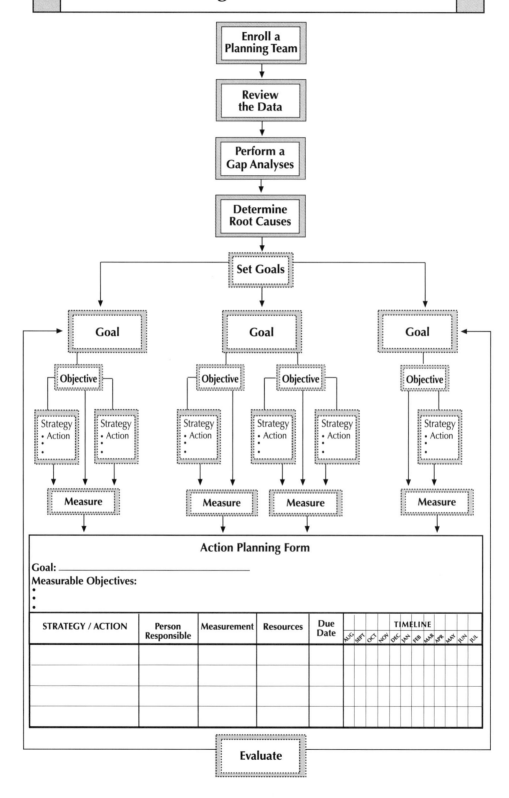

▼ Enroll a Planning Team

Creating the action plan with a large number of people is hardly ever feasible. Therefore, we suggest that the school enroll a team to develop the plan, to monitor the implementation of the plan, and to update it over time. We recommend starting out with a representative group of staff members, not just those who think alike, and not just the leadership team. Include stakeholders such as parents, community, and students. This team will lead the development and draft the parts of the plan, then bring the parts back to the whole staff to review and suggest changes. Although five to eight people is a good size for a functioning team, the more change required of staff to implement the vision, the more individuals need to be involved at the plan creation level.

▼ Review the Data

The action planning team reviews the multiple measures of data (that the entire staff analyzed together) that answer the question "Where are we now?," using *The School Portfolio Continuous Improvement Continuums,* perceptions data, demographics, student learning results, and process analyses (as described in Information and Analysis and Chapter 4).

▼ Perform a Gap Analysis

The action team compares the gap between *where we are now* (the synthesis of the school results, strengths, and weaknesses) and *where we want to be* (the vision). This gap leads to a summary of areas needing improvement (described in Chapters 4 and 5).

▼ Determine Root Causes

Analyze the underlying reasons for the problems or needs that emerge from the gap analysis. Root causes are the deep underlying reasons for a specific situation. (Root causes are discussed in Chapter 4.)

An *action plan* is the part of Continuous School Improvement Planning that describes the tasks that must be performed, the responsibilities that must be assigned, the resources that must be allocated, and the schedules that must be met in order to implement the strategies.

> **Goals** are how the school generally intends to address needs or gaps between where they are now and where they want to be.

> **Objectives** are goals that are redrafted in terms that are clearly tangible.

▼ *Set Goals*

Schoolwide goals need to be set with the whole staff before the actual writing of the plan commences. Goals are statements of the intended outcomes of the vision. They are stated in broad, general, abstract, and non-measurable terms. Doug Reeves (2000) advises that we should have only two or three school goals. Write each broad goal on the top of a piece of chart pad paper. Example: *All students will demonstrate continuous improvement in the areas of math, reading, and writing.* (See *Goal Setting Activity*.)

▼ *Identify Objectives*

Draft objectives that will close the gap for each of the goals. Objectives are goals that are redrafted in clearly tangible terms. Objective statements are narrow, specific, concrete, and measurable. When writing objectives, it is important to describe the intended results, rather than the process or means to accomplish them. Example: *The percentage of students achieving the reading comprehension standard will increase from 50 to 60 by Spring 2002.* Write each objective on a large post-it and place under the appropriate goal that is written on the chart pad paper.

▼ *Determine How the Objectives Will Be Measured*

Objectives are measurable statements. Determine what assessment tools and strategies will be used to know if the objectives are being met or have been met. Example: *The percentage of students achieving the reading comprehension standard will increase from 50 to 60 by Spring 2002, as measured by the state reading assessment exam at each grade level.*

▼ *Identify and Group Strategies to Achieve the Objectives*

Brainstorm and discuss different strategies to reach the objectives, making sure root causes of the gap(s) have been analyzed. Group the strategies under the objectives. Example: *To increase the number of students reading on grade level by ten percent, the strategies might include:*
- *professional development in teaching reading for all teachers*
- *study how reading is successfully taught in other locations*
- *coach each other to implement new strategies*
- *determine how to implement standards at every grade level*

▼ *Actions Required to Implement the Strategies*

Below each strategy, list the actions that need to be accomplished to implement the strategy (i.e., *study the learning standards, study the research on reading, and increase reading time*).

▼ *Arrange Strategies and Activities*

Begin to arrange the strategies and activities in chronological order. (Keep this version for later reference and fine-tune the plan in chronological summary form, starting with the action to be taken first.)

▼ *Determine How the Actions Will Be Evaluated*

For each activity, determine how you will know if the action is being implemented and the impact of its implementation.

▼ *Use a Planning Form*

Using a planning form 💿 or a planning program, label columns—strategy/action, person responsible, measurement, resources, due date, and timeline. Place the reorganized strategies and actions in the action column in a manner that is easiest for staff to utilize later. In the column next to each action, identify the person ultimately responsible for the action. Try not to use team names like *Language Arts Action Team* in the "person responsible" column. Accountability is most effective if the responsibility is delegated to an individual. Responsible persons determine how accountability reviews are conducted and how to talk with one another about fostering and demonstrating accountability.

▼ *Establish Due Date*

In the column next to person responsible, write in the due date. For each strategy or activity (depends on the topic and structure for implementation), determine when the activity absolutely must be completed. In the columns that represent months, weeks, and sometimes days, make notations that will indicate when each activity will begin and when it will be completed by showing an "X" in the cell. Indicate the duration by marking a line between the "X's" across the months.

▼ Determine Resources

Using the action plan, determine the costs associated with each action. This budget, developed in conjunction with the action plan, will determine the financial feasibility of the actions for the year. Alterations are made simultaneously and balanced back and forth, while looking for items that can leverage other items. Dollars sometimes limit activities. School staff are often surprised, however, to discover that many times what they have to spend is equivalent to what they can do in a year's time. If the latter does not hold true, the school staff has important and specific information (i.e., the action plan and budget plan) to utilize in seeking additional support for their efforts. Note that the budget plan is a part of the action plan and that all school funds are used with the one resulting school plan. Everything in the school should be working toward that one plan and the school vision. All school money is a part of this plan. The planning team must have a clear understanding of all budget resources.

Collapsing funding sources for implementing professional development is also possible. This strategy serves to focus professional development efforts, for example, and reinforces collaboration for design implementation and evaluation because funds are utilized more wisely to serve a wider sector.

▼ Evaluate

The entire continuous school improvement plan must be evaluated with the vision as the target. This comprehensive evaluation will evaluate the parts and the whole of the plan to indicate if the goals, objectives, and strategies are leading to the attainment of the vision.

▼ Refine the Plan

With the first draft of the plan complete, review the elements and the big picture of the plan. Below are some guiding questions:

- ◆ Will this plan lead to improved student learning?
- ◆ Are the objectives about improved student learning for all students?
- ◆ What evidence do you need to know if the objectives are being met?
- ◆ Will the strategies lead to attainment of the objectives?

- Do the strategies address root causes?
- Are there strategies/actions that can be further collapsed?
- Will staff know what is expected of them?
- Does the plan include new learnings required of staff? If so, has training and support been incorporated for each area?
- Are the time frames realistic?
- How will you keep the ultimate goal of improved student learning for all students at the forefront of everything you do?
- How often will the plan and strategies be monitored?
- Whose job is it to monitor the implementation of the plan?
- How will new staff members learn about the plan?

▼ Report

Determine how the action plan will be documented, communicated, reported, and updated. Communicate progress toward the attainment of the school improvement goals and objectives in newsletters, staff bulletins, websites, and bulletin boards.

EXAMPLE PLAN

The Central City Plan

Working together to create an action plan the staff would use to accomplish the shared direction.

In the following example, *Central City Elementary School Action Plan,* the entire vision of the school is in the plan. This school wanted meaningful documentation of the vision. They wanted every word to represent action to be taken within the school. They wanted a plan that showed all the actions needed to accomplish the vision. Everything happening in the school is in the plan. Anything that is not in the plan should not be happening at this school.

The Central City Plan was drafted by the Leadership Team which included representatives from each grade level and year-round track. The team used data, the values and beliefs, purpose, and shared direction they developed as a whole staff in order to create the plan the staff would use to accomplish the shared direction. This staff started this process without a vision in place. These parts are shown starting on the opposite page.

This example serves to show how one school staff created all dimensions of a plan together. This plan is not meant to be replicated for the sake of putting a plan in place. Rather, this example serves to show how important a plan is and how collaborative thinking results in detailed steps for implementing the plan.

FIGURE 6.2

Central City Elementary School Values and Beliefs
(Brainstormed)

We believe...
- Curriculum, instruction, and assessment should be aligned to meet the needs of *all* students.
- Teachers must have high expectations of all students — all staff personnel must have high expectations of academic performance and social behavior (each student must be able to reach her / his full potential).
- Assessment needs to be efficient, workable, regular, manageable, understandable to everyone, quick (fast), and inform and drive instruction (making students responsible for ongoing assessment of their own work, as appropriate).
- Students should feel safe, emotionally and physically, both inside and outside of the classroom. Students and teachers respect and positively interact with each other.
- Curriculum and instruction must be standards-driven, uniform within grade level, and articulated across grade levels.
- Grade-level meetings need to be focused on curriculum, instruction, and assessment and reflective of teachers' needs.
- Communication should occur at all levels, bottom to top, top to bottom, and between programs.
- Flexible grouping of students support instruction at each students' instructional level.
- Shared decision making will support a quality school.
- All teachers, including those with low-performing and incoming students, need support with inservices, materials, and programs.
- Communicating with parents about curriculum instruction and assessment will assist with students' learning.
- All teachers need time, resources, and training to achieve successful student learning.
- All students are entitled to a well-rounded curriculum.
- Instruction must fit different student learning styles.
- Instruction must:
  * incorporate (enrich) students' real-life experiences and connect to relevant, creative instruction
  * provide for new experiences that students may not get otherwise
  * diversify and focus on basic skills in grades K-3

FIGURE 6.3

PURPOSE

The purpose of Central City Elementary School is to educate our students to their fullest potential of academic knowledge and social competence, thereby, developing productive individuals who contribute responsibly to society.

QUALITY PLANNING

FIGURE 6.4

MISSION

The mission of Central City Elementary School,
by addressing the needs of the total child,
is to develop academically and socially successful students,
and to help create literate life-long learners
who are caring and contributing citizens.

Shared Vision
(Brainstormed, first draft)

▼ Curriculum

- ◆ Emphasis in basic skills K-3
- ◆ Additional, specific remediation curriculum
- ◆ Supplemental resources (technology, independent reading libraries, field trips, guest speakers)
- ◆ Extended learning time needs curriculums that are different, but aligned in their approach to standard classroom curriculum in literacy
- ◆ Teacher input in selection of curriculum materials
- ◆ Standards-driven
- ◆ Teacher support in implementing new curriculums taking into account different teacher needs (ongoing and timely support, not single day training)
- ◆ Communicate curriculum and essential standards (for grade level) to parents
- ◆ Timely delivery of curriculum materials for year round
- ◆ Pacing/timeline for literacy, and math curriculums that take into account classes with large percentage of students below grade level
- ◆ Provide/select curriculum materials that include strategies for different skill levels in the same classroom
- ◆ Single grade classrooms that allow for the teaching of a single grade curriculum

▼ Instruction

- ◆ Systematic skills instruction within a meaningful context for students—hands-on learning, literature-based, real world experiences—supports student success
- ◆ Consistent use of effective research-based instructional practices across grade levels supports student mastery
- ◆ Instruction needs to meet the diverse needs of students and, therefore, include a variety of strategies and modalities
- ◆ Integrated, thematic instruction supports student learning and retention
- ◆ Flexible grouping based on periodic assessments, within or across classrooms, for different student skill levels is essential for timely mastery of skills
- ◆ Initial instruction needs to be followed by consistent practice (including homework) of new skills
- ◆ Productive, academic use of the entire school day is essential to student success
- ◆ The grade level (team) meeting is the essential support system for an articulated general curriculum, systematic instructional practices, and collaborative instructional decisions related to underperforming students
- ◆ Instructional time needs to be sacred and uninterrupted
- ◆ Everyone sticks to the program and focuses on the district and state standards

▼ Assessment

- ◆ Assessment needs to be systematic, efficient, ongoing and inform productive instruction
- ◆ Assessment has to be at meaningful instructional points during the year
- ◆ Bilingual assessment will be more formalized and used to frame curriculum
- ◆ Assessment has to take into account the actual levels of student attainment upon entering the grade level
- ◆ Assessment needs to be regularly summarized to inform and improve classroom grade level and schoolwide practice
- ◆ Align assessment to the standards and report card

- Authentic assessment based on student work and performance
- Pre-test—to understand academic level of class (helps to plan curriculum)
- Post-test, see growth (can be used for next grade level's pre-test)
- Grades two through six integrate test-taking skills into the curriculum
- Assessments are regularly reported to parents in a variety of ways

▼ Learning Environment

Safe and healthy room:
- all ideas valid and respected
- chance to speak without hurting others
- chance to listen (responsibly)
- right to teach/learn
- right to make mistakes and to learn from them
- right to have materials, supplies, appropriate teaching and learning tools (in working order)
- freedom from disturbances
- right to feel safe—physically and emotionally

School grounds:
- high quality, trained supervisors
- quality play area (sufficient space)
- physically safe

Our school should have—
- Student Council
- Student Safety Patrol
- Safer parking lot
- Uniforms – enforced consistently
- Restrooms

▼ Support Systems
- Systematic professional development, including training, collaborative curricular planning, and peer coaching that supports effective classroom practice.
- Weekly, informal observations of classroom instructional practices by site administrators to support continuous improvement of the school educational program.

- Instructional reform needs to be focused, efficiently implemented, and maximize teacher time for curricular and instructional planning.
- Information related to school programs needs to be communicated in an ongoing, systematic, and accessible fashion.

Central City Vision Narrative

When the Central City vision is implemented, all students will be meeting the state learning standards and will be speaking English and Spanish. Students will be learning in context in meaningful ways through hands-on, literature-based strategies, and real-world experiences. Teachers will reach out to meet the diverse needs of students through a variety of strategies, such as integrated, thematic instruction, flexible grouping, and effective and regular assessments. All students will feel safe, physically and emotionally. All students will be encouraged to do the best they can do, learning from mistakes and successes. Teachers will work together, communicate often about student learning, and implement a continuum of learning that makes sense for all students.

Strategies, Goals, and Objectives

The leadership team pulled implied strategies out of the vision to accomplish each objective. The Central City goals, and objectives for each goal, are:

Goal 1	*Improve learning for all students.*
Objective:	Improve the achievement of students in all content areas by June 2003, as measured by SAT9, SABE2, ADEPT, ongoing classroom assessments, and the Academic Performance Index.
Goal 2	*Improve the way we operate on a continuous basis.*
Objective 1:	Staff will support and ensure the implementation of the shared direction in each classroom and throughout the school, as shown by a five-rating on the shared direction self-assessment tool, by Spring 2003.
Objective 2:	Staff will improve the learning organization, as measured by the Continuous Improvement Continuums, questionnaires, and other evaluations by 2003.

For each major strategy item in the vision, the leadership team listed on post-it notes all the actions implied in the item. For example, for —

Integrated, thematic instruction supports student learning and retention

the team made a list that included the following:

Professional development
Grade-level meetings/cross grade-level meetings
Peer coaching

This list was a first iteration of implementation needs and issues. Their next steps were to continue to refine their thinking and then begin to combine the actions across the strategies.

Testing the Plan

After much dialogue and many drafts of steps around each shared vision item, the team resorted to answering the question: *What would a day look like when I implement the vision and the standards in my grade level?* Although difficult to do, each grade-level representative drafted a day, minute by minute. The discussion focused the plan more and more. Several drafts later, they had a concrete plan. A proud staff appreciated the clarity of the vision.

Evaluating the Central City Elementary School Plan

The evaluation of the Central City Elementary School action plan is designed around the goals of the plan, which are to:

▼ Improve learning for all students

▼ Improve the way we operate on a continuous basis for increased student learning and achievement

Evaluating the implementation of the vision requires effort and collaboration. No existing tools will tell you if your specific vision is being implemented in ways your staff intended it to be implemented. Each action step might have a different way of knowing if it is on-course. How each action step will be evaluated is a required part of the action planning process and will be fairly easy to develop. After the action plan is completed, it is wise to combine the evaluation components into one document to collapse common assessments, such as the Central City Elementary School evaluation plan.

An outline of the first goal of the evaluation plan follows (Figure 6.5). The complete evaluation plan ⊙ is on the CD.

FIGURE 6.5

Central City Elementary School Evaluation Plan Outline

Goal 1: *Improve learning for all students*
Objective: Improve the achievement of students in all content areas by June 2003, as measured by SAT9, SABE2, ADEPT, ongoing classroom assessment, and the Academic Performance Index (API).

The improvement of curriculum and instructional strategies to improve student achievement will be measured by:

♦ Continued progress of cohorts of students from one grade to the next as measured by the SAT9, SABE2 over time
♦ Gains of over 25 points in the Academic Performance Index using the SAT9, ten points using the SABE2
♦ Increase in numbers of students becoming fluent in English Language earlier than in the past
  • Disaggregate data based on number of years in educational program (bilingual /English-only)
    * SABE 2 = 2nd and 3rd grade students and pre-transitional students in intermediate grades
    * SAT 9 = transitional and post-transitional students in bilingual and English-only classes
    * Multiple measures = based on language of instruction K-6th grades
  • Disaggregate data based on entry level skills (at grade level, number of years below grade level)
  • Disaggregate SAT 9 scores based on appropriateness
    * English language learning students in English-only versus English-dominant students in English-only
    * 4th, 5th, 6th grades disaggregate based on pre-transitional, transition,post-transitional
  • Number of students meeting bilingual benchmarks in a timely manner
    * 90 points/one level ADEPT
    * adding English reading at the end of 3rd grade for those who began a bilingual program in kindergarten
    * reaching redesignation in 5th or 6th grade if entered bilingual program in kindergarten or 1st grade
♦ On-going assessments in the classroom in subject areas
  • Running Records
  • District Reading Rubric
  • Scholastic
♦ Increases in attendance and decreases in tardiness of students

EVALUATING THE IMPLEMENTATION OF THE VISION

In addition to the overall evaluation plan, one can design a tool by laying out the major actions and strategies of the vision and asking staff to indicate the degree of implementation. These tools can help our concrete learners understand the *abstract* vision in terms they can understand and will assist visual learners with *pictures* of the vision.

Central City staff wanted to find a way to reinforce the implementation of the school vision (see Figure 6.6 below). These teachers felt that a Likert scale would be most appropriate for them.

FIGURE 6.6

Teacher Assessment Tool Related to Central City Vision

To what degree are you implementing these processes and strategies in your classroom?
Circle the number that represents the degree of implementation right now. Add comments.
(1 = not at all; 2 = not all the time; 3 = about half the time; 4 = almost all the time; 5 = all the time)

Implementation *Language Arts Curriculum*	*Classroom*	*Comments*
1. Develop a K-3 focus on Language Arts, Mathematics, and Second Language Development in K-3, by integrating Science, Social Science, and the Arts into these three areas.	1 2 3 4 5	
2. Include a systematic process for Language Arts instruction in a 1-1.5 hour block for kindergarten, 2.5 hour block for grades 1-3, and a 2 hour block for grades 4-6.	1 2 3 4 5	
3. Include systematic skills instruction along with a literature-based integrated thematic program aligned to the standards and curriculum guides.	1 2 3 4 5	
4. Teach through different modalities.	1 2 3 4 5	
5. Adapt to different learning styles.	1 2 3 4 5	
6. Be adaptable to a wide range of abilities and levels.	1 2 3 4 5	
7. Provide a program with specific strategies for instructing low-performing	1 2 3 4 5	
8. Include Accelerated Reader.	1 2 3 4 5	
9. Maintain a writing program that includes the specific skills based on the writing rubric and the standards for each grade level.	1 2 3 4 5	

This tool shows the elements of the school vision and asks staff to independently determine where they are with respect to implementing each of the vision elements. Teachers' assessments on the tool help them share where they are as a grade level and what they need to do to support each other's implementation. Grade-level teams take their collective results to cross-grade-level meetings to discuss how the staff is doing within and across grade levels. Professional development needs and support required for the whole staff are then recorded and addressed in the next professional development training, or the next professional development training is adjusted to meet immediate needs. The Central City example and a template for building a similar tool is found on the CD.

For evaluating the implementation of the vision, some schools build rubrics. The highest level of the rubric is critical. It would clarify what it would look like, sound like, and feel like with respect to the environment, curriculum, instruction, assessment, and outcomes if the vision is truly being implemented. The one level shows the first steps that staff believe will get them started on the vision. Levels two through four are identifiable points along the way to full implementation of the vision. The example staff-developed rubric (also see Figure 6.7 below for level five example), a template, and an activity for creating such a template appear on the CD.

FIGURE 6.7

Frank Paul School:
Brain Compatible Education Rubric

LEVEL FIVE*
Physical & Social Values of Environment
• The sense of responsibility for others and the feeling of the community are the most important values • Classroom has calming colors, music, plants, and potpourri • The calmness of the teacher's voice contributes to a settled classroom environment • Students are working in cooperative clusters with individual access to work tools • Yearlong theme is evident throughout classroom environment and life skills are an integral part of the class
Curriculum
• Teacher develops and implements a yearlong theme which integrates the three science areas, all content areas, key points, and inquiries for the entire year • 100% of science curriculum is planned
Instructional Strategies
• Teacher implements integrated thematic instruction all day, all year • Collaborative groupings for students • Students make choices about the inquiries they do • Students help in the selection of key points and take part in writing inquiries
Assessment
• Culminating performances chosen by the student that demonstrate mastery and application of key points • Performance task assesses original, creative, and problem-solving thinking • Students/peers self-assessment • Students select best work for showcase portfolio • Ongoing student/teacher assessment conferences with the use of rubrics • Student/teacher/parent interaction and conferences about portfolio
Outcomes
• Students participate in the design and evaluation of outcomes • Students take control of their learning and act in a self-directed manner for the entire day • Students demonstrate more shared leadership while doing collaborative activities • Students participate in peer and cross-age tutoring • Students can connect what they are learning in school to real life • Students can creatively solve real-life problems through interrelating and connecting what they have learned in various subject areas and the real world • Students use life skills as the basis for interacting with others

(*Level Five was developed for older learners.)

The staff knew that there was a developmental approach to implementing their vision. In other words, there were definite steps required in implementing the vision that built on the previous steps, so the rubric approach was appropriate for them. In other locations, the vision and plan may be established so that implementing a part of the vision is not an option, such as with the Central City Plan. In this case, the staff did not want a rubric that would show staff how to implement the plan incorrectly or halfway.

Some visions might not lend themselves to a "developmental" approach such as this example. In that case, a degree of implementation measurement tool, such as the Central City tool mentioned above, might be more useful.

These self-assessment tools would be used by individual teachers whose assessments are discussed at grade-level meetings. The grade-level assessments are then discussed at cross-grade-level meetings, etc. The results will clarify where implementation is bogging down, what professional development is needed, and where support needs to be focused. It will also invite additional questions leading to ongoing inquiry for clarification and reinforce the fact that we are indeed implementing the vision. A *Sharing Progress Activity* was designed for staff subgroups to share their progress toward implementing the vision and is on the CD.

SUMMARY

Once the vision has been created, the end targets, or goals, can be identified. Vision and goals represent *where the school wants to be*. The data analysis of strengths and weaknesses clarify *where the school is now*. An analysis of the difference between *where the school is now* and *where the school wants to be* is identified as the gap. One or more measurable objectives to achieve each goal describe how this gap will be closed.

The action plan to achieve the goals and objectives includes strategies/actions, person responsible, measurement, resources, due date, and timeline. All parts of the action plan are evaluated. Implementation assessment and monitoring tools and leadership structures will assist with ongoing implementation.

FREQUENTLY ASKED QUESTIONS ABOUT QUALITY PLANNING 💿
CD-ROM

▼ **What is the difference between a goal and an objective?**

Goals are achievements or end results. Goals are broad; objectives are narrow. Goals are general intentions; objectives are precise. Goals are intangible; objectives are tangible. Goals are abstract; objectives are concrete. Goals can't be validated as is; objectives can be validated. Goal statements describe the intended outcome of the vision and are stated in terms that are broad, general, abstract, and non-measurable. Example: *Our school's goal is to have all students meet the state learning standards.*

Objectives are goals that are redrafted in terms that are clearly tangible. Objective statements are narrow, specific, concrete, and measurable. When writing the objectives, it is important to describe the intended results, rather than the process or means to accomplish them, and state the time frame. Example: *The percentage of students achieving the math problem-solving standard will increase from 50 percent to 60 percent by Spring 2002, as measured by the state math exams.*

▼ **Who initiates the planning process?**

Most often plans are mandated by a state, district, or school improvement design. However, staffs or administrators can initiate the planning process when they believe the vision is not clear to everyone on staff, or when the processes are not achieving the intended results.

▼ **How do you narrow the focus in planning?**

This is an important question with a complicated answer. The important thing to remember when creating a comprehensive quality plan is that one must start with the vision and work backward. In that sense, a narrowing of the focus to work on math one-year only is not appropriate. On the other hand, when one starts with the vision, works backward to create action steps to achieve the plan, the focus begins to narrow immediately. How things can collapse becomes clear. What gets done first is clear. In that sense, the focus is being narrowed.

▼ How do you align the plan and processes?

The plan should include the processes for implementing the vision. Besides the obvious instruction and assessment strategies, this would include a leadership structure, times for meeting, and a method for assessing classroom implementation.

▼ How do you keep action and visions aligned?

The leadership structure, effective meetings, assessment tools, and colleagues will help keep the action and vision in alignment. So will the school portfolio.

▼ How do you bring staff along?

If the visioning process is done in a manner where every voice is heard and included, and the planning process allows everyone to be a part, or to review along the way in a safe environment, the staff will have ownership. The leadership structure must also support the change process and include regular meetings to clarify communication.

▼ How do deficiencies get addressed in a comprehensive action plan?

A comprehensive action plan starts with a review of data, specifically to synthesize needs and to understand the gap between the vision (where the school wants to be) and where the school is currently (data, strengths, and weaknesses). The purpose of the plan is to determine strategies to eliminate the gaps or deficiencies. This multi-year plan gets narrowed down to an immediate one-year plan. That comprehensive plan and the immediate one-year plan must focus on parts which are most deficient. These are the areas that get the highest priority. The data deficiencies will also point to most needed professional development.

▼ How do we determine what instructional strategies and programs are best?

Staff must study different instructional approaches and programs and read what other schools have found to make a difference with similar populations or with similar deficiencies. If staffs do not study different approaches, all they can do is implement the status quo. The analysis of current strategies and the results, along with the results other schools are getting, will help.

You may want to consult your Regional Professional Development Center (RPDC), Regional Service Center (RSC), Local Education Agency (LEA), or State Department of Education for references and additional assistance.

▼ **How can I be sure that staff will not get bogged down in the process?**

The process of planning is arduous. A facilitator must make the process fast-paced and fun. Team building activities interspersed in this work can help. For the long haul, the plan must include structures for implementation and monitoring.

YOUR QUESTIONS

Do you have the following in your continuous school improvement plan?

▼ Data analysis

▼ Values and beliefs

▼ Purpose

▼ Mission

▼ Vision

▼ Goals

▼ Objectives

▼ Strategies to implement the vision

▼ Actions to implement the strategies

▼ Person responsible

▼ Due date

▼ Timelines

▼ Evaluation

How will you evaluate the plan and keep it alive with staff and school community members?

ON THE CD RELATED TO QUALITY PLANNING TO ACCOMPLISH THE VISION

▼ Items to Include in the Quality Planning Section of the School Portfolio

▼ Quality Planning Continuous Improvement Continuum

▼ Frequently Asked Questions about Quality Planning

▼ Planning to Implement the Vision

- ◆ Steps in Creating an Action Plan
- ◆ Developing an Action Plan Activity
- ◆ Gap Analysis to Objectives Activity
- ◆ Root Cause Analysis Activity
- ◆ Goal Setting Activity
- ◆ Action Plan Form
- ◆ Questions to Guide the Refinement of the Continuous Schoolwide Improvement Plan
- ◆ Central City Elementary School Action Plan
- ◆ Central City Elementary School Shared Vision
- ◆ Central City Elementary School Evaluation Plan
- ◆ Teacher Assessment Tool Related to the Central City School Vision
- ◆ Teacher Assessment Tool Related to Our School Vision
- ◆ Staff Developed Vision Implementation Rubric Example
- ◆ Our School Shared Vision Implementation Rubric
- ◆ Staff Developed Rubric Activity
- ◆ Sharing Progress Activity

▼ Quality Planning Section Template

CHAPTER 7

PROFESSIONAL DEVELOPMENT:

Implementing the Vision

Chapter Objective: TO EMPHASIZE THE USE OF ONE SCHOOL IMPROVEMENT PLAN THAT EMBEDS PROFESSIONAL DEVELOPMENT IN THE PLAN

Quality professional development is like...

An engine, not the hood ornament. (Bob Chase, NEA)

Exercise, food, and water for the mind. It nourishes competence and confidence.

A glove that fits the hand of the school plan.

A box of tools given to school personnel that allows them to accomplish their assigned tasks and reach their goals of improved student achievement.

Learning to play a musical instrument—it takes instruction and ongoing practice, sounds best when collaborated with the rest of the orchestra (job-embedded); becomes better when the quality of performance is measured and improved; results in skills/abilities that performers take with them and patrons appreciate.

Music. It works to synchronize many instruments in a school — it blends ideas; bleeds passion; builds harmony in knowledge. It takes us beyond the vision.

A never-ending journey through adolescence, full of highs and lows. You change and grow. You want to belong, yet maintain your individuality. You know where you want to go, and it's a struggle to get there. It's hard. It's worth it.

Kindergarten—fun; new ideas; all should get along; naps and snacks; and how to grow.

A journey—should inspire; requires planning, packing, a map, a destination; willingness to go on a road less traveled; find excitement, must be flexible for surprises, good food. Professional development is the traveling, not the end destination.

A large, landlocked, extended family, all agreeing to learn to sail a schooner to Tierra del Fuego and survive the trip!

The School Portfolio Toolkit Reviewers

In this era of improving schools for student performance results, professional development for educators is being redefined for purposes of enhancing student performance. The skills of school leaders, including teachers at all levels, must continually improve if student learning is to improve. For ongoing continuous improvement, there must be ongoing, continuous professional development.

Professional development for educators cannot be perceived as a luxury for only the few who want to take advantage of the variety of interesting opportunities that are offered by local districts as professional development. As Bob Chase, National Education Association President, has stated:

Professional development is not the hood ornament; it is the engine of school improvement.

Professional development must be aligned to a thoughtful, shared school vision, as well as the overall district vision for student success. Professional development must be embedded into the workday of educators, constructivist in design, and contain a systemic component to implement the vision.

REDEFINING PROFESSIONAL DEVELOPMENT FOR CONTINUOUS SCHOOL IMPROVEMENT

Two decades ago, districts that could afford the time and money included professional development as part of their overall school improvement plan, usually basing their offerings on perceived needs or desires. Whatever teachers or administrators thought they needed or wanted to learn, they could choose. Often, due to limited funding, the monies were divided equally among a few. For administrators, an annual association conference often translated into their professional development choice. For educators, tuition reimbursement for graduate credit translated into their choice for professional development. Regardless of how either the conference or the graduate class might impact learning, teaching, or leadership processes, staff at all levels were given these choices without much more.

In the mid to late 1980's, many states instituted mentoring programs designed especially to assist new and/or first year teachers. Mentoring often resulted in a veteran teacher taking the new teacher under her/his wing in an advisor-advisee relationship. Mentors were, in some cases, and still are, paid to serve in this role. The relationship is always key to the success of mentoring with some mentoring experiences being more effective than others.

When mentoring does not provide the ongoing growth or enhancement of one's repertoire of skills or instructional strategies, or provide the motivation for the mentee to become an integral part of the school community team, isolation will result at best and burnout can more easily occur at worst! Many staff members work as hard as they know how to work. It is when staff perceives that they are working hard but not getting the results expected from students that frustration, discouragement, and blame occur.

One-shot workshops and schoolwide presentations with "outside experts" of new methods not necessarily connected to what teachers are experiencing in the classroom have been a steady approach to professional development over the years. Teachers have been able to choose which workshops they would like to attend and/or have been "pulled away" from their regular teaching duties to attend—without regard to other staff or a school vision.

There is little evidence that any of these approaches to professional development ever led to school improvement or improved student learning. Recent research in professional development is clear that "Improving teacher knowledge and teaching skills is essential to raising student performance…what teachers know and can do directly affects the quality of student learning" (Sparks and Hirsh, 1999).

Now we know that the ultimate purpose of professional development is to implement the vision to help all students learn. To accomplish this purpose in a systemic and systematic manner, all members of the learning organization must be learning and working in congruence with each other. No longer can schools simply allow individuals to choose what they want to learn. Professional development must provide for individual *and* organizational development, with student learning as the focus.

The National Partnership for Excellence and Accountability in Teaching (NPEAT) issued a report in 1999 entitled, *Revisioning professional development: What learner-centered professional development looks like* (1999). In this report, NPEAT defines research-based principles for professional development that ultimately improves student learning as follows:

▼ The content of professional development focuses on what students are to learn and how to address the different problems students may have in learning the material.

▼ Professional development should be based on analyses of the differences between (a) actual student performance and (b) goals and standards for student learning.

▼ Professional development should involve teachers in identifying what they need to learn and in developing the learning experiences in which they will be involved.

▼ Professional development should be primarily school-based and built into the day-to-day work of teaching.

▼ Most professional development should be organized around collaborative problem solving.

▼ Professional development should be continuous and ongoing, involving follow-up and support for further learning — including support from sources external to the school that can provide necessary resources and new perspectives.

▼ Professional development should incorporate evaluation of multiple sources of information on (a) outcomes for students and (b) the instruction and other processes involved in implementing lessons learned through professional development.

▼ Professional development should provide opportunities to understand the theory underlying the knowledge of skills being learned.

▼ Professional development should be connected to a comprehensive change process focused on improving student learning.

Reinventing professional development for educators requires redefining what effective professional development really is. Joellen Killion, National Staff Development Council Director of Special Projects, defines professional/staff development as the:

Development and exchange of professional ideas, values, beliefs, practices, and strategies designed to improve student achievement.

This definition supports the NPEAT principles, and the National Staff Development Standards for Staff Development, shown below in Figure 7.1. 💿
CD-ROM

FIGURE 7.1

2001 National Staff Development Council Standards for Staff Development

Context Standards

Staff development that improves the learning of all students:

- Organizes adults into learning communities whose goals are aligned with those of the school and district. (*Learning Communities*)
- Requires skillful school and district leaders who guide continuous instructional improvement. (*Leadership*)
- Requires resources to support adult learning and collaboration. (*Resources*)

Process Standards

Staff development that improves the learning of all students:

- Uses disaggregated student data to determine adult learning priorities, monitor progress, and help sustain continuous improvement. (*Data-driven*)
- Uses multiple sources of information to guide improvement and demonstrate its impact. (*Evaluation*)
- Prepares educators to apply research in decision making. (*Research-based*)
- Uses learning strategies appropriate to the intended goal. (*Design*)
- Applies knowledge about human learning and change. (*Learning*)
- Provides educators with the knowledge and skills to collaborate. (*Collaboration*)

Content Standards

Staff development that improves the learning of all students:

- Prepares educators to understand and appreciate all students; create safe, orderly, and supportive learning environments; and hold high expectations for students' academic achievement. (*Equity*)
- Deepens educators' content knowledge, provides them with research-based instructional strategies to assist students in meeting rigorous types of classroom assessments. (*Teaching Quality*)
- Provides educators with knowledge and skills to appropriately involve families and other stakeholders. (*Family Involvement*)

Source: *http://www.nsdc.org/standards.htm*

THE PROFESSIONAL DEVELOPMENT LEADER

Schools committed to improvement must reculture themselves for change. They must establish new systems for teamwork, communication, and collaboration. They must become, and continue to be, communities of learners in which the administrator is the *head learner* of the school. These schools must create new norms of behavior, and they must develop leadership and continuous improvement skills in all employees. This process of creating a new school culture requires that teachers, the principal, and staff be able to work well together—to communicate clearly and effectively with each other, and to trust and respect each other. Trusting relationships are key to reculturing. When staff is trustworthy as stewards of the vision and keepers of the dream, behaviors will change, as will communication and conversations.

The effective instructional leader, the model staff developer of the school, the building-level principal, must consistently understand, motivate, and lead her/his staff and students through successful school improvement transitions by being the steward of the vision and by providing the necessary support structures for school improvement teams to self-assess, look at data, plan together, make decisions, set measurable goals, and celebrate success. (Also see Chapter 8 on Leadership.)

The school leader has the responsibility to inspire results-driven staff development; that is staff development that is purposeful, aligned to the school vision, and is a foundational driving force in accomplishing the plan of action for implementing the vision. This responsibility includes developing and supporting systems and structures that foster collaboration.

Leaders must lead the implementation of professional development through the implementation of the vision. According to the Interstate School Leaders Licensure Consortium (ISLLC, 2000), school leaders at all levels need the skills to facilitate the process of establishing a shared vision. School administrators, in particular, must understand what effective professional development is; be the instructional leader to facilitate the resources for it; and also be committed to ongoing, quality professional development for her/his leadership in collaboration with school teams.

> *An organization's commitment to and capacity for learning can be no greater than that of its members.*
>
> **Peter Senge**

ISLLC bases its standards, shown in Chapter 8, 🔘 on these principles related to professional development:

▼ Conventional concepts of professional development need to be broadened.

▼ Professional development should focus on the personal and professional needs of the school leader. The school leader, not a supervisor, must be responsible for defining, implementing, and reflecting on the professional development process.

▼ Professional development must occur within the context of schools and must be directly connected to the specific and most critical needs for the improvement of schools.

▼ The ultimate goal of a school leader's professional development is to expand necessary leadership abilities in order to enhance teaching and learning in schools.

For school leaders who are committed to leading local professional development efforts, the school portfolio implementation process is ongoing, systemic, job-embedded professional development for staff at all levels. The process often changes the focus of school improvement from one of sporadic innovations and program implementation to one of quality planning based on results and multiple measures of important school, staff, student, and community data. The continuous analysis of data supports the learning community at all levels in its efforts to grow and strengthen its members.

DESIGNING PROFESSIONAL DEVELOPMENT TO IMPLEMENT THE VISION

Improving teacher knowledge and teaching skills is essential to raising student performance. With our knowledge base doubling every few years, and with the rapid change in the technological world, it is no wonder that the people whose job it is to prepare our next generations for the world of work must constantly be learning and developing new skills for improving student performance.

Effective professional development training to implement a vision for successful school improvement and real change in the classroom needs to be ongoing, job-embedded, constructivist in design, and contain a systemic component to implement the vision.

On-the-job learning or job-embedded learning is learning that occurs during daily work and includes methods and activities for sharing with each other, reflecting on experiences, and listening to best practices (Wood & McQuarrie, 1999). Job-embedded professional development is not only necessary, it can be much more valuable than sporadic, one-shot internal or external staff development (Sparks and Hirsch, 1997). Having teachers work together is job embedded professional development that is critical to increasing student learning (Joyce and Showers, 1988).

When staff development is constructivist in nature, those participating have ongoing opportunities to assist in the design and, just like student learners, are more likely to enroll in the process and stay focused and committed to the process of professional growth. When teachers can see their own growth lead to improved student outcomes, commitment becomes evident.

The school portfolio and continuous school improvement context provide many opportunities to embed professional development, designed by school staff, to implement the vision and to ensure the alignment of all the parts of the system to achieve increases in student learning. Some powerful professional development designs that are job-embedded, constructivist in design, and contain a systemic component to implement the vision, if designed that way, are summarized in Figure 7.2, shown on the following pages.

Figure 7.2 names the design and provides a brief definition of the traditional notion of the design along with references. Activities that describe how each design can be used in the context of the school portfolio and continuous school improvement appear on the CD. 💿
CD-ROM

When teachers can see their own growth lead to improved student outcomes, commitment becomes evident.

PROFESSIONAL DEVELOPMENT

FIGURE 7.2

Powerful Professional Development Designs

Name	Description	References
Action Research	Teachers and/or administrators raise questions about the best way to improve teaching and learning, systematically study the literature to answer the questions, implement the best approach, and analyze the results. **(CD)**	Calhoun, 1993 & 1994; Glanz, 1999; Loucks-Horsley, 1998; Sagor, 2000; Sagor, 1993; Stringer, 1996; Wood & McQuarrie, 1999
Cadre or Action Teams	Teaming allows for the delegation of responsibilities so teams of educators can study new approaches, plan for implementation of new strategies or programs, and get work done without every staff member's involvement. **(CD)**	Rappaport, 1999; Stiggins, 1999; Wood & McQuarrie, 1999.
Case Studies	Staff members review case studies of student work, and/or of another teacher's example lessons, which can lead to quality discussions and improved practices. **(CD)**	Barnett, 1999; Barnett, 1998; Colbert, 1996; Merseth, 1996; Shulman, 1992; Wasserman, 1993
Coaching	Teachers form teams of two or three to observe each other, plan together, and to talk and encourage each other in meaningful ways while reflecting on continuously improving instructional practices. **(CD)**	Costa & Garmston, 1994; Harwell-Kee, 1999; Showers & Joyce, 1996; Sparks, 1990
Curriculum Development	Curriculum is the way content is designed and delivered. Teachers must think deeply about the content, student learning standards, and how it must be managed and delivered.	Ball & Cohen, 1996; Killion, 1993; Loucks-Horsley, 1998
Curriculum Mapping	Curriculum mapping and webbing are approaches that require teachers to align the curriculum and student-learning standards and look across grade levels to ensure a continuum of learning that makes sense for all students.	Fitzharris, 1999; Jacobs, 1997; Martinello & Cook, 1994
Curriculum Implementation	Curriculum implementation is putting curriculum into practice.	Guskey, 1996; LoucksHorsley, 1997
Demonstration Lessons	Teachers demonstrate lessons for other teachers wishing to see what a quality lesson in a particular area would look like, sound like, and feel like. The lesson can be demonstrated to colleagues in the classroom with students, or outside of the classroom.	
Examining Student Data	Examining student data consists of conversations around individual student data resuls and the processes that created the results. This approach can be a significant form of professional development when skilled team members facilitate the dialogue. **(CD)**	Bernhardt, 2000
Examining Student Work	Examining student work as professional development ensures that what students learn is aligned to the learning standards. It also shows teachers the impact of their actions. **(CD)**	Loucks-Horsley, 1998; Mitchell, 1999

FIGURE 7.2 (Continued)

Powerful Professional Development Designs (Continued)

Name	Description	References
Example Lessons	Some teachers need to see what a lesson that implements all aspects of the school vision would look like. Providing examples for all teachers to see can reward the teacher who is doing a good job of implementing the vision and provide a template for other teachers. It is very effective to store sumary examples in a binder for everyone to peruse at any time. Example on CD. **(CD)**	Morton, Mendocino Grammar School
Immersion	Immersion is a method for getting teachers immersed in different content through hands-on experiences as a learner. **(CD)**	Lappan, 1999; Loucks-Horsley, 1998
Journaling	Journal writing helps teachers contruct meaning for, and reflect on, what they are teching and learning. **(CD)**	Killion, 1999; Killion & Todnem, 1991
Listening to Students	Students' perceptions of the learning environment are very important for continuous improvement. Focus groups, interviews, and questionnaires can be used to discover what students are perceiving. **(CD)**	Bernhardt, 1998; Hord & Robertson, 1999; Kushman, 1997
Mentoring	Mentoring pairs an experienced teacher with a teacher with less experience.	Loucks-Horsley, 1998; Robbins, 1999; Showers & Joyce, 1996; Shulman & Colbert, eds., 1987
Needs Assessment	Needs assessments help staff understand the professional development needs of staff. If used well, a needs assessment tool can lead to quality staff conversations and sharing of knowledge. Example tool on CD. **(CD)**	
Networks	Purposeful grouping of individuals/schools to further a cause or commitment. **(CD)**	Lieberman, 1999; ; Lieberman & Grolnick, 1996; Loucks-Horsley, et al., 1997
Observation	Teacher and observer agree on what is being observed, the type of information to be recorded, when the observation will take place, and how the information will be anlayzed. Observer might be a colleague, a supervisor, or a visitor from another location.	Collins, 1997
Partnerships	Teacher partnering with businesses in the community, scientists, and/or university professors can result in real-world applications for student learning and deeper understandings of content for the teacher. **(CD)**	Bernhardt, 1999; Loucks-Horsley, 1998
Process Mapping	School processes are instruction, curriculum, and assessment strategies used to ensure the learning of all students. Mapping or flowcharting school processes can help staff objectively look at how students are being taught. **(CD)**	Bernhardt, 1998
Reflective Logs	Reflective logs are recordings of key events in the educators work days to reflect for improvement and/or to share learnings with colleagues. **(CD)**	Wood & McQuarrie, 1999

FIGURE 7.2 (Continued)

Powerful Professional Development Designs (Continued)

Name	Description	References
Scheduling: What a Day Would Look Like	A real test for whether or not a vision is realistic is to have teachers develop a day's schedule. This would tell them immediately if it is doable, or what needs to change in the vision and plan to make it doable. (CD)	
School Improvement Planning	Planning to implement the vision requires studying the research, determining strategies that will work with the students, and determining what the vision would look like, sound like, and feel like when implemented, and how to get all staff members implementing the vision.	See Chapter 6
School Meetings	Staff, department, grade level, and cross-grade level meetings can promote learning through study, communicating, and practices while focusing on the implementation of the vision. (CD)	Wood & McQuarrie, 1999
School Portfolio	*The School Portfolio* is a professional development tool that gathers evidence about the way work is done in the school and a self-assessment tool to ensure the alignment of all parts to the vision. A school portfolio can also serve as a principal portfolio.	Bernhardt, 1999; Bernhardt, et al., 2000
Self-Assessments	Staff self-assessments are tools to measure progress toward the vision, such as the *Continuous Improvement Continuums*, will help staff see where their school is as a system and what needs to improve for better results. Examples on CD. (CD)	Chapter 3; Bernhardt, 1999
Shadowing Students	Purposefully following students and systematically recording the students' instructional experiences is a wonderful job-embedded approach to understanding what students are experiencing in school. (CD)	Wilson & Corbett, 1999
Specialty Area Leaders	When implementing a vision requiring teachers to implement strategies they have never used before, teachers or specialists who understand and use these processes regularly can provide support for those trying strategies for the first time. Subject focused teams can be part of the leadership structure.	
Storyboarding	Storyboarding is an activity that will allow participants to share previous knowledge, while reflecting on a topic. It is a structure for facilitating conversations. (CD)	NCREL, 2000
Student-Led Conferences	Student-teacher-parent conferences led by the student can give the student an opportunity to describe what she/he is learning and take ownership in what she/he is learning. The teacher and students would have to prepare for the conference together, allowing the teacher to gain more intimate knowledge of what the student is thinking and learning.	

FIGURE 7.2 (Continued)

Powerful Professional Development Designs (Continued)

Name	Description	References
Study Groups	Groups of educators meet to learn new strategies and programs, to review new publications, or to review student work together. (CD)	Murphy, 1999; Murphy, 1997; Murphy, 1995; Murphy & Lick, 2001; Murphy & Lick, 1998, Wood & McQuarrie, 1999
Supervision and Evaluation	Both of these strategies include pre-conferences, observations, and post-conferences for feedback and dialogue that can determine needs and lead to improved instruction and continuous school improvement.	Wood & McQuarrie, 1999
Teacher Portfolios	Portfolios document a teacher as learner, reflections, observations, and evidence. Portfolios can be used for many things including self-asessment, employment, supervision to replace traditional teacher evaluation, and for peer collaboration. (CD)	Dietz, 1999; Dietz, 1995; Green & Smyser, 1996; Wolf & Dietz, 1998
Team Development	Team development builds collegiality and can change the school culture. Norms of behavior, team meeting protocols, teambuilding training, and structures to work together develop teams. Many of the tools on the CD support team development. (CD)	Stiggins, 1999
Team Planning and Teaching	Actual planning, teaching, and sharing plans and results with colleagues can lead to rich discussions of practices and possibilities.	Stiggins, 1999; Wood & McQuarrie, 1999
Train the Trainers	Train the trainers is an approach to saving time and money. Individuals are trained and return to the school or school district to train others. (CD)	Griffin, 1999; Guskey, 1995; Joyce & Showers, 1995; Loucks-Horsley, et al., 1997
Training	Training as professional development is common. Training assists with the understanding of theory, and is most effective when modeling, demonstrations, and/or practice are included.	Collins, 1997; Joyce & Showers, 1995
Tuning Protocols	A tuning protocol is a formal process for reviewing, honoring, and fine-tuning colleagues' work through presentation and reflection. (CD)	Allen, 1995; Allen & McDonald, 1993; Kushman, 1995; Easton, 1999
Workshops	Workshops as professional development are a common approach for gaining new knowledge of content areas. It is a way to learn from experts, or others with more expertise.	Fullan, 1991; Joyce & Showers, 1998; Loucks-Horsley, et al., 1997

PROFESSIONAL DEVELOPMENT

PLANNING FOR PROFESSIONAL DEVELOPMENT

Planning for effective professional development in congruence with the school vision, goals, plan, and calendar provides staff with opportunities to improve personal performance while learning new skills for reforming the school culture and supporting the development of a true learning organization around a shared vision.

For professional development to be the engine of school improvement, it must be designed backwards from the vision, with improved student learning as the goal. Professional development can become a part of everything a staff does. Creating time for this ongoing work is embedding it into the culture of the school.

Creating the Professional Development Plan During Action Planning

More often than not, the professional development plan will be developed as a part of the action planning process. Figure 7.3 shows questions and recommendations for creating a professional development plan that is job-embedded, ongoing, and constructivist in nature.

In the action planning process, described in Chapter 6, a planning team would start by creating a vision, identifying two to three school goals (the outcomes of the vision), and analyzing the school data. The team would then determine the gaps between where the school wants to be (vision and goals), where it is right now (strengths and areas for improvement), and analyze root causes for the gaps so the true problems can be solved and not just treat the symptoms. From the root cause analysis, strategies would be identified, as well as actions to implement the strategies. This is the point where comprehensive professional development planning comes into play. The planning team could build the professional development plan through a series of questions and use Figures 7.2 and 7.3 to determine which job-embedded strategies will become the way the school does business. The important questions appear below as steps in professional development planning. A tool for recording this information is found on the CD. An example follows the questions.

▼ *What skills and knowledge are needed to close the gap between where we want to be and where we are right now?*

General areas for improvement in teaching practices will surface when analyzing student achievement data and when looking at the gaps between where the school wants to be in the future and

Planning for quality professional development.

FIGURE 7.3

Planning for Quality Professional Development

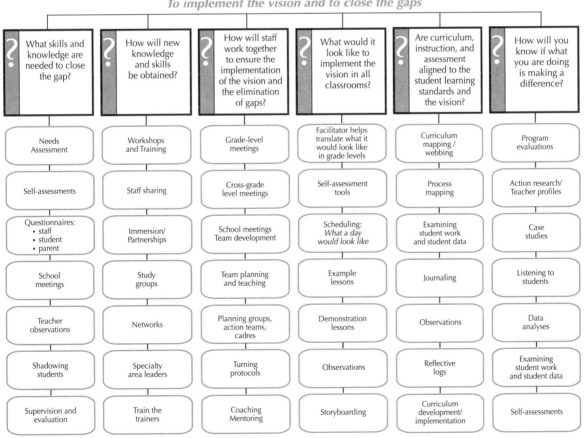

VISION

School Goals

Gaps Between Vision and Reality

Root Cause Analysis

Professional Development Plan
To implement the vision and to close the gaps

What skills and knowledge are needed to close the gap?	How will new knowledge and skills be obtained?	How will staff work together to ensure the implementation of the vision and the elimination of gaps?	What would it look like to implement the vision in all classrooms?	Are curriculum, instruction, and assessment aligned to the student learning standards and the vision?	How will you know if what you are doing is making a difference?
Needs Assessment	Workshops and Training	Grade-level meetings	Facilitator helps translate what it would look like in grade levels	Curriculum mapping / webbing	Program evaluations
Self-assessments	Staff sharing	Cross-grade level meetings	Self-assessment tools	Process mapping	Action research/ Teacher profiles
Questionnaires: • staff • student • parent	Immersion/ Partnerships	School meetings Team development	Scheduling: *What a day would look like*	Examining student work and student data	Case studies
School meetings	Study groups	Team planning and teaching	Example lessons	Journaling	Listening to students
Teacher observations	Networks	Planning groups, action teams, cadres	Demonstration lessons	Observations	Data analyses
Shadowing students	Specialty area leaders	Turning protocols	Observations	Reflective logs	Examining student work and student data
Supervision and evaluation	Train the trainers	Coaching Mentoring	Storyboarding	Curriculum development/ implementation	Self-assessments

where it is right now. For example, if the goal of the school is to have all students reading at the grade level reading standard and only forty percent of the students are reading at this level, one might expect that new knowledge and skills for teachers will surface as an issue. The data analysis work will help staff understand which students are not learning and in which areas, so the knowledge and skills can be targeted to the appropriate group and in the appropriate content and context. It could be that most students are very close to achieving mastery. It might be that students are not mastering one sub area, only, or one could find that the lowest two deciles are struggling with all concepts. Either way, this is important information for designing professional development activities. In addition to analyzing comprehensive student achievement data, staff might want or need to gather more data to know specifically the skills and knowledge that are necessary for closing the gap. Using Figure 7.2, tools for understanding needed knowledge and skills could include:

- Needs assessment
- Self-assessment using a vision rubric
- Self-assessment using a five-point scale
- Questionnaires
- School meetings
- Teacher observations
- Shadowing students
- Supervision and evaluation

▼ *How will the knowledge and skills be obtained to implement the vision?*

When it is known which skills and knowledge will be targeted for professional development, the professional development planning committee can recommend to the full staff (or the whole staff can brainstorm) how the knowledge and skills will be obtained. Some job-embedded approaches, which do not stand alone, include (but not limited to):

- Workshops and/or training
- Staff sharing
- Immersion
- Partnerships
- Study groups
- Networks
- Specialty area leaders
- Train the trainers

▼ *How will staff work together to ensure the implementation of the vision and the elimination of gaps?*

Each of the approaches for obtaining the skills and knowledge will need a support and practice strategy to ensure implementation in each classroom as well as throughout the school. Some of these strategies include:

- Grade level meetings
- Cross grade level meetings
- School meetings with team development
- Team planning and teaching
- Planning groups, action teams, and cadres
- Tuning protocols
- Coaching
- Mentoring

▼ *What would it look like to implement the vision in all classrooms?*

Many times teachers say they are happy to implement the vision in their classrooms, they just need help in understanding what it would look like. Some strategies include:

- Workshop facilitator helping with the translation of what it would look like in grade levels
- Self assessment tools
- Scheduling: What a day would look like
- Example Lessons
- Demonstration lessons
- Observations
- Storyboarding

▼ *Are curriculum, instruction, and assessment aligned to the student learning standards and the vision?*

As a part of understanding the skills and knowledge needed, and/or for determining the impact of implemented strategies, curriculum mapping can help staffs see if what they are doing is helping students achieve the learning standards. Some job-embedded approaches, which do not stand alone, include:

- Curriculum mapping/webbing
- Process mapping
- Examining student work
- Examining student data
- Journaling
- Observations

- Reflective logs
- Supervision/evaluation
- Curriculum development/implementation

▼ *How will you know if what you are doing is making a difference?*

Some job-embedded approaches to understanding if what the teachers are implementing in their classrooms is making a difference include:

- Program evaluations
- Action research
- Teacher portfolios
- Case studies
- Listening to students
- Data analyses
- School portfolio
- Examining student work
- Examining student data
- Self-assessment

An example of a first draft of one part of a professional development plan, using this approach, follows as Figure 7.4.

Pulling a Professional Development Plan from the School Plan

If a continuous school improvement plan has been developed as described in Chapter 6, major professional development pieces will already be identified. It will be necessary for the leadership team, the school improvement leader, or professional development coordinator to pull out the professional development pieces and begin to organize around them, and/or with their knowledge of powerful professional development designs, enhance the professional development plan to include time for appropriate ongoing, job-embedded, constructivist professional development.

With respect to the Central City plan shown in Chapter 6, the Central City planning team knew that staff was clear about what the school would look like, sound like, feel like when the vision was implemented since their vision was developed from staff values and beliefs. They incorporated strategies in their plan that would ensure that every staff member had the skills and knowledge to implement the vision and the support and tools to know how to improve and when to improve.

FIGURE 7.4

Page 1 of Draft Professional Development Planning Example

Goal 1: All students learning at high levels.

Objectives:
- To increase the number of students meeting and exceeding mastery in all subject areas, by 10 percent, by the end of 2003.
- To ensure that students in all parts of the scoring distribution improve

Gaps	Knowledge and Skills Needed	Design Strategies	Time Line	Measurement	Resource Needs
In analyzing math scores, math problem solving was low. Other math subtests were excellent. Only 47 percent of the student population met mastery in math problem solving, about the same as the previous two years. Math problem solving disaggregated by gender shows that fewer boys scored at mastery or above than girls—for five years. Looking at deciles, one can see that there are many students right below the mastery cut score.	From the analysis of data, we can see that we have been doing the same thing over and over and expecting different results. We must change our practice. Curriculum review showed that our math curriculum is not aligned to the standards. Students are being tested on concepts not yet taught. The staff questionnaire showed that staff feel they need more knowledge about teaching math problem solving, and would like to see what good lessons look like.	Curriculum development Training Observe other teachers teaching Example lessons Curriculum alignment Study student work Follow-up in grade level, cross-grade level, and staff meetings Self-assessment tool	Curriculum development and training in August and September, with follow-up throughout the year Observations and example lessons: once per month Study student work officially quarterly Staff meetings—Tuesdays Self-assessment monthly and report at meetings	Improved test scores Increases in implementation of aligned curriculum as measured by our vision self-assessment tool, observa-tions, example lessons, and student work Administrative observations	Roving substitutes for observa-tions New curriculum materials Facilitator for trainings Release time to plan and implement new curriculum

Central City staff wanted every staff member to implement the vision to its fullest. Using the school portfolio framework, the staff discussed embedding professional development in all parts of their learning organization.

Staff determined they would use training with implementation strategies when new knowledge and skills were needed. Teachers on staff could even be the training facilitators. They would use a leadership structure that would clarify roles and responsibilities, while creating time for collaboration, communication, team building, and support for implementing the vision. Staff committed to meeting from 2:30 to 4:30 every Tuesday afternoon to work in grade level, cross-grade level, focus group, or whole staff teams. During these meetings, staff would discuss staff assessments on the vision implementation tool they developed. This discussion would inform all staff of the difficulties they were having implementing the vision and of additional support required and desired. To support the implementation of the vision directly in the classroom, staff would observe each other, demonstrate quality lessons, plan together, share action research findings, review data analysis, share case studies, put together a binder of exemplary lessons that illustrate implementing the vision, conduct program evaluation, and examine student work and student data.

The school planning team selected from the action plan all references to professional development by school goal, being careful to include strategies that are not traditionally considered professional development. In their second step, they grouped common elements, or those that needed to be together, and organized them around a school calendar. (An example of page one of the *Central City Elementary School Professional Development Plan* is on the CD.)

CREATING THE TIME FOR PROFESSIONAL DEVELOPMENT

Most teachers and administrators say that the hardest thing to find around schools is time. Time is commonly stated as the reason specific school improvement efforts are rejected or not implemented. Unfortunately, time will not find us; we have to find the time (Barkley, 1999). Sometimes we might even need to lose time in order to gain time (Wiggins, 1990).

No doubt we must become more creative about making time. Some suggestions include:

▼ Team teaching, releasing one or more teachers to attend professional development training or to observe another teacher teaching

▼ Banking time by adding ten minutes of instruction to four days a week and having an early release time one day a week that is dedicated to staff planning and vision implementation

▼ Structuring the day so teachers get an hour to plan each day, preferably with a targeted team member (i.e., coach, mentor, partner)

▼ Working with church or community partner groups to plan educational activities for students for a day or half-day so teachers can learn and plan together

▼ Dedicating school meeting times to learning and implementing the vision

▼ Adding time to the beginning and/or end of the day or school year for staff learning

▼ Videotaping excellent lessons for teachers to review on their own time

▼ Meeting as a study group for breakfast, lunch, or dinner on a regular basis

▼ Utilizing student teachers, substitutes, instructional assistants, resource specialists, community partners, the assistant principal, and/or the principal to release classroom teachers to engage in job-embedded professional development

▼ Requiring course-related projects and community service that gets students out in the community with chaperones, while teachers learn together

▼ Scheduling lunches and planning periods for teachers working together

▼ Establishing special days or partial days of activities or assemblies for students that release some of the teachers for a block of time, who then release other teachers for a later block of time.

▼ Implementing block scheduling

▼ Rethinking the number of supplementary staff

▼ Staggering teachers' teaching schedules

RESOURCES FOR PROFESSIONAL DEVELOPMENT

The National Staff Development Council and school improvement specialists recommend that school districts devote at least ten percent of their operating budgets to professional development and that teachers devote at least twenty-five percent of their work time to personal learning. When school districts calculate their professional development expenses, they often include only the cost of paying tuition and covering the cost of substitute teachers. As staff development becomes more sophisticated and necessary for improving student achievement, school districts will need to calculate the cost of time for team meetings, school improvement planning, peer coaching, classroom observations, developing curriculum, and other powerful designs for professional development.

REPORTING ON PROFESSIONAL DEVELOPMENT TRAININGS

There will be times when staff members want to attend professional development out of the mainstream of other staff members. It would behoove a school or district to have a system in place that would ensure that any professional development must help the staff member implement the vision. One system might require staff to complete a report form (Figure 7.5) describing what topics they plan to attend, and ways that it will have a positive impact on student learning.

FIGURE 7.5

Staff Development Proposal
(To be submitted to the Office of Staff Development PRIOR to the proposed date.)

Date(s) of proposed session or series: _____

Check ALL that apply:

❑ Districtwide in-service	❑ Building level in-service
❑ Single session	❑ Register for each session separately
❑ Series of related sessions	❑ List this in-service in the next district booklet
❑ Same session repeated on different dates	❑ Do not list in the district booklet
❑ Must attend all sessions to receive credit	

Location of staff development: _____ Room: _____

Audience: _____ May others attend? _____

Maximum number of attendees: _____

Title of session: _____

Facilitators(s) *(for out-of-district facilitators, please include position and address):*
_____
_____

Brief description of sessions/series as it should appear in the booklet *(attach additional pages, if needed):* _____
_____
_____
_____

Relationship of in-service to district's school improvement (SI) objectives, assessed needs, and/or student data *(check ALL that apply):*

District SI objectives

❑ SI 1: All students in the district will be proficient readers by the end of grade three.

❑ SI 2: The number of students in the proficient and advanced levels on the statewide assessment will increase by five percent yearly.

❑ SI 3: District results on nationally standardized tests will be at or above state and national averages.

❑ SI 4: The district will achieve a 95 percent average daily attendance rate.

❑ SI 5: The district will reduce the dropout rate to five percent or below by the 2004 school year.

❑ SI 6: 100 percent of all graduates will be prepared to enter post-secondary education/training programs or productive occupations related to their educational training.

Top 20 districtwide needs

❑ Dealing with disruptive students	❑ Parental support and involvement
❑ Lack of basic skills	❑ Authentic (real-world) learning
❑ Discipline	❑ Using computers in the classroom
❑ Stress management for student/teachers	❑ Oppositional and defiant disorders
❑ Positive behavior programs	❑ Internet research skills
❑ Working with difficult parents	❑ Student motivation and involvement
❑ Content-specific computer-assisted instruction	❑ Instructional strategies for special-needs students
❑ Brain-based learning/how people think	❑ Dropout prevention
❑ Word-processing, spreadsheets, databases	❑ Classroom management
❑ Developing assessments/rubrics	❑ Authentic assessment

Adapted from Columbia Public Schools, Columbia, Missouri

EVALUATING THE SCHOOL'S PROFESSIONAL DEVELOPMENT PROGRAM

The quality and impact of professional development is one of the hardest elements of school improvement to understand. There will not be just one tool available to evaluate the impact of any professional development. Instead, a combination of tools and student achievement analyses will be required. It is best to think through the whole design before forging ahead.

FIGURE 7.5 (Continued)

Staff Development Proposal (Continued)
(To be submitted to the Office of Staff Development PRIOR to the proposed date.)

Building level goal or objective: _____

Need based on the following student data: _____
_____

Special information to be noted in the description:
(i.e., material or meal costs, credit restrictions, etc.)

_____

_____

_____

_____

Any expenditure of district funds will require prior approval.

Person responsible for the in-service: _____
(to receive and return sign-in sheets to Staff Development Office)

Person completing this form: _____

_____

Signature for approval:

_____   or   _____
District Director/Coordinator/Supervisor   Principal
(for districtwide inservices only)   *(for building-level inservices only)*

Staff Development Office approval:

_____

Adapted from Columbia Public Schools, Columbia, Missouri

Many people believe that evaluations require control groups and a research design. We want to avoid thinking that one must have control groups in order to understand program impact. That is not only impractical; it is unethical at times in the world of education (i.e., we cannot give a classroom of students technology and not give another classroom of students access to technology in order to understand the impact of technology on student learning). In education, we study what we think will make a difference for the students we have, and then we implement those strategies. When we evaluate the implementation of those strategies, we do not want a yes-no answer to the question of *Did it work?* Instead, we want to know which strategies worked and to examine the elements of implementation to understand how to continue to ensure and support further successful implementation.

Putting together an evaluation design can be quite logical. Basically, think about when you need feedback on training and implementation and how you are going to get that feedback. An example of a comprehensive evaluation design for understanding the impact of on-going professional development for implementing technology is shown in Figure 7.6. The design is set up in terms of questions teachers want answered about the implementation of technology throughout the school. For each question, methods for answering the question and the purpose of the method are outlined. The tools mentioned in the example are referenced to the locations in which they are discussed in the chapter.

An activity for evaluating a professional development program is on the CD.

Evaluating Impact with Hypotheses

An evaluation design can also be written around hypotheses in place of questions. When teachers determine to implement a special vision or process schoolwide, they have ideas about the impact it could make. They might believe that implementing technology, for instance, will improve student writing, reading, and problem-solving skills. They might also believe that technology will help with attendance and discipline. When the vision is written, it is important to lay out these hypotheses, along with why they believe the strategies will impact student learning, and how the impact will be measured. Action research, mentioned earlier as a powerful professional development design, can also be used as an evaluation component.

FIGURE 7.6

Evaluation Design: Implementing Technology

Where is staff with respect to understanding how to implement technology in the classroom?	**Needs Assessment Tool** 🌼 *Purpose*: To discover exactly where the teachers are with respect to implementing technology and to know what professional development they need and want. (Might be given more than once.)
What is the quality of the Professional Development Training?	**Formative Evaluations (Figure 7.7 and 7.8)** *Purpose*: To have teachers reflect on the quality of the first day of multi-day training, and to provide input into the next day(s) training.
To what degree is technology (and/or the vision) being implemented?	**Questions at end of sessions (Figure 7.9 and** 🌼 **)** *Purpose*: To reflect on the quality of the professional development session and to think about implementing the content in the classroom.
How do we support the implementation of the vision, provide feedback on the implementation, and provide models for others to see?	**Self-Assessment/Observation Tool (Figure 6.6)** *Purpose*: To have teachers self-assess using a tool that spells out what they need to be implementing. The results will show the degree of implementation, and training and support needs. It also reinforces implementation.
How do we support the implementation of the vision, provide feedback on the implementation, and provide models for others to see?	**Self-Assessment (Figure 6.6)** *Purpose*: This tool can monitor the implementation of the vision and clarify professional development needs. **Unit Description (Figure 7.3)** *Purpose*: To show each other what a unit that implements technology (and the vision) might look like and to provide reflection and feedback with respect to making it better. If done well, this can be used as a celebration tool (e.g., the units can be placed in a binder for review or on the school website as excellent examples.)
How do we support the implementation of the standards?	**Standards-based Assessment Tool (Table 7.10)** *Purpose*: To keep the standards in focus at all times. Can be used in conjunction with the implementation of technology, but changing the tool a bit, to ask the question, *How are you using technology to implement the standards?* These results can provide needed information about professional development needs.
What is the impact of the professional development training over the long haul?	**Professional Development Follow-up Questionnaires (Figure 7.11 and 7.12)** *Purpose*: To keep the professional development training in mind and to check on additional support needs.
What is the impact on student learning?	**Student Achievement Results (Chapter 4)** *Purpose*: To understand if there are student learning increases that are attributable to professional development.

The Formative Questionnaire

If a formal professional development workshop on training is more than one day, a formative questionnaire can be given at the end of the first day, such as Figure 7.7 or 7.8. The feedback will allow participants to reflect on the content of the day and how the new information can help them implement the concepts, while providing valuable feedback to the professional development trainer. The questions can be few and simple. The facilitator could also just ask participants to write on index cards what they really want to cover the next day.

FIGURE 7.7

FIGURE 7.8

Formative Evaluation 1

Name *(optional)* _____

What was the most effective part of today?

What would have made the day more effective?

What do you definitely want to cover tomorrow?

Formative Evaluation 2

Name *(optional)* _____

What was the focus?

What were the strengths?

What would you do differently (tomorrow)?

The most common tools for evaluating the immediate impression of professional development trainings are summative in nature and ask questions about the quality of the training. The more these evaluation tools ask the recipients to think about using the information for their own implementation, the better.

Certainly, the self-assessment of the implementation on the vision tools (shown in Chapter 6 and described in Figure 7.2 as a powerful professional development design) would also provide information related to the quality of the professional development received by staff with respect to the implementation of the concepts. Each individual's developmental issues must be kept in mind; however, as staff members will not be at the same place at the same time.

A tool for understanding the immediate impact of the professional development workshops or trainings is shown in Figure 7.9. Figure 7.9 and three additional summative instruments are provided on the CD.

FIGURE 7.9

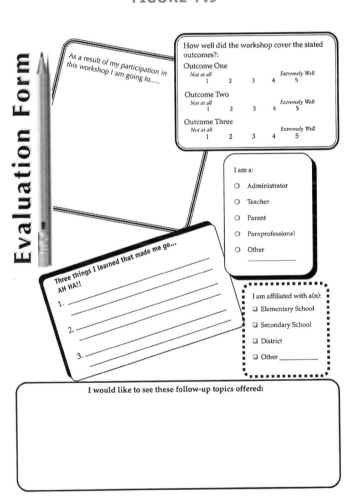

The Learning Standards Implementation Questionnaire

Schools must support and ensure the teaching of student learning standards at each grade level. Quality professional development will include implementation of these standards. A tool such as the one in Figure 7.10 could query staff about the implementation of standards. The questionnaire must be made more useful by putting in specific standards. This tool could also be adjusted to become an observation tool and could include vision elements as well.

FIGURE 7.10

Standards Implementation Questionnaire		
Teacher:		
Grade Level:		
To what degree are you implementing the standards in your classroom?		Examples of Standards-Based Activity
Language Arts	1 2 3 4 5	
Reading	1 2 3 4 5	
Writing	1 2 3 4 5	
Mathematics	1 2 3 4 5	
Science	1 2 3 4 5	
Social Science	1 2 3 4 5	

Self-Assessment of NSDC Standards Implementation

The CD contains a tool developed by the National Staff Development Council (*www.nsdc.org*) for schools to assess their professional development program to the NSDC Standards. The assessment will help schools determine where they are and determine strengths and areas for improvement.

The Follow-Up Questionnaire

To keep the professional development training fresh in staff members' minds and to check on additional support needs, a follow-up questionnaire, similar to Figure 7.11 and 7.12, could be given to all participating staff members. The questionnaire asks about how the professional development training assisted them with implementation.

FIGURE 7.11

FIGURE 7.12

Professional Development Follow-up Questionnaire 1

Name: _____

We would like to know the impact of the professional development you have been receiving. Your responses will be greatly appreciated. Please be as honest as possible.

1. What did you do differently in your classroom following the workshop?

2. From your perspective, what was the impact or benefit of using these new ideas?

3. Are you working on/with a team to implement these concepts?

4. If you decided *not* to implement anything different after the workshop, what type of ongoing support would have helped you implement the concepts?

On a scale of 1-5, please rate your progress in implementing each of the following elements:

No progress   Excellent Progress
1   2   3   4   5

Add specific elements from the professional development training	1 2 3 4 5		1 2 3 4 5
	1 2 3 4 5		1 2 3 4 5
	1 2 3 4 5		1 2 3 4 5
	1 2 3 4 5		1 2 3 4 5

5. What specific additional support, if any, do you need to implement these concepts?

5. What additional support do you need to continue studying and implementing the concepts and key skills?

6. Would you be interested in a follow-up workshop?   Yes ☐   No ☐

Comments:

Professional Development Follow-up Questionnaire 2

Name: _____

We would like to know the impact of the professional development you have been receiving with respect to student learning. Please complete the statements below.

1. Regarding student achievement in my classroom/building/district, I attended this session to gain knowledge about:

2. Students in my classroom/building/district will ultimately benefit from this session and my new learning because:

3. I plan to use the key concepts and new skills by:

4. I will share my learning with students and staff during:

5. The system in which I work will need to consider:

   in order for me to continue improving my skills on:

Comments:

DESIGN YOUR OWN QUESTIONNAIRE

If the examples provided here do not quite fit your needs, you could design your own questionnaire. An activity to help you create a questionnaire is provided on the CD.

LOOKING AT THE IMPACT OF PROFESSIONAL DEVELOPMENT ON STUDENT LEARNING

The tools mentioned above are considered "soft" evaluation, subjective, or qualitative. While they might not have a "hard" feel to them, they can be pretty good indicators of what happened in the classroom after the trainings or workshops. To take the evaluation to a "harder" level, or the quantitative level, we would have to understand the impact of professional development on student learning. To do this, one would need to look at student achievement results in conjunction with teaching processes. Many of the analyses described in Chapter 4 provide information about the quality of professional development designs, with the implication being that if the designs are effective, the processes will be implemented and student learning would improve. To really understand the impact on student learning, student achievement data need to be gathered before and after the training. If standardized test scores are used, the year or two before the training and implementation will give a baseline perspective. The year of the training and the years after will show how trends shifted because of the implementation.

To follow individual students, look at the distribution of test scores in Figure 4.6 in Chapter 4. This type of distribution will reveal information about the implementation of different processes, if you follow students who are in classrooms that implemented the processes in question. In other words, find the students who were in grade two before the program was implemented, who then had teachers who implemented the professional development training when they became third graders and fourth graders, etc. Following students in all the combinations and permutations of implementation, one can begin to see if there were gains over the years that could be attributed to the professional development training and/or the implementation of the vision. This is where the understanding of processes being implemented is so crucial and where focused professional development to implement the vision is key.

The average analyses shown in Figure 4.4 in Chapter 4 can also indicate gains attributed to different processes. Instead of disaggregating (initially) by gender, one could disaggregate by whether or not the students were in classrooms with teachers implementing a specific professional development process. Using normal curve equivalent (NCE) scores, where 50 NCE is who one would expect as an average year's growth, one could see if the students that are in classrooms implementing the strategies grew at a steady rate, or at a rate different from those in classrooms not implementing the vision. With the NCE, there should be steady increases for all students. At least their scores should not be decreasing. If the processes are making the intended impact, the growth of students in classrooms implementing the process should be greater than the growth of students in classrooms not implementing the processes.

Sometimes actual student work can show the impact of implementing a new process, vision, or technique. For example, if teachers begin to use e-mail as a means of improving writing, they might look at the writing samples they received before using e-mail (i.e., in previous years) and compare the results with the writing they are receiving after implementing e-mail as a writing tool.

SUMMARY

Professional development is the *engine of school improvement* and the key to implementing the vision. Professional development must be planned in advance, be ongoing, job-embedded, systemic, and focus on implementing the vision. Professional development must be evaluated to understand its impact on classroom practices and, ultimately, student achievement.

FREQUENTLY ASKED QUESTIONS ABOUT PROFESSIONAL DEVELOPMENT

▼ **What is effective (or quality) professional development?**

Quality professional development is the *development and exchange of professional ideas, values, beliefs, practices, and strategies designed to improve student achievement* (Killion, NSDC).

Effective professional development training helps staffs implement a vision for successful school improvement and improved student learning. Effective professional development that leads to real change in the classroom needs to be ongoing, job-embedded, constructivist in design, and contain a systemic component to implement the vision.

▼ **How do you reculture a school for change?**

Reculturing the school for change is very difficult, but essential for moving an entire school to a vision. Reculturing a school requires leaders who understand their job is to move the entire staff to implement the school vision; staff members who understand their roles and responsibilities with respect to implementing the vision; commitment from the entire staff to implement the vision; staff members knowing how to delegate and expect work to be completed; and assurance that the vision is shared by all staff members. Job-embedded professional development in all these aspects will help with the reculturing task. So will achieving a shared vision through values and beliefs.

▼ How do we get the whole staff to believe that everybody needs to be doing the same professional development work?

Getting everybody working and learning together is definitely a goal and a challenge. Before this can happen, a school must have a vision that is shared by all staff members. The work of getting to a shared vision has to be done together and commitment built and rebuilt along the way for that vision to be truly shared. When it is clear what the vision will look like, sound like, and feel like, staff will realize that everyone needs many of the same skills and instructional strategies, and at the same time. As the structure of the school begins to incorporate the route to the vision, job-embedded professional development will become a way of life. The plan will organize it, the leadership structure, including staff meetings and grade-level meetings, will be job-embedded professional development, and lead staff to work together to build a continuum of learning that makes sense for all students. Ongoing, embedded professional development will become the way business is done in the school.

YOUR QUESTIONS

What do you have in place to assess the implementation of the vision?

What do you need to put into place if you do not have something now?

What professional development strategies will help you implement your vision?

How will you evaluate the impact of professional development?

ON THE CD RELATED TO PROFESSIONAL DEVELOPMENT 💿

▼ Items to include in the Professional Development Section of the School Portfolio

▼ Professional Development Continuous Improvement Continuum

▼ Frequently Asked Questions About Professional Development

▼ National Partnership for Excellence and Accountability in Teaching (NPEAT) Report

▼ National Staff Development Council Standards

▼ Interstate School Leaders Licensure Consortium (ISLLC) Standards

▼ Powerful Professional Development Designs
  ◆ Action Research Activity
  ◆ Cadres or Action Teams Activity
  ◆ Case Studies Activity
  ◆ Coaching Activity
  ◆ Examining Student Data: Teacher Analysis of Test Scores Table One
  ◆ Examining Student Work Activity
  ◆ Example Lessons:
    • Birds of a Feather Unit Example
    • Unit Template
  ◆ Immersion Activity
  ◆ Journaling Activity
  ◆ Listening to Students Activity
  ◆ Needs Assessment:
    • Professional Development Needs Related to Technology
    • Professional Development Plan Related to Technology
  ◆ Networks Activity
  ◆ Partnerships: Creating Partnerships Activity
  ◆ Process Mapping: Charting School Processes Activity
  ◆ Reflective Logs Activity
  ◆ Scheduling Activity
  ◆ School Meetings: Running Efficient Meetings
  ◆ Self-Assessments:
    • Teacher Assessment Tool Related to the Central City School Vision
    • Teacher Assessment Tool Related to Our School Vision

CHAPTER 8

LEADERSHIP: Building a Leadership Structure to Implement the Vision

Chapter Objective: TO DISCUSS AND SHOW HOW LEADERSHIP STRUCTURES CAN BE ALIGNED TO THE VISION AND HOW LEADERS MUST NURTURE THAT ALIGNMENT

Quality leadership is like...

The dawn, certain, ordered, precise, full of unlimited possibilities.

A beehive. Each person has a role to support the bee community. All have one shared vision, to produce large amounts of honey. The community promotes togetherness and hard work to accomplish a common goal.

A flock of migrating geese that have a willingness to share the lead while working toward a common destination.

The School Portfolio Toolkit Reviewers

THE LEADERSHIP CHALLENGE

Kouzes and Posner, authors of *The Leadership Challenge* (1995), conducted years of research on leaders and uncovered five fundamental practices that enable leaders to get extraordinary things done. The leaders they studied were able to—

▼ Challenge the process
▼ Inspire a shared vision
▼ Enable others to act
▼ Model the way
▼ Encourage the heart

The leadership processes spelled out in *The School Portfolio: A Comprehensive Framework for School Improvement* (Bernhardt, 1999) and the Interstate School Leaders Licensure Consortium (ISLLC) standards require these features, as well. Let's dig into what it would look like if we apply these five fundamental practices to the school portfolio process.

Challenge the Process

By using data, leaders of the school portfolio process must challenge the status quo in order to innovate and get new processes implemented.

Leaders must be willing to take risks and to find better ways to do things. Effective leaders know that in order to get different results, they must change the processes for curriculum, instruction, and assessment, that create the results. Effective leaders also understand the processes that are being used now and are able to look at the results with respect to these processes. This understanding of current processes and results is the fastest way for leaders to understand which processes to challenge to achieve different results. The Information and Analysis section of the school portfolio is the canon for principals who "challenge the process."

Inspire a Shared Vision

The process to a shared vision, spelled out in Chapter 5, begins with the values and beliefs of the individuals in the learning organization. An effective leader would listen to these beliefs, as they will tell her/him what is possible and what it will take to get the individuals to own a new vision. The individuals must also know that the leader is listening and understands them, their needs, beliefs, and ideas.

Leaders see what it will look like, sound like, and feel like when the processes that will result in improved achievement are implemented. They can visualize the results that the different processes will achieve, even before the processes are implemented. Kouzes and Posner state that "in some ways, leaders live their lives backwards." In other words, they can play through the scenarios and know that different innovations will make a difference. Good leaders also know what it will take to implement the innovation. The leaders cannot be the only ones to see the vision, however.

These leaders must make sure everyone in the organization understands the vision and her/his role in implementing it. This clear, shared vision must be inspired, never commanded. The leader must communicate her/his enthusiasm for the vision. It is the leader's enthusiasm and staff's belief in the vision that will "inspire a shared vision." Articulating the vision, asking key questions in light of the vision, and reporting on progress toward the vision are all skills that effective instructional leaders possess.

Enable others to act

Exemplary leaders enlist the support and assistance of all those who must implement the vision, all those who have a stake in the vision, and all those who must live with the results. These leaders make it possible for others to act, to take risks, and to feel ownership of the results.

> *Leaders breathe life into the hopes and dreams of others and enable them to see the exciting possibilities that the future holds.*
>
> **Kouzes and Posner**
> **The Leadership Challenge**

A solid leadership structure that allows others to participate in the day-to-day direction of the vision is necessary, as is quality professional development, to help each person gain the skills needed to implement the vision. (A discussion on building a leadership structure appears later in this chapter.)

Model the way

When staffs agree to work differently, they look to leaders to verify actions. Leaders go first. Leaders must show by example how to implement the vision and how to carry out agreements. Exemplary leaders concentrate on producing small wins that lead to implementation and, therefore, strengthen the commitment to the vision. A well thought through quality plan can ensure that there are accomplishments and celebrations of accomplishments all along the way.

Strong leaders make sure that all the times together with staff are used to model the implementation of the vision and to move that implementation forward. Leaders must show what it looks like to act in congruence with beliefs, purpose, and vision. Effective staff meetings are a wonderful way to show by example how to implement the vision (discussed later in this chapter).

Encourage the Heart

Leaders must keep everyone aiming for the vision at all times. They must be the vision torch-bearers; "stewards of the vision;" the modelers of the vision; and the cheerleaders and inspirers for individuals who implement the vision daily. A leadership structure that includes everyone in the organization and in which they agree will support the implementation of the vision will ensure that implementation. Effective staff meetings are another way. And, finally, how leaders visibly and behaviorally link rewards with performance gives them their credibility. Credibility of action is the single most significant determinant of whether a leader will be followed over time. *Does your leader walk the walk, or just talk the talk?*

Greater Community and Political Social Contexts

In addition to the five fundamental practices that enable leaders to get extra ordinary things done, Interstate School Leaders Licensure Consortium (ISLLC) standards and the school portfolio include sections on including the "greater community" in the vision and understanding the "political, social contexts." Strong leaders must work from the context of the greater community, as well as from the political and social contexts. Strong leaders engage parents, the community, businesses, and the district in win-win partnerships. (This is discussed further in Chapter 9.) The ISLLC standards are outlined below, appear on the CD by themselves, and are cross-referenced with *The School Portfolio* requirements.

Interstate School Leaders Licensure Consortium (ISLLC) Standards

Standard 1

A school administrator is an educational leader who promotes the success of all students by *facilitating the development, articulation, implementation, and stewardship of a vision of learning that is shared and supported by the school community.*

Standard 2

A school administrator is an educational leader who promotes the success of all students by *advocating, nurturing, and sustaining a school culture and instructional program conducive to student learning and staff professional growth.*

Standard 3

A school administrator is an educational leader who promotes the success of all students by *ensuring management of the organization, operations, and resources for a safe, efficient, and effective learning environment.*

Standard 4

A school administrator is an educational leader who promotes the success of all students by *collaborating with families and community members, responding to diverse community interests and needs, and mobilizing community resources.*

Standard 5

A school administrator is an educational leader who promotes the success of all students by *acting with integrity, fairness, and in an ethical manner.*

Standard 6

A school administrator is an educational leader who promotes the success of all students by *understanding, responding to, and influencing the larger political, social, economic, legal, and cultural context.*

BUILDING A LEADERSHIP STRUCTURE

A quality leadership structure defines how decisions will be made: basically who will make what decisions and when. *The Leadership Responsibility Matrix Activity* can be used to determine who makes what decisions when. These structures allow everyone to share in the decision making. The key to effective shared decision making and a quality leadership structure is to clarify—

▼ processes and procedures for the decision-making work

▼ roles and responsibilities of everyone in the organization to implement the vision

▼ a truly shared vision

The benefits of shared decision making include an empowered staff, commitment, ownership, professionalism, and the building of leadership capacity. Most importantly, the people who must implement the decisions are the ones who should make them. The downsides of shared decision making that put it at-risk for the long-haul focus are time and skills, for example; finding the time to do the research behind each decision; finding the time to meet as a team to make the decisions; and learning the skills to run effective meetings are challenges.

It takes time to develop a shared decision-making structure responsive to the needs of an individual school. The intent is to have staff determine the structure—not the principal in isolation of staff. It is also intended that the shared decision-making structure will comprehensively replace old structures—not merely be an addition. Shared decision making will ideally become the norm.

Many different structures can work to involve principals, teachers, staff, students, and even the community, in shared decision making. The *action team* approach is commonly utilized as the shared decision-making structure of choice when there are changes to be made throughout the school. Action teams are established to—

▼ study new approaches to improving the school processes for meeting students needs

▼ implement the recommended changes

▼ lead the improvement process and day-to-day school events

▼ perform specific work details on an ad hoc basis

Study Teams

Most shared decision-making schools use a system of action study teams or committees that take responsibility for researching and making recommendations about specific approaches to achieving the school vision and goals. Study teams conduct vital research activities, such as:

▼ investigating new instructional strategies or programs for potential implementation

▼ visiting schools that have implemented new strategies and programs

▼ formulating an overall timeline for implementation

▼ analyzing costs and efficiency of implementation at the school

▼ correlating the impact or use of new strategies with the needs of the school population

▼ determining what it would take to implement the strategies

Ideas for study can come from any direction. They can come from the teams themselves, from principals, district staff, from teachers on other teams, or from external resources such as Regional Professional Development Center staffs. It is very important that all teachers feel that the input process is open and that everyone's opinion is helpful and appreciated. Study teams usually include representatives of every section of the school community, such as grade level teachers, subject matter teachers, classified staff, school and district administrators, students, parents, and community members.

Implementation Teams

Study teams are often disbanded when their recommendations have been approved for implementation. (In other words, when the team's work is done, the team does not continue to meet just because the team has been established.) After a comprehensive school-level action plan is developed from study team recommendations, implementation teams are formed to give the recommendations substance and to guide implementation within their jurisdiction (i.e., subject area and student groupings). Implementation teams monitor the timelines and quality of implementation in a supportive fashion.

The structure of implementation teams is very important for realizing the vision and the school goals. For example, if the vision for a high school is to integrate subject matter with team teaching across the disciplines, the implementation teams should consist of integrated team members and not be set up by subject matter areas. Having the interdisciplinary team plan together, and coach and monitor each other, will greatly assist the implementation of new strategies throughout the school.

Having a leadership team integrate recommendations from the action study teams helps ensure congruence with the school vision, mission, beliefs, and values. The leadership team, most often made up of team leaders from the implementation action teams, administrators, and school community representatives, ensures that the implementation of the new strategies is articulated, timely, ongoing, and measurable.

The leadership team is accountable to the full staff. The amount of decision-making power granted to the team by the staff varies from school to school. At the point when final decisions need to be made, some schools rely on whole staff meetings; others use town-hall-style meetings, and still others give authority to the leadership team to make the final decisions. In the former case, the leadership team works as a liaison between the study and implementation teams and the full staff, with final decision-making power held by the full staff. In the latter case, the leadership team takes the recommendations of the action teams, integrates the input, makes the decisions, and then communicates those decisions to the staff.

An example of how action teams evolved at Pelican High School follows (excerpted from *The School Portfolio: A Comprehensive Framework for School Improvement* [Bernhardt, 1999], pages 129-131):

> *After thoroughly analyzing student achievement results over time, students' evaluations of school processes, and the newly developed school vision, Pelican High School teaching staff felt they could better meet the needs of their students if they could decrease the number of students teachers saw every day. They also knew they could provide instruction in an integrated fashion with more real-world applications. Staff determined that they needed to look into a school-within-a-school approach; they needed to understand more about the behavior and developmental issues of high-school-age students, as well as new approaches to instruction and assessment, including utilizing technology. The staff divided into teams (as shown in Figure 8.1) to study these issues with respect to the school's vision and mission. Each study team was structured to have representation from each grade level*

and subject area in the school. Additionally, a leadership team (made up of the leaders of each study team and of school administrators) was developed to monitor and encourage the study teams.

As they worked, study teams reported progress regularly to the leadership team who listened carefully to ensure congruence of each team's focus with the school mission and vision; to make sure the teams were not overlapping efforts when inappropriate and that they were overlapping efforts when appropriate; to gently redirect the teams in meaningful ways when necessary. When the study teams finished their research, they made recommendations to the leadership team and then to full staff. The leadership team was given the charge by the full staff to synthesize the study teams' recommendations and make a comprehensive overall recommendation with an action plan. After the overall recommendation and action plan were approved through total staff consensus, the leadership team developed a continuous school improvement plan, which was then reviewed, revised,

FIGURE 8.1

Study Team Structure

and approved by the full staff for implementation. A new shared decision-making structure with implementation action teams (as shown in Figure 8.2) was established, congruent with the continuous school improvement plan and the new school structure described in the school vision.

Each implementation team established its own vision and mission within the context of the overall school vision. With respect to shared decision making, the teams determined which decisions would be appropriate for each team to make, which decisions needed full staff consensus, and which decisions could and should be made by the leadership team or the principal alone. Times for meeting were established around the timelines for implementation, and accountability was spelled out in the continuous school improvement plan.

FIGURE 8.2

Implementation Team Structure

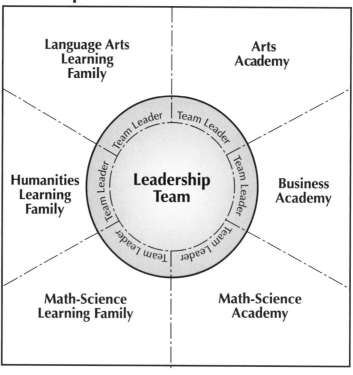

Figure 8.3 shows *Central City's Leadership Structure* that emerged from the vision and plan that you saw in the previous chapters.

FIGURE 8.3

Central City Elementary School Leadership Structure

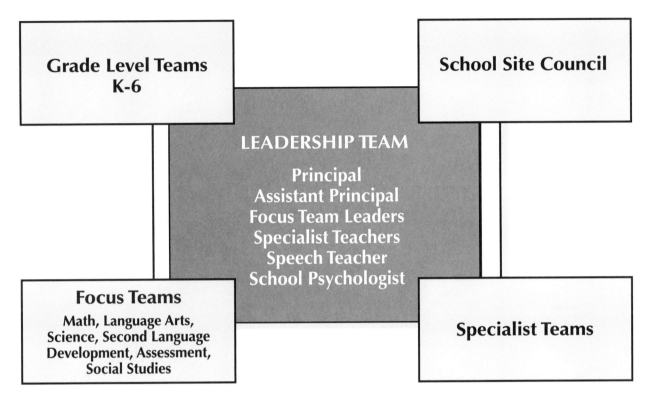

This leadership structure will supercede all other leadership structures existing at Central City Elementary School.

The Central City Leadership Team will be made up of grade-level leaders and focus team leaders:

- Two leaders will be named for each grade level and each focus team from different tracks
- Only one will act as leader each six weeks
- Leaders will serve two-year terms, which will be staggered to ensure that the next track leader is prepared to take over:
  - Principal and Assistant Principal
  - Specialty Teachers
  - Speech Teacher and Psychologist, as available

The leadership team will meet one Monday each month.

Meeting Times for Staff

All staff will be expected to meet every Tuesday from 3:30 to 5 pm, as follows:

Week 1 Staff Meeting

Week 2 Grade-Level Meeting

Week 3 Staff Meeting

Week 4 Focus Team Meeting

Week 5 Staff Meeting—Focus Teams report-out agenda

Week 6 Grade-Level Meeting

Staff meetings will be focused on whole school change (15 minutes on logistics, e-mail will be used at other times).

A part of the leadership structure is meeting time for grade levels and focus teams, as follows:

◆ Grade-level teams will meet twice every six weeks to discuss improvement of curriculum, instruction, and assessment.

◆ Focus teams will meet once every six weeks. The focus teams include:

- Math Focus Team
- Language Arts Focus Team
- Science-Second Language Development
- Assessment Focus Team
- Later add Social Studies Team—we first want to keep focus on the areas tested

Roles and Responsibilities

Grade-level Teams

◆ Every teacher will participate with her/his grade level.

◆ The purpose is to maintain unity of curriculum, instruction, and assessment at each grade level.

◆ Teachers will coach and support the vision in classrooms.

◆ Grade-level leaders will bring in support from focus teams as needed.

◆ Grade-level representatives or the whole team will attend district training as appropriate.

Focus Teams

- Every teacher will participate on one focus team (each team will be represented by a mix of grade levels, experience, tracks)
- Each teacher will serve on a focus team for one year
- There will be two leaders, who are also grade-level leaders, each from different tracks
- The purposes are to:
  - improve instruction in these areas by solving schoolwide curricula issues
  - implement the vision within and across grade levels of content standards, curriculum, instruction, and assessment
  - advise the leadership team of progress and concerns
  - coach and support the implementation of content areas
  - be a resource for teachers in each content area
  - review data, plan for improvement
  - disseminate content information from district, state, textbook adoptions, etc.
  - respond to content issues from staff

Grade-level leaders and focus team leaders are responsible for:

- Articulation of vision between and across grade levels
- Advising the leadership team of progress and concerns
- District meetings on their subjects

Ad Hoc Teams

As shared decision making becomes institutionalized, more sophisticated forms of teamwork evolve for making decisions on specific items or to perform specific regular school tasks and then disband. (They must do the work and not take on a life of their own.) Specific tasks that schools do every year can be delegated to ad hoc teams—items that do not require full staff approval and do not directly impact the school improvement efforts, such as staff holiday parties, regulatory program renewals, sports supervision, and parents' night. Ad hoc teams are great for helping to organize the year in advance and to enable staff to plan and perform their work in a proactive manner throughout the year.

Action Team Benefits

The action team approach provides many benefits, as described above. Action teams help schools "divide and conquer" the work by creating a system for dialogue, planning, and research in which everyone can take part and contribute based upon the abilities and interests of each person. They create ownership of the process because everyone is involved. Action teams provide a system for sharing the research work so that individual teachers do not need to become "experts" in everything. They provide leadership opportunities and provide individuals with the opportunity to express opinions in small groups rather than in front of the entire school community, so more opinions are heard. Action teams provide a forum for staff members who may have particular concerns but are afraid to address them to school administrators. They give teachers of different student groupings and subject areas opportunities to work together, ending years of relative isolation, and reinforce the fact that everyone is committed to implementing the vision. Action teams help schools focus on purpose, student learning standards, student achievement, achievable goals, and articulation across student groupings. Action teams help schools establish a new culture of collaboration.

Action Team Downsides

There are downsides to the action team approach, including the amount of time required to hold meetings, to research issues, to share information, and to reach consensus. There may be scheduling conflicts until the team structure is institutionalized and a lack of participation by some staff members. Sometimes, there is a lack of support by the district. The logistical difficulty in communicating effectively with everybody in the school is a challenge at all schools, but communicating may be a special problem at schools with year-round and multiple-track schedules. However, the results that are produced by using the action team approach are definitely worth the effort.

Leader of the Leadership Team

Because of the enormity of the task of establishing a shared decision-making structure and of implementing school improvement, things will run much smoother if someone is assigned, or elected by staff, to coordinate the efforts. This leader or coordinator is usually not the principal; although, in some situations, the principal may be the most appropriate person. This person also plays a key leadership role as a keeper of the school vision and mission, ensuring that everyone stays involved, on track, and committed to improvement. Overall, leaders must be well-organized, capable of visualizing the big picture, dedicated to improvement, thick-skinned, and approachable. The leader's responsibilities might include the following tasks:

▼ serve as primary communication contact within the school and outside of the school—serve as public and community relations officer for the improvement effort

▼ keep the "big picture"—school vision, mission, values and beliefs—at the forefront

▼ monitor the shared decision-making structure, develop agendas, and facilitate leadership team meetings

▼ supervise and coach action teams

▼ coordinate the budget

▼ attend district meetings to keep the two-way communication flowing

▼ plan retreats

▼ schedule and monitor staff development activities

▼ assist with the recruiting of partnerships with business and community groups

▼ delegate tasks to share the work that staff and leadership determine is needed

▼ downplay personal viewpoints and agendas and work to consolidate ideas

▼ be a good listener and sounding board for ideas

▼ communicate with the principal

The role of leader requires tremendous time and energy; although, as the school community becomes more familiar with the principles of shared decision making, the leader's role becomes less strenuous. Some schools use co-leaders to ease the time constraints for individuals who may also have classroom teaching duties. Other schools have restructured their staff workload to have at least one teacher on special assignment who can lead their school improvement efforts. The shared decision-making leader is such an important person for school improvement that reallocating money within the school budget to institutionalize the position would be smart for schools that plan to improve continuously.

ESTABLISHING MEETINGS THAT MAKE A DIFFERENCE

Staffs are limited by the amount of quality time they have together to talk about their work and to build that continuum of learning for students. This is why those times together must be used to their fullest potential. The items discussed during a staff meeting should consist only of items that have outcomes based on full group participation. Much of what is done during typical staff meetings can be handled in other ways (e.g., information items disseminated through written staff bulletins and e-mails, and interest inventories for special programs through written surveys). A guide for effective meetings ⊙ appears below.

A quality organization uses every minute together to effectively move the organization closer to its vision. Group processes make the most of limited-time meetings and encourage individuals to work with peers they may not know well or with whom they do not normally have an opportunity to share ideas. Creating vertical teams by mixing and separating grade level and subject area staff can also help.

To run quality meetings, it is helpful to establish norms of behaviors for meetings in terms of ground rules and meeting etiquette, and to use quality procedures for brainstorming and coming to consensus—examples ⊙ are shown on the opposite page (Figures 8.4 and 8.5).

FIGURE 8.4

GROUND RULES
This is a safe room
There is no rank in this room
All ideas are valid
Each person gets a chance to speak
Each person gets a chance to listen
We are here to focus on the future
Our purpose is improvement, not blame

FIGURE 8.5

MEETING ETIQUETTE

Raise your hand and be recognized before speaking
Be brief and to the point
Make your point calmly
Keep an open mind
Listen without bias
Understand what is said
Avoid side conversations
Respect others' opinions
Avoid personal agendas
Come prepared to do what is good for the organization
Have fun

Running Effective Staff Meetings

The time that shared decision making requires is the most frequently cited disadvantage of the process. Here are some tips on running efficient meetings to help ease the time crunch:

▼ formalize a meeting date, time, and place (e.g., first Monday of every month at 7:30 a.m. in the cafeteria)

▼ create and distribute the agenda before the actual meeting day

▼ set a time limit for each item on the agenda

▼ set up a process to address only the most important issues (school vision, mission, and goals) instead of spending time on issues that can be dealt with by one or two people

▼ assign a facilitator, timekeeper, and record-keeper at each meeting; rotate roles from meeting to meeting

▼ decisions should be made on the basis of data collected on the issue rather than hunches or "gut feelings," which differentiates between treating the problem or the symptom

▼ stay on schedule

▼ determine next steps and individual assignments for follow-up

LEADERSHIP

There are times when it is necessary for all individuals to agree on, and implement, a crucial next step. Voting is not an adequate procedure to determine which way to go. Consensus is a more appropriate method, as spelled out below.

COMING TO CONSENSUS

Any team's goal should be to reach decisions that best reflect the thinking of all team members. Use consensus when you want input and support of every member of the team. *Consensus means finding a proposal that everyone can support and no one opposes.* It does *not* mean: *a unanimous vote* (consensus may not represent everyone's first priorities); *a majority vote* (in a majority, only the majority get something with which they are happy, while those in the minority may get something they don't want at all); or with which everyone is *totally satisfied*. For coming to consensus you need:

▼ time to discuss ideas

▼ the active participation of all group members

▼ good communication skills (listening, clarification, conflict resolution, and facilitation for both discussion and dialogue)

▼ creative thinking and open-mindedness

Decide ahead of time when you will push for consensus. Decisions that have a major impact on the direction of the school must belong to the whole team and be supported by consensus. Again, the vision should drive the process of reaching consensus. *Coming to Consensus* appears on the CD.

Brainstorming for Consensus

One of the most effective tools for beginning the consensus process is brainstorming. This technique is especially helpful because it allows team members to examine a wide range of options before making a final decision. It also encourages people to be as creative as possible without restricting their ideas in any way. The goal of brainstorming is to generate as many ideas as possible. No value judgements are made at the brainstorming stage. Rules to follow in brainstorming (Figure 8.6) include:

▼ Review the topic; define the subject of the brainstorm; ask why, how, and what questions

- ▼ Encourage everyone to freewheel; don't hold back any ideas even if they seem silly — the more ideas the better
- ▼ No discussion during the brainstorm; save it for later
- ▼ No judgment or criticism is allowed of another's ideas, not even with a groan or grimace
- ▼ Allow people to "hitch-hike" by building upon ideas generated by others

FIGURE 8.6

GROUND RULES FOR BRAINSTORMING
Every idea is a good one **No idea is ever criticized** **No person is ever criticized** **Ideas are written down so everyone can see** **Ideas are not discussed until brainstorming is complete**

PERSONNEL EVALUATIONS THAT ASSIST A SCHOOL IN IMPLEMENTING THE VISION

Effective leaders make sure people benefit when behaviors are aligned to values and beliefs, mission, and vision. Many of our school portfolio schools that have built rubrics for assisting with the implementation of the vision ultimately use these rubrics to replace old ways of "evaluating personnel." In other words, the rubric for implementing the vision that appears in Chapter 5, and is discussed in the evaluation of the action plan, could become a self-assessment/evaluation tool for teachers. Teachers can assess where they are with respect to each element on the rubric and set goals with their principal for moving up on the continuum. This is a wonderful, consistent alignment tool that ties rewards to vision implementation.

SUMMARY

Leadership is an important component of the action plan for implementing the vision. Strong leaders must challenge the process, inspire a shared vision, enable others to act, model the way, encourage the heart, and include the greater community. A structure for leadership must be aligned with the vision and help everyone understand her/his role and responsibilities in *implementing* the vision. Action teams help with the implementation of shared decision making. Most of these teams, made up of representative staff members, have a purpose, do their jobs, make recommendations, and then are done. Implementation action teams support the implementation of the vision in all parts of the school over the long haul.

FREQUENTLY ASKED QUESTIONS ABOUT LEADERSHIP

▼ **How do we encourage our principal to help us establish shared decision making?**

First of all, you must be very clear with yourselves about why you want shared decision making. If you want to share decisions as a benefit for implementing the vision, that argument will most probably encourage the principal to participate. If it is for an ulterior reason, you might need to reconsider.

▼ **What do we do if we have a principal who is not willing to change?**

That is definitely a tough question. If you have a principal not willing to allow staff to get involved with decision making and to support change, staff has two options: 1) wait until the principal moves on; or, 2) move ahead and hope the principal catches on. Just make sure your efforts are focused on a vision you all believe in and know will make a difference for the students.

▼ **What do we do if the district talks about shared decision making but does not support it in their actions?**

This is another tough question. One of the best ways to prevent a district from undoing everything a school is trying to do is to keep district leaders involved and understanding what it is you are trying to do and what you are finding along the way; in fact, your school portfolio will help you with this. They can see your ultimate goals, your progress, the benefits of your work, and it is less threatening to them. It might be wise to look for a champion within the district office who could be your "school coach." Ask a district staff member you trust, who does quality work, and who can ultimately influence a warranted change at the district level, to be your school coach. By bringing her/him into some of your inservice days and staff meetings, she/he can begin to see what is going on and also be the messenger of information you want to have delivered back to the district office. *A district office can change.*

▼ **How do we set up a shared decision-making structure?**

First of all, for a shared decision-making structure to implement the vision, you have to be very clear on a vision. Once you are clear on a vision it is much easier to play through the scenario of how decisions should be made throughout the organization. Try drawing a picture of a leadership structure that would align with the way the vision must be implemented before people are identified to be on the team, and before the vision is implemented. This can desensitize the whole process and can be a very good way to make the vision actually happen.

One of the reasons schools have difficulty creating a leadership structure for implementation is that they might be thinking about leadership deciding dollars and management issues. It becomes a relief when they learn this structure is to lead the implementation of the vision.

▼ **How does one determine if consensus has been reached?**

Each consensus-building approach has its own method of knowing that consensus has been reached. The method we use for assessing on the *Continuous Improvement Continuums* is basically to ask if there is anyone who "could not live with this assessment." Other times, after the discussion starts sounding as if the group has reached consensus, we often just ask if we can have a thumbs up, thumbs down, or thumbs parallel to the ground indication to make sure we are really there.

YOUR QUESTIONS

Draw a picture of your current leadership structure. Is this leadership structure aligned with your school vision? Does it help you achieve your goals and implement your action plan?

If the answer to the question above is a "no," draw a leadership structure that will help you implement the vision.

ON THE CD RELATED TO LEADERSHIP

▼ Items to Include in the Leadership Section of the School Portfolio

▼ Leadership Continuous Improvement Continuum

▼ Frequently Asked Questions About Leadership

▼ Interstate School Leaders Licensure Consortium (ISLLC) Standards

▼ Cross Reference Matrix of The School Portfolio with ISLLC

▼ Leadership Responsibility Matrix Activity

▼ Central City Leadership Structure Example

▼ Group Process Tools
   ◆ Running Efficient Meetings
   ◆ Issue Bin/Parking Lot
   ◆ Ground Rules
   ◆ Meeting Etiquette
   ◆ Norms of Behavior
   ◆ Coming to Consensus
   ◆ Guidelines for Brainstorming

▼ Example Leadership Section Template

CHAPTER 9

PARTNERSHIP DEVELOPMENT:
Involving Partners to Implement the Vision

Chapter Objective: TO DESCRIBE HOW TO PLAN FOR EFFECTIVE PARTNERSHIP INVOLVEMENT

> *Quality partnership development is like...*
>
> A herd of wild mustangs, full of vibrancy and energy—charging and interchanging leaders, all for the sake of greener pastures.
>
> Winning the super bowl. It requires hard work, practice, providing leadership, enthusiastic support to create a team of players, coaches, and fans to bring home a victory.
>
> Missouri School Portfolio Awareness Session, February 2001

Schools that seek to prepare students to live and work in the communication age would do well to establish partnerships with businesses, the community, parents, the district, and university teacher and administrator preparation programs. When established and implemented, these partnerships can make instructional programs exciting and relevant to the purpose of developing all students into successful citizens and quality workers. Partnerships help to reinforce learning at home and may help provide solutions to some of the problems teachers face when trying to teach children who are not prepared to learn. Effective partnerships help schools implement the vision and achieve student learning standards.

Partnerships can provide schools with information to guide curriculum and instruction and can help schools set priorities and achieve goals. Businesses, community groups, and parents are all clients of the school. Involving clients in the continuous improvement of the product (student learning) enables schools to make use of talents, resources, and advice from people who have a vested interest. University teacher and administration preparation programs and the district can learn how to support the school in their implementation of student standards through their partnership with the school. They can also see what types of personnel are required to implement the state's learning standards.

School portfolios are an excellent way to begin discussions with potential partners. The portfolio provides the context of the school, who the students and staff are, the vision, the plan to implement the vision, the impact the school hopes the vision will make, and how the implementation will be evaluated. Partners can see how and where their support can help the school succeed. The key is to let all partners benefit and contribute meaningfully and to celebrate successes, together. Another place to start is to use the *Partnership Development Continuous Improvement Continuum* ⊕ and self-assess where staff believes the school is with regard to partnerships.

ESTABLISHING A PARTNERSHIP PLAN

If your school has not worked with partners in meaningful ways to implement the vision, you will need to plan to do so. Below are the steps in creating partnerships ⊕ that will become a part of the continuous school improvement plan.

❶ Determine, as a staff, the vision for the school.

❷ Develop a continuous school improvement plan to implement the vision.

❸ Within the continuous school improvement plan, include partnership involvement to help meet student learning standards.

❹ Either before or after the plan is completed, establish a team to research, coordinate, create, and implement partnerships.

❺ Contact prospective partners to determine interest.

❻ Meet with interested prospective partners to exchange information about student learning standards, the school vision, and the potential partners' organizations:

  ◆ Prospective partners describe why they want a partnership with the school and how they would like to partner.

  ◆ Partnership team utilizes the school portfolio to describe the school's values and beliefs, mission, vision, student learning standards, current operations and processes, and to describe what they need from partners.

Effective partnerships help schools implement the vision and achieve student learning standards.

⑦ Prepare an agreement, establish outcomes, and determine how the partnership will be monitored and improved on a continuous basis:

- ◆ Regular meeting times are established.
- ◆ Cost and personnel requirements for the partnership are identified.

⑧ Implement the partnership.

⑨ Celebrate and thank the partners for their contributions.

Implementing the Partnership Plan

Partnerships must be researched and organized to be beneficial to the school, to the partners, and especially to students. It is best to start small and to continually reinforce the reasons for the partnership. In any partnership, large or small, partners must agree first on the specific goals of the partnership, the vision and the plan, and on what constitutes progress and reasonable evidence of success.

Most schools serious about partnerships create a team to coordinate partnerships. With the overall school improvement plan in hand, this team conducts research on how partnerships will help the school achieve its goals and benefit student achievement. Initially, the team learns about effective partnerships in other schools, and they think about creative ways in which partners could work with their school. Although it is important to have a comprehensive plan for partnerships, it is also important to keep the plan flexible enough to accommodate input from the partners after they are identified.

Once staff gives input and approves the plan, the partnership team contacts, interviews, meets with, or sends questionnaires with letters to potential partners. The team learns about the prospective partners' interests and capabilities, informs the partners about the kinds of partnerships that are related to the school vision in which the school is interested, and arranges for a face-to-face meeting and on-site visit.

Whether the prospective partners come to the school for a site visit, or host meetings at their offices, the school portfolio can quickly orient them to the school—its values and beliefs , mission, vision, student learning standards, goals, current operations, the improvement process, and the school culture. The school portfolio can help the school team present a clear message about the school in order to make it easy for prospective partners to see where their contributions might benefit students. In negotiating creative partnership possibilities, the partnership team must be as oriented to the partners' needs and goals for a partnership as they are to their own.

When establishing a partnership agreement, the organizations lay out goals, identify desired outcomes, and determine approaches to measure the success of the partnership. All partnerships must be evaluated on an ongoing basis to ensure the attainment of the overall objectives and to ensure that both parties are getting what they expect out of the partnership. Additionally, schools should always encourage, acknowledge, and publicly thank the partners for their contributions, and, together, celebrate accomplishments.

The sample partnership plan below (Figure 9.1), pulled from a continuous school improvement plan, shows the first steps in getting partnerships started in a school. A template is available on the CD. Another plan would need to be developed to show steps in implementing the partnerships.

FIGURE 9.1

Example of Planning for Partnerships

Action	Jan	Feb	Mar	Apr	May	Jun	Jul	Aug
Establish Partnership Team	X							
Determine roles and responsibilities		X						
Review and refine roles and responsibilities with staff		X						
Partnership Team studies approaches to bringing in partners			X	X	X			
Partnership Team visits potential partners to discuss the school vision				X	X	X		
Partnership Team creates plan for partnerships for staff approval								X

TOOL FOR CREATING PARTNERSHIPS RELATED TO STUDENT LEARNING STANDARDS

When establishing a partnership plan, it is helpful for staff to brainstorm the types of partnerships that would help students meet learning standards, within the context of the school vision. An activity for creating partnerships related to student learning standards and to help focus your partnerships to the standards appears on the CD. The accompanying tool (Figure 9.2) can be adjusted to include your specific standards.

To use the tool, staff need to agree on the standards that are the most appropriate for partnerships, not limiting them to the most obvious. The tool can be adjusted for use at the overall school level, or at each grade level or department.

FIGURE 9.2

Partnership Brainstorming Tool
Grade Level: First

Student learning standards	How business can help	How parents can help
At the first grade level, we want students to learn to read, write, and begin to use technology.	Become e-mail buddies to write to students daily so they have a reason to read and write and a reason to use technology.	Encourage students to write thank you notes, letters to relatives, to read signs, and to use different programs on the computer. Students need to see parents modeling these behaviors.

CLARIFYING NEEDS

As stated in *The School Portfolio*, for a partnership to be successful, both parties must contribute and both parties must benefit (Jere Jacobs, Pacific Telesis Foundation). In order to contribute, partners need to understand how to contribute. Certainly the vision, the continuous school improvement action plan, and the student learning standards can help; as can the completed brainstorming tool. Beyond the standards-related contributions, potential partners might want to volunteer other services: grade papers, read with students after school, instruct on specific issues that relate to the vision, or play a musical instrument. Some schools post volunteer sign-ups in classrooms and/or in the front office. Other schools send out questionnaires (Figure 9.3) asking parents if and how they would like to contribute.

FIGURE 9.3

Parent Partner Resource Questionnaire

Parent Information:	Children:		
Name: _____	**Name**	**Grade**	**School**
Address: _____	1) _____		
City: _____ Zip: _____	2) _____		
Phone (hm): _____	3) _____		
Phone (wk): _____	4) _____		
Phone (cell): _____	5) _____		
E-mail: _____	6) _____		
Best time to call:			

What skills, interests, hobbies, or talents do you have which you would be willing to share with the school community to enhance student learning? Please check all that apply.

❏ Carpentry ❏ Landscaping ❏ Videotaping ❏ Web Page Design
❏ Word Processing ❏ Technology ❏ Literature ❏ Wallpapering
❏ Sewing Costumes ❏ Telephoning ❏ Tutoring ❏ Fundraising
❏ Page Layout/Graphics ❏ Gardening ❏ Photography ❏ Database Design
❏ _____ ❏ _____ ❏ _____ ❏ _____

Do you have any special life experiences which you would be willing to share with our students?

Yes ❏ *Short description:*_____

Do you speak languages other than English? Yes ❏ _____

Would you be willing to volunteer to support students, or do you know a ❏ neighbor, ❏ friend, ❏ relative, or ❏ retiree, who would be interested? What would you or they be interested in doing?

_____

If you are already involved at our school, in what capacity? ❏ _____
❏ _____ ❏ _____ ❏ _____

Do you belong to a company or any community organizations that might be willing to donate any of the following? Please check and describe all that apply.

❏ Materials _____ ❏ Services _____
❏ Resources _____ ❏ Funding _____

Would your employer be interested in a mutually beneficial community partnership? Yes ❏
Does your employer have a matching grant program? Yes ❏

Does your employer have a support/donation program that might be beneficial to our students?

Yes ❏ *Short description:*_____

Company Info:	Company Name: _____	Phone: _____
	Address: _____	Contact
	City: _____ Zip: _____	Person:

Would you or your company like more information regarding how you can become our school partner?
Yes ❏

EVALUATING PARTNERSHIPS

Evaluating partnerships is not much different from evaluating professional development programs. One must identify the intent, state hypotheses about the partnership, and then search for evidence to prove or disprove the hypotheses. An example tool to evaluate partners ⊙ appears on the CD.

SUMMARY

Successful partnerships are those that are specific to implementing student learning standards and the vision, and are stated clearly so that both parties know the aim of the partnership. We want both parties to contribute and both parties to benefit from the partnership.

FREQUENTLY ASKED QUESTIONS ABOUT PARTNERSHIPS ⊙

▼ **How do you define partnerships?**

One simple definition of partnerships is: Two or more agencies working together for a common cause. In this case, the school, parents, community, and businesses working together to help all students meet student learning standards. Joyce Epstein (1995), defines partnerships as practices that schools, families, and communities conduct to influence children's learning and development.

▼ **How do you go about getting business partners?**

The first thing to concentrate on is getting a clear vision and a plan that has the steps to get to the vision, if what you are looking for is support for actually implementing the plan and student learning standards. If you are looking for partners who can help contribute to understanding the needs of the future and to developing a vision, you need to approach potential partners in your area and ask them to work with you. Your school portfolio will help you with the initial discussions.

Undoubtedly, some parents work for businesses in the area and they can tell you if their businesses want to actively support schools. For more parent involvement, staff has to be clear about what they expect parents to do. What does parent involvement *mean* at your site? If you had a busload of parents pull up in your school's driveway tomorrow morning, what would you do with them? Parents want to be a part of visioning, determining outcomes, and making decisions about the school and what happens in the classroom. Many schools concentrate on all-school functions for parents. Grade-level functions, related to standards, can also be effective and productive. Networking is a key to making partners feel welcome at school.

▼ What does it mean that both parties need to contribute?

It means that the businesses and parents want to help schools in whatever way they can. They do not want to just give money or correct papers. To just give donations or be a "go-fer" is not satisfying. These potentially powerful partners want to think through ideas with your school, and they want to make a difference. Most of the time, schools are contributing to the businesses when they let the businesses contribute to the schools. Ask your partners what they want out of the partnership and how they want to contribute—and then thank them.

YOUR QUESTIONS

List the partnerships you have at your school and how they impact student learning.

If they are not impacting student learning, can they? How?

What other partnerships do you want to establish?

ON THE CD RELATED TO
PARTNERSHIP DEVELOPMENT

▼ Items to Include in the Partnership Development Section of the School Portfolio

▼ Frequently Asked Questions About Partnership Development

▼ Partnership Continuous Improvement Continuum

▼ Establishing a Partnership Plan
   ◆ Partnership Team Plan Example
   ◆ Partnership Team Planning Template
   ◆ Creating Partnerships Activity

▼ Partnership Resource Questionnaire

▼ Partnership Evaluation Questionnaire

▼ Partnership Development Section Template

CHAPTER 10

CONTINUOUS IMPROVEMENT AND EVALUATION:
Evaluating the Implementation of the Vision

Chapter Objective: HOW TO EVALUATE AND TROUBLESHOOT THE CONTINUOUS SCHOOL IMPROVEMENT PROCESS

Quality continuous improvement and evaluation is like...

Perfecting your favorite recipe. Over time, each preparation leads to something that is shared, enjoyed, and critiqued with ideas for future changes.

A flowing river – always moving, always changing, but forever constant. A reflection of where we've been and a guide towards where we are going.

Mirrors, reflecting the programs being assessed. The powers that be ponder the value of this sight. And when the conditions are right, the hard-earned efforts are blessed by a heavenly rainbow. But, alas, this too shall pass. The rainbow fades.

The raindrops evaporate. The programs and processes are renewed. And sometimes—it just rains.

A pine tree, always growing, generation after generation, losing outdated growth, branching out and up toward the sky; providing strength, shelter, and opportunity for those who approach it, while the roots are firmly grounded in values and beliefs, which do not change.

The first reluctant raindrops falling from the sky; idyllic gems and instructional thought each striving for perfection. More thoughts and data gather to form puddles in our minds.

Missouri School Portfolio Awareness Workshop
and Reviewers of *The School Portfolio Toolkit*

Continuous improvement and evaluation is the process of:

▼ analyzing strengths and weaknesses

▼ developing a vision and guiding philosophies

▼ determining what needs to improve

▼ obtaining the skills and knowledge to implement the vision

▼ developing a plan to implement the vision

▼ implementing the plan

▼ evaluating and assessing progress toward the vision

▼ improving implementation based on the continuous evaluation of processes and parts

These are the key concepts of data-driven decision making. We need to gather data to know if we are meeting our targets; our targets being our values and beliefs, purpose, mission, vision, and student learning standards. Everything we plan must be focused on these targets. Everything we implement and evaluate must be aimed at these targets. And, finally, everything that we improve on the basis of our evaluation work must be focused on the targets. Figure 10.1 shows how these pieces work in a continuous cycle to accomplish the vision.

FIGURE 10.1

Note. From *The School Portfolio: A Comprehensive Framework for School Improvement* (p.163), by Victoria L. Bernhardt, 1999, Larchmont, NY: Eye on Education. Copyright © 1999 Eye on Education, Inc. Reprinted with permission.

CONTINUOUS IMPROVEMENT CONTINUUMS

The key to the successful application of continuous improvement concepts to the school improvement process is the active use of data. Measuring the school's progress against identified criteria—such as the *Education for the Future Initiative Continuous Improvement Continuums*—provides a benchmark that schools can use to see if their actions have created the results they intended. These measures are supported by analyzing data gathered through interviews with clients of the school, questionnaires, performance measures, and observations of the learning environment. When these measures are used on a regular basis, the data clearly document trends and provide information that assist schools in deciding next steps for improvement. Again, the school's guiding principles must be kept in mind to understand the true impact of the data. The *Continuous Improvement Continuums, Assessing on the Continuous Improvement Continuums (CICs) Activity,* a sample CICs report, and CICs reporting and charting templates appear on the CD. (A discussion related to assessing on the CICs appears in Chapter 3.)

THE SCHOOL AS A SYSTEM

The school is a system made up of many parts—each part affecting all other parts. We must look at the school as a whole system as we plan, implement, evaluate, and improve. The school portfolio is a tool to this end. To focus on one part at a time may lead to improvement of that part; however, it will never lead to the improvement of the whole system. Paul Preuss, (based upon comments made by Dr. Russell Ackoff at the Goal/QPC Conference in Boston, 1992), eloquently summarizes the following:

▼ a system consists of a set of parts—each part affects all other parts; no part has an independent effect on the whole

▼ the system as a whole cannot be divided into independent parts

▼ if you focus on optimalization of parts, you will not improve the system

▼ performance of the system depends on how the parts fit, not on how good the parts are

▼ systems are not the sum of their parts but rather the product of the interaction of the parts

▼ systems thinking is understanding the connections between people and processes in organizations so that we can continuously improve our work

▼ systems thinking is about seeing the whole and understanding the relationships among the parts

The *Education for the Future Continuous Improvement Continuums* assess the whole system. Student achievement analyses and utilizing demographic, school process, and perceptions data can also give information about the school as a system. These comprehensive analyses are critical for ensuring a look at the whole system, since the majority of the time true school problems, or the root causes of these problems, are system related.

PLANS FOR CONTINUOUS IMPROVEMENT AND EVALUATION

Schools need to *plan* for continuous improvement and evaluation or continuous improvement will not happen. A continuous improvement plan can be very logical. Figure 10.2, shown on the following pages, outlines thinking through system evaluation questions. (The outline is available on the CD, as well as a template of the form for your use in thinking through your continuous improvement and evaluation plan.) Two other tools are on the CD that will help evaluate your continuous improvement efforts. They are: *Troubleshooting Your Continuous Improvement Efforts* and *What Would It Be Like If....*

FIGURE 10.2

EVALUATION QUESTIONS OUTLINE

	ACTIVITY	PURPOSE	OUTCOME	EVALUATION QUESTIONS	APPROACH
PLAN	Seek input from students, parents, business, and community.	Make sure all clients of the school are a part of defining the current and future needs of students and the school.	Commitment of school community to work together to rethink how student needs will be met in the future. Ownership of the process.	What constituencies need to be involved? Who is involved? Is the involvement representative of all constituencies? Does everyone feel she/he is truly involved and has a say? Is there a commitment to study new approaches to meeting student needs? Does each person understand his or her role?	Questionnaires to constituents; interviews.
	Define the philosophical underpinnings of the organization.	Values and beliefs provide the context behind the mission, vision, purpose of school, and student learning, and serve as guides for the improvement efforts.	A shared purpose, mission, and vision built from the values and beliefs of the school community so everyone has the same understanding of, and motivation for, the change. A shared vision to establish the same visual image of what is to be accomplished.	Were individuals' values, beliefs, and opinions sought, understood, and respected? Are the values and beliefs of the individuals congruent? Do they represent what the individuals actually believe? Are they shared? How were shared values and beliefs established? Was the sharing accomplished in such a way that individuals were not "talked out" of their personal values and beliefs, and did the shared vision emerge from personal values and beliefs? Is the mission an accurate representation of the purpose of the school? Is it built on the values and beliefs of the individuals of the school community? Is it a clear, compelling, and a proactive goal that can serve to unify and challenge the organization? Can outsiders understand it with little explanation? Do insiders have a precise understanding of it? Does the vision describe what the school will be like when the mission is achieved? Is the vision congruent with the values and beliefs of the school community? Does it bring the mission to life? Is the vision truly shared? Was the vision built from personal visions and meeting the future needs of students? Are all individuals committed to the vision?	Facilitated group meeting or training sessions; interviews.

FIGURE 10.2 (Continued)

EVALUATION QUESTIONS OUTLINE

	ACTIVITY	PURPOSE	OUTCOME	EVALUATION QUESTIONS	APPROACH
PLAN	Determine the needs and challenges of the students, community, and the school.	Understand current and future needs of students, the community, and the school to focus the school improvement efforts on preparing students for the future within the context.	Clear understanding of the clients, their needs, root causes of problems, the impact of current processes on the clients, and identification of essential student learnings.	Who are the students, parents, teachers, and administrators? What are their needs? What are their skills? How effective are current processes in meeting student needs from every constituent's perspective and from existing school data? Who are the future students? What will they face in the future? How do they learn best? What are the overall challenges, needs, pressing issues, and/or opportunities? What are the root causes of the problems and challenges? What is the current process of schooling? How effective is it in meeting the overall challenges and needs? What does the school want students to know and be able to do when they leave? What are the elements of school that must be changed? How are all of these understandings communicated to everyone in the school community?	Needs assessment questionnaires; student, teacher, parent questionnaires, demographic data; review of literature; flow-chart of current processes, with student achievement results.
	Establish plan for school improvement.	Analyze needs, challenges, and current structure to plan an approach to studying and sustaining improvement.	A decision-making structure/comprehensive data-based plan for developing a strategic action plan for systemic school improvement.	Given the needs, challenges, pressing issues, and identified student outcomes, is the plan and structure for study and day-to-day decision making appropriate? Is each structure congruent with the philosophical underpinnings of the organization? What information needs to be tracked for improvement? Does the new study and decision-making structure sufficiently represent all points of view? Does the structure allow for effective communication with all members of the school community?	Analyses of data, including current processes; review of literature; brainstorming.
	Build skills for change.	Obtain new skills that will allow the school community to work in ways different from current processes and structures.	Abilities to share decisions; work in teams; build consensus; communicate; run efficient meetings; plan; and continuously improve operations.	What skills are present in the school community and needed for individuals to work together to establish a new structure to share in decision making and studying new approaches to meeting the needs of students? How are current skills assessed and new skills obtained? How effective is the training received for building new skills? Is the training appropriate and sufficient? How will new skills be monitored, supported, and implemented? How effective are individual, team, and staff interactions that require use of these new skills? How can they be improved?	Interviews; facilitated meetings; literature reviews; questionnaires; brainstorming.

Note. From *The School Portfolio: A Comprehensive Framework for School Improvement* (pages 168-171), by Victoria L. Bernhardt, 1999, Larchmont, NY: Eye on Education. Copyright © 1999 Eye on Education, Inc. Reprinted with permission.

CONTINUOUS IMPROVEMENT

FIGURE 10.2 (Continued)

EVALUATION QUESTIONS OUTLINE

	ACTIVITY	PURPOSE	OUTCOME	EVALUATION QUESTIONS	APPROACH
P L A N	Study new approaches to meeting the needs of students.	Understand how students in this school learn, and new approaches for ensuring student success that leads to recommendations for new ways of operating to meet student needs.	Well-researched recommendations for the systemic improvement of every aspect of the school, based on the comprehensive study of pressing issues and how students learn that will lead to a strategic plan for implementation.	Is each study team comprised of representative members of the community? Are the teams effective in their study of new approaches? Do all team members participate? Is there consensus? Is the study in-depth or cursory? Are the items being considered for implementation potentially effective in meeting the needs of this student population, or do they represent the latest fad? Is the communication within and between teams appropriate, sufficient, and effective? Is the plan for study appropriate, effective, and efficient? Are the timelines for study sufficient? Do teams offer sufficient rationale for why they believe their recommendations will work?	Team meetings; questionnaires; interviews; review of the literature; visits to other schools.
	Develop an overall strategic plan for school improvement.	Establish a comprehensive strategic plan that integrates the in-depth research of the study teams and guides the implementation of the new approach throughout the period.	A strategic plan that will lead to the congruent and articulated implementation of new structures, strategies, and their continuous improvement, congruent with the mission, vision, and outcomes.	Is the decision-making body appropriate for integrating the study team recommendations? Is everybody aware of the approach to be used? Do they understand how to provide input to the process? Are they committed to the implementation of the integrated plan? Does the strategic plan have a comprehensive list of tasks to be implemented, skills needed for implementation, timelines, responsible persons, and due dates? Is the plan challenging, yet doable? Does the plan reflect the latest research on effective implementation strategies? Does the strategic plan appropriately reflect the intent of the study team recommendations, as well as the outcomes and philosophical underpinnings of the school? Does the plan provide a clear and efficient method of implementing the vision? Will the plan really lead to change that can be sustained? Is there more than one school plan?	Interviews; facilitated meetings; literature reviews; questionnaires; brainstorming; review of plan.
	Establish a structure to implement the plan and vision.	Establish a structure for implementation and decision making congruent with the strategic plan and vision.	Appropriate teams and effective decision-making structure are established to implement the overall strategic plan.	Are the teams appropriate for implementing the vision? Do all members understand their roles and responsibilities? Does each team have a plan and have they identified student outcomes? Are consensus-building and communication strategies used appropriately and effectively? Does each team understand how to run effective and efficient meetings? Do appropriate support, monitoring, skill-building, and accountability components exist for implementing the vision? Are they effective?	Team meetings; questionnaires; interviews; review of the literature.

Note. From *The School Portfolio: A Comprehensive Framework for School Improvement* (pages 168-171), by Victoria L. Bernhardt, 1999, Larchmont, NY: Eye on Education, Inc. Copyright © 1999 Eye on Education, Inc. Reprinted with permission.

FIGURE 10.2 (Continued)

EVALUATION QUESTIONS OUTLINE

	ACTIVITY	PURPOSE	OUTCOME	EVALUATION QUESTIONS	APPROACH
IMPLEMENT	Implement new strategies.	To achieve student outcomes and realize the vision, new strategies, defined in the strategic plan must be implemented, not merely adopted.	A vision congruent with the mission of the school is implemented in every aspect of the organization. Student outcomes are achieved and the school becomes a true learning organization.	Is the structure effective for implementing the strategic plan? Is it effective for decision making? What elements are most effective? What elements are least effective? Is communication effective for teams and full staff? Is professional development training for implementing the vision appropriate, ongoing, supportive, and effective? Are new strategies really being implemented? Are the new strategies appropriate? Is there enough support and accountability? What is the impact of implementation on staff, teachers, students, administrators, parents, and the community? Is everyone informed of implementation strategies and expected outcomes? Are partnerships appropriate and effective? What are the benefits of the new strategies?	Team meetings; questionnaires; interviews; review of the literature; data analysis.
EVALUATE	Evaluate.	Analyze the intent and implementation of all processes, procedures, and products with respect to the philosophical underpinnings of the organization.	Understanding of the impact and effectiveness of implemented processes, procedure and products on students and other members of the school community.	Does a real learning organization exist? Is there an understanding of implementation through leverage points? Is communication effective in every element of the organization and across elements? Are all elements of the organization congruent with the mission, vision, values, beliefs, and outcomes? How can any or each of the elements be improved? Why are some things not improving? What elements impact other elements? Is there a clear understanding of the interrelationships of the elements? What is the status of the pressing issues? Were the root causes and serious problems effectively attended to? Is the vision implemented? Can the vision be implemented within the current structure?	Interviews; questionnaires; student achievement analysis; observations; assess on Continuous Improvement Continuums.
IMPROVE	Continuously improve.	Act on the results and information obtained through the ongoing evaluation process to continuously improve the organization.	An organization that is sensitive to the impacts of its actions on its clients, and is capable of data-based decision making and implementing change for improvement.	Based on the evaluation report recommendations, what changes need to be made to improve operations? What processes need to change to ensure the school community that the vision is being implemented? What elements of the vision need to change based on new information received while implementing the vision? Does the mission, vision, and purpose need to be revisited and improved? Does the school community understand the interrelationship of elements and on this basis know how changing one element will impact other elements? What is the impact of the changes made?	Interviews; questionnaires; student achievement analysis; observations.

Note. From *The School Portfolio: A Comprehensive Framework for School Improvement* (pages 168-171), by Victoria L. Bernhardt, 1999, Larchmont, NY: Eye on Education. Copyright © 1999 Eye on Education, Inc. Reprinted with permission.

SUMMARY

The school portfolio is a process and framework for continuous school improvement. Throughout the development and implementation of the school portfolio process, data will be collected and analyzed to understand if the processes are making the intended differences with student learning. A benefit of using the school portfolio for continuous improvement and evaluation is that it allows one to see the school as the system it is; understanding the alignment of the parts to create the healthy-whole school.

Continuous improvement is a never-ending cycle of planning, implementing, evaluating, and improving; using the school's guiding principles—purpose, mission, vision, and student learning standards—as the core of the effort.

FREQUENTLY ASKED QUESTIONS ABOUT CONTINUOUS IMPROVEMENT AND EVALUATION ⊙ CD-ROM

▼ **Do the *Continuous Improvement Continuums* fall into the Continuous Improvement and Evaluation section?**

The Continuous Improvement and Evaluation section is an excellent place to put the school's assessments on the seven *Continuous Improvement Continuums* to get a comprehensive feel for the health and alignment of the parts of the learning organization.

Note that while you are discussing your assessments, what you document in each section of the portfolio becomes obvious. The discussion will focus at some point on *What do we have for information and analysis?* The next piece of the discussion and documentation would be *What other things do we need to gather or do?* and *What do we need to do to move up the continuum?* These pieces of evidence become relevant information to put into the specific sections of the portfolio.

▼ **What if we didn't get enough time to really discuss each continuum during our first assessment?**

That is okay, as long as you came to consensus on where you are. You can start implementing the ideas and come back to the assessments in six months or sooner. Many schools that say they didn't have enough time to discuss are trying to come to solutions. Actually, assessment time is *not* a time to discuss solutions—just determine *Where are we now?* and *What do we need to do next?*—which might be to thoroughly study the issues and possible solutions.

▼ **What if we cannot come to consensus using the *Continuous Improvement Continuums*?**

Listen to the conversation taking place. Is the discussion really starting to focus on solutions? Many times, the lack of consensus, and a discussion that goes on and on is because the discussion did not focus on what the school has for evidence and what other things the school needs. Understanding what the school has for evidence will shorten most discussions and assist with consensus.

YOUR QUESTIONS

How will you evaluate your continuous school improvement plan?

How often will you evaluate your continuous school improvement plan?

ON THE CD RELATED TO CONTINUOUS IMPROVEMENT & EVALUATION

▼ Items to Include in the Continuous Improvement and Evaluation Section of the School Portfolio

▼ Continuous Improvement and Evaluation Continuous Improvement Continuum

▼ Frequently Asked Questions About Continuous Improvement

▼ Education for the Future Continuous Improvement Continuums

▼ Continuous Improvement Continuums Assessment Activity

▼ Continuous Improvement Continuums Baseline Report Example

▼ Continuous Improvement Continuums Follow-up Report Example

▼ Continuous Improvement Continuums Baseline Report Template

▼ Continuous Improvement Continuums Graphing Templates

▼ Evaluation Questions Outline Example

▼ Evaluation Questions Outline Template

▼ Troubleshooting Your Continuous Improvement Efforts

▼ What Would It Be Like If …

▼ Continuous Improvement and Evaluation Section Template

CHAPTER 11

UPDATING THE SCHOOL PORTFOLIO:
Maintaining the Momentum

Chapter Objective: TO PROVIDE SUGGESTIONS AND TOOLS FOR MAINTAINING THE SCHOOL PORTFOLIO AND KEEPING IT ALIVE WITH STAFF

Completing a school portfolio is like...

Creating a family album.

Climbing a mountain — it is strenuous and even a bit scary at times; yet, when you reach the destination, a wonderful feeling of exhilaration is your reward.

The dashboard on a car—it should contain all the information and controls you need to successfully operate the system.

Finishing a good novel, knowing there is a great sequel right around the corner.

A birthday celebration—noting what has been accomplished while looking ahead.

The birth of a child—culminating months of planning and work—requiring continuous care and nurturing to grow.

Writing the second draft of a book whose publisher will require at least six drafts.

Organizing your junk drawer—you know in your heart that you need to do it; everything that you need is already there; you have to be motivated to do it; once it is completed, you feel sooooo good!

Dedicating a new bridge—creates passages to new destinations; comes after planning and hard work; requires continuous care, repair, and use to be an effective avenue to student achievement.

Putting together a puzzle so that all pieces contribute to a clear picture. As students, staff, and requirements change, puzzle pieces must be replaced to reflect the new picture.

Going to heaven; it's what you did on the way that counts.

Missouri School Portfolio Awareness Workshop
and Reviewers of *The School Portfolio Toolkit*

It is a real spirit booster when a school staff first sees its hard work on school improvement reflected in a "finished" school portfolio. Usually a small group of people have taken the responsibility for putting the portfolio together, although the staff has been involved in collecting data, including questionnaires, samples of student work, and student achievement results. The usefulness of the portfolio for getting grants, introducing the school to visitors, and accreditation is obvious. However, the portfolio has the potential to be far more than a public relations document. When used well, it is a tool for ongoing assessment of progress toward the school's vision and goals. Reflection of the content can help everyone understand what steps need to be taken to move forward. And most importantly, the documentation and ongoing assessment of school improvement efforts will keep staffs targeted and committed to change.

Leni von Blanckensee
Adjunct Education for the Future Initiative Associate

KEEPING THE PORTFOLIO UP-TO-DATE

Schools create their own ways to gather the evidence and to keep their portfolios up to date. Below are common considerations.

▼ *Determine Who is Going to do the Work*

Staff will have to decide who takes the lead in updating the school portfolio. In many cases, the school improvement coordinator or the principal takes responsibility for updating the portfolio. That does not mean that they do all the work. It just means that they take the lead and may delegate parts to different teams or individuals in the school who would then be responsible for making sure that the portfolio is up-to-date for major events such as open houses, program reviews, and important visitors. Everyone knows this person or these people are keeping the evidence and will route appropriate materials to them as they crop up.

Whoever is collecting the evidence needs to have a system for keeping the evidence safe from being inadvertently thrown away or becoming soiled. Hanging files, boxes, in-baskets, or binders, labeled appropriately, can hold the evidence until it is time to work on placing the evidence in the school portfolio binder.

What and when to add to the school portfolio depends upon the type and purpose of the evidence and information being gathered. Staff should outline how evidence will be treated and when it will be updated to ensure that others understand the timeline. A system within the school portfolio (e.g., subsection indices) can be helpful in clarifying what will be added when. (For example: professional development by year.)

School staff seldom rewrite their entire school portfolio each year. While the exception and not the rule, some sections do lend themselves to being rewritten each year (e.g., context of the school, its enrollment, the demographics of its population, student achievement results). The school will want to work with historical graphs in order to follow cohorts of students and to track increases in student achievement and enrollment over time. As new scores are added, new graphs must be created to replace the outdated graphs. These are sections that the school will want to have ready for use at all times. They are important for committees to have and are the boilerplates for grants, state and regional reviews, and for federal program reporting. These are mostly sections that blend historical data with current data.

The frequency of adding new material to the school portfolio varies from section to section. Most sections will probably need updating once or twice a year. For example, questionnaire results will likely be added once a year (you might want these graphs to show progress over time), and self-assessments on the *Education for the Future Initiative Continuous Improvement Continuums* will likely be added twice a year.

Since the portfolio documents the school's continuous improvement process and progress, and since continuous improvement is an ongoing process, not a year-end activity, relevant newspaper articles and other evidence need to be added as they become available. Another section that might need to be updated on an ongoing basis is the school plan. As things are accomplished and new information is obtained with respect to implementing the school vision, the plan must be updated to reflect the progress and changes.

When implementing a system for updating the school portfolio, it is important to remember that one of the original purposes of the school portfolio is to create one document that describes the school and can be used for multiple purposes. Be sure to keep those purposes in mind and the objectives clear throughout the updating process.

▼ *Set Up an Archival Process*

The school portfolio will eventually hold all historical data, analytical data, and other evidence important to the school. Consequently, the physical size of your portfolio can become very big and too cumbersome to handle. It is recommended that you establish an annual process to archive the old evidence that may no longer be current, but still of value to keep.

Your old evidence may have historical significance in the years ahead. Your old statistical data will serve to cement the school's progress and growth as you look back in time. Create graphs that consolidate data over time and write up summaries of events that occurred during the year. This process makes the maintenance of a lot of additional evidence unnecessary. You might choose to add adjunct binders to hold graphs and other supporting material.

COMBINING SELF-ASSESSMENT WITH EVIDENCE GATHERING

So how can we keep the momentum going? School staffs can most easily understand how a school portfolio can be used for continuous assessment and improvement by drawing parallels between its use and the use of student portfolios. For any portfolio to be effective, it is important for the work it documents—the work of the school in this case—to be assessed against some criteria. Schools can create their own rubrics or can choose from ones already developed, such as the *Education for the Future Continuous Improvement Continuums*. Whatever rubrics are chosen, it is important that the highest level of the rubrics are consistent with the vision, plan, and goals of the school and indicate the targets the school wishes to reach.

Self-assessment is a process that should occur at least twice a year. Since the purpose is continuous improvement, it makes sense to assess in the fall, and to assess early enough in the spring to see the effect of changes which were made at the beginning of the year to be able to make more corrections. Some schools find that assessing themselves more than twice a year is what they need to keep everyone together and on-track in the change process.

The school portfolio self-assessment process is one of evidence-gathering and reflection. Evidence can be anything concrete that the school can show to demonstrate that the self-assessment is correct. A staff can use a variety of ways to go about self-assessing and gathering evidence after the first school assessment.

The simplest approach would be to indicate as the self-assessment is done what the school has as evidence to justify a rating, and then assign someone to place it in the portfolio.

Another scenario that can be used after the first assessment of the *Continuous Improvement Continuums*, is the *Treasure Hunt*. (We believe it is important to have the whole staff assess at least the first time.)

1 Prior to the assessment, encourage staff to examine the portfolio which contains the evidence and data gathered to-date.

2 Working in small groups assigned a rubric, have each group discuss the rubric, highlighting the areas on the rubrics which best describe the school.

3 Have each group list evidence that it believes supports its assessment.

4 Have each group report to the whole staff.

5 Discuss the assessments with the whole staff and come to consensus on a number for *Approach*, *Implementation*, and *Outcome*. (Don't forget to take notes to include in the portfolio as evidence of your continuous improvement process.)

6 Over the next week or two, conduct a "treasure hunt" for actual artifacts which relate to the descriptors in the rubrics.

7 At the next meeting, examine the artifacts and discuss the significance of what staff has found.

8 Have staff confirm or change the assessment on the rubrics, based on actual evidence. (Or you can let the original assessment stand and use this evidence to support an increase in progress for the next assessment.)

❾ The staff adjusts its school plan for reaching the vision as necessary, based on the evidence.

❿ Selected evidence is included in the portfolio, along with the assessment on the rubrics, justifications for the assessment, and a summary of the next steps.

The process for updating the school portfolio is very similar, except that the staff might be asked to bring evidence and review the *Continuous Improvement Continuums* ahead of time. Eventually, collecting evidence becomes an ongoing process. Staff become familiar and comfortable with "look for's."

Another process that will involve most, if not all, staff members in the maintenance of the school portfolio is to set up a *School Portfolio Maintenance Vine* (Figure 11.1).

FIGURE 11.1

SCHOOL PORTFOLIO MAINTENANCE VINE

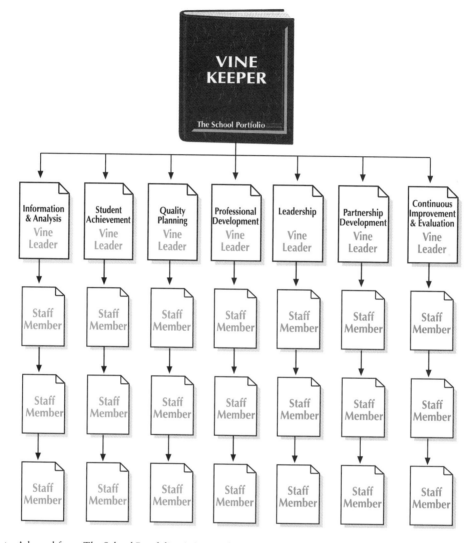

Note. Adapted from *The School Portfolio: A Comprehensive Framework for School Improvement* (p.198), by Victoria L. Bernhardt, 1999, Larchmont, NY: Eye on Education. Copyright © 1999 Eye on Education, Inc. Reprinted with permission.

Set up the vine by agreeing on who will be the primary school portfolio vinekeeper. It should be an energetic, dynamic, respected, and not-afraid-to-ask staff member. This person may or may not be the principal. Next, staff members are divided into small groups or "vines." Staff members should be grouped based upon interests in particular sections of the school portfolio, collegiality, access to one another, break times, early birds, late workers, proximity, and any other criteria that bring people together.

The vine leaders coordinate maintenance activities with the School Portfolio Vinekeeper. Each vine leader will have staff members on its vine, and each staff member will be responsible for collecting or writing specific pieces of evidence, determined by that vine. The vine leaders, as well as the vine keeper, must actively participate in this process. By keeping in communication with her/his staff members, the vine leaders will make sure that the target dates for collecting all evidence will be met.

The success of each vine, and the entire vineyard, depends upon how well each member meets her/his responsibilities for data collection evidence. Once the vine leaders collect all the evidence, they will meet with the vine keeper to update the school portfolio.

Tools useful for maintaining the school portfolio are the *School Portfolio Summary Update Worksheet* and the *School Portfolio Summary Chart* (mentioned in Chapter 3). Staff use these worksheets to think through the updating of the portfolio sections when they conduct their assessments on the *Education for the Future Initiative Continuous Improvement Continuums*. Again, the easiest time to update the school portfolio is when staff assesses on the *Continuous Improvement Continuums*.

WHAT EVIDENCE SHOULD BE INCLUDED?

In addition to the data being collected, such as standardized achievement and demographic data, the following are examples of what might be included in a portfolio as evidence:

▼ Photos showing:

- ◆ teachers using vision related instructional strategies and students at work
- ◆ examples of finished student work that would not fit easily into a binder
- ◆ students presenting their work
- ◆ students assessing their work
- ◆ use of technology as part of the curriculum
- ◆ the staff examining student work
- ◆ professional development experiences
- ◆ parents and other school partners participating in leadership meetings or significant activities with students
- ◆ the staff and community involved in the planning or evaluation process
- ◆ the impact of grants or partnerships on student learning
- ◆ community celebrations of student achievement increases
- ◆ community celebrations of the school portfolio

▼ Questionnaire data, disaggregated by subgroups (ethnicity, gender, grade, etc.), what was learned from the data, follow-ups needed or conducted, and the impact of the data on the school plan.

▼ Student work that demonstrates the results of instructional strategies that are described in the vision and plan. Samples should also reflect the range of students, not only the best students.

▼ Documents showing the professional work which supports the change process.

The previous list is not in any way meant to be exhaustive. Whenever meaningful data is collected, it should be included in the portfolio. In addition, almost any artifact that is meaningful to the school can be evidence *if it is presented with an explanation of its significance* to an outside reader.

Organizing Evidence

Within each section of the portfolio, the school will want to trace evidence which shows the approach that has been adopted, the degree of implementation, and its effect on students. By following this trail of evidence, staff is able to assess what has worked well and what implementation approaches need to be changed. For example:

▼ Evidence of the school's alternative assessment practices might include:

  ◆ any rubrics, continuums, or benchmarks which have been developed as the criteria for assessing student work

  ◆ samples from student portfolios with the student's reflections attached

  ◆ a summary of feedback from students and parents about their perceptions of the assessment process

▼ Evidence that the school is improving instructional practices, leading to student achievement gains might include:

  ◆ a description of the strategies which the school has adopted

  ◆ the plan for a cross-curricular unit of study that uses these strategies, developed by a team of teachers

  ◆ a unit description for students

  ◆ pictures taken in class which show the instructional strategies in use

  ◆ samples of completed student work with student reflections attached

  ◆ written feedback from students about the unit

  ◆ written responses to student-led conferences from the parent and student

  ◆ planned improvements for the future

  ◆ evidence that this unit is not an isolated case

  ◆ assessment results from a vision implementation assessment tool

▼ Evidence that professional development activities are impacting the classroom might include:

  ◆ a schedule of professional development activities for the year

  ◆ photos from the workshops

- case study results
- action research results
- examination of student work
- a list of expected outcomes
- photos of classrooms with students working in congruency with professional development themes
- samples or photos of finished work, along with student reflections of how well they met expected outcomes
- implementation date logs or reflection forms

GUIDELINES FOR KEEPING THE SCHOOL PORTFOLIO CURRENT

Continuous Improvement is an ongoing process, not a year-end activity. Since the portfolio documents your continuous improvement process, relevant documents need to be added as they are developed. The following is meant as a guideline which can be modified to fit your school:

▼ Add the notes from self-assessments two to three times a year, whenever you self-assess.

▼ Add the most pertinent samples of evidence collected in conjunction with the self-assessment at the same time, making sure that the trail of evidence is clear.

▼ Add changes to your school plan whenever progress, modifications, or additions are made.

▼ Add questionnaire data and other hard data as soon as you debrief the data, along with information about what you learned, and next steps.

After the first year, the original narrative will be out of date, but the notes from your rubric assessments and the data you have collected throughout the year will be a good record of your progress. The end of the school year is a good time to write a brief summary updating each section of the portfolio based on the data you have been collecting and analyzing. Year-end updates are especially helpful to the outside reader and any new staff members who were not there as the evidence was collected. You may want to have yearly dividers behind each section divider of the portfolio for ease in finding information.

MOVING FORWARD

While one person is responsible for keeping the portfolio current, everyone needs to be involved in the collection and examination of evidence. When the school portfolio maintenance is wedded to the staff's reflection of progress based on actual evidence, the portfolio greatly enriches that reflection and helps everyone understand her or his part in moving forward to reach the school's vision.

Year Two

If year one of the school portfolio is about putting the pieces in place, such as:

▼ Gathering, analyzing, and interpreting the data

▼ Creating a vision for the learning organization

▼ Planning for the implementation of the vision

▼ Learning new knowledge and skills to implement the vision

▼ Creating a leadership structure to implement the vision

▼ Involving partners to implement the vision

▼ Evaluating the implementation of the vision

Year two is about ensuring the alignment of all the elements of the learning organization to the vision, showing progress, and taking the data and the vision to deeper levels of understanding. In year two and beyond, we need to answer questions such as:

▼ Is the vision meeting the needs of the students we have?

▼ Is the plan getting us to the vision?

▼ To what degree have we truly implemented the vision?

▼ What is the impact of implementing the vision?

▼ Is the professional development we are engaging in assisting us in implementing the vision and meeting the needs of our students?

▼ Which instructional strategies help us meet the needs of which students?

▼ How will we keep this work going over time?

The continuous work on the school portfolio is about making everything count and understanding the impact of staff actions on student achievement. Are we doing only the things that make a difference for students? Are there things that we should not be doing? Are there things everybody should be doing? Are we truly implementing that continuum of learning that makes sense for students?

WAYS TO KEEP THE SCHOOL PORTFOLIO ALIVE

In districts with all schools completing a school portfolio, it is wonderful to have a districtwide portfolio celebration for the community to view the finished products. The celebration can honor the school staff for their hard work and dedication to continuous school improvement, while informing the community of what the schools are doing and what they are achieving. Another way to get the word out to the community is to have a different school, each month, present to the Board of Education an update to the community and the board.

There is nothing like positive newspaper coverage to help staff feel accomplished and appreciated. A partnership with the local media is a way to highlight/spotlight schools and their growth.

A single school could present to the Board of Education also, and share with parents at a Back-to-School Night or other times parents are at the school.

BENEFITS AND CONCERNS

What do most people see as the benefits, and what are their concerns as they begin putting a school portfolio together, and how do these perceptions change over time?

At the end of many school portfolio workshops, Education for the Future staff ask participants what they feel are the *Benefits and Concerns* (offered as an activity on the CD), related to developing a school portfolio. For benefits they typically say:

▼ The school portfolio helps our school focus on existing status, analyze data to determine gaps and root causes of problems, and develop plans for improvement.

▼ The school portfolio helps us, as a staff, know where we are going and to define our vision. It also sets us up with a grant proposal.

▼ The portfolio process is logical school improvement!

▼ The school portfolio provides an effective model for documentation.

▼ Going through this process benefits the district, the individual schools, and the individual educators.

▼ The portfolio helps us achieve a more in-depth picture of our school.

▼ We can put this information together once and use it for many things—grants, accreditation, and state school improvement reviews.

▼ The school portfolio assists with keeping all staff informed—a great communication tool.

▼ The school portfolio is documentation of where we are in relationship to where we want to be and will keep us moving forward.

▼ The school portfolio process can help with consistency of expectations (vision): we keep backing up, then down, going back and forth. A shared vision will drive all "programs" from now on.

▼ The portfolio is a concrete example of what we have accomplished and an awareness of what is missing.

▼ The school portfolio will definitely lead to improved teaching and learning.

▼ The portfolio will help us with streamlining education programs (less is more).

▼ The school portfolio shows growth to all constituents and is positive public relations.

▼ The portfolio guides all actions to the benefit of students.

▼ A school portfolio will allow everyone to have a shared sense of vision and a focus.

Listed as their first concern in almost every workshop is time, followed by getting teachers to "buy in" to these ideas. Other concerns often expressed are:

▼ Resources—how will we get the time and dollars to do this?

▼ Teachers might see this as another innovation, rather than a structure or framework for programs already being implemented.

- ▼ Teachers will need new skills, mostly in technology.
- ▼ Need more support to implement, gather, and review information.
- ▼ The perception of teachers might be that this is one more thing that will go away.
- ▼ Being able to include everything that everyone is doing (however, this would become more streamlined as our vision becomes more specific.)
- ▼ How do you get people to reach a vision and get on board?
- ▼ How do we get started?
- ▼ Quality and availability of data is a huge concern.
- ▼ Putting this all together seems overwhelming but worth doing.

Over time, the *benefits* of keeping up a school portfolio are:

- ▼ The schoolwide focus and everyone knowing what we are doing is making a difference.
- ▼ It is a positive communication tool that keeps all staff knowing what is going on and what the next steps are and why.
- ▼ So much more proactive than any other school improvement effort we have engaged in.
- ▼ We are more proactive now and we are getting grants—so many that we have had to turn some away; we cannot re-plan fast enough to show our growth and get ready for the next steps that a new grant implies. (Also, by the time some of the grants come through, we have already finished that piece.)

Over time, the *concerns* of keeping up a school portfolio are:

- ▼ Keeping it going at this level of quality over time takes organization and support.
- ▼ Our school is not used to sticking to the same design for this long…
- ▼ Assuring staff that the school portfolio is not the latest fad in education; rather, it is an ongoing process for improving schools.

SUMMARY

Staff will be very proud when the first draft of their school portfolio is completely put together. It might be together, but it is not finished. A school portfolio must be maintained over time. If done well, the maintenance activities will also be continuous improvement and assessment activities. Over time, staff will see that maintaining a school portfolio will make a difference in the results they are getting and in how the school approaches its work in a more proactive way.

FREQUENTLY ASKED QUESTIONS ABOUT MAINTAINING THE MOMENTUM 💿
CD-ROM

▼ **Our superintendent wants to use our school portfolio to evaluate the principal and teachers at our school. What do you think about that?**

First of all, the intent of the school portfolio is for the self assessment and continuous improvement of the school. When used by another party, it remains a truthful document for continuous improvement only if that portfolio is used in a nonjudgmental way or in a manner agreed-upon by the reviewee. If a school's work is going to be judged by someone else, all of a sudden the way the document is written becomes more a highlight of the positive elements that are in place—what we want the portfolio to do is to encourage changes in those areas that typically are not dealt with.

Secondly, we would like to see school portfolios used to replace the typical personnel evaluation process in this way: the portfolio can remain an honest document that describes what is going on right now at the school, the assessment of the school, and plans for improvement. In this respect, the evaluation would be more of a discussion between the principal and her/his supervisor about goals for improvement, how she/he is leading staff through improvement, and about reviewing progress to date. The terms of this approach should be agreed-upon before it is used for evaluation.

Thirdly, the school portfolio could serve as a "principal portfolio," required by some licensure groups. The portfolio might have to be slanted more towards "what I have done to lead staff to data-driven decision making, etc." It is okay to have two variations of the same portfolio.

▼ How do we keep the momentum to maintain a school portfolio going over time?

Usually, staff is so excited to see the documentation of their progress through a school portfolio that it builds the momentum for the change. The change leads to more documentation of progress. Wonderful things happen and staff finds that they have to work very hard to continuously revise their plan; things happen very fast once they are clear on a vision and a plan. (Presenting to the Board of Education at least annually, as described in this chapter, could help keep the momentum going.)

We recommend, when possible, that schools work together in a network with other schools, with regularly scheduled meetings throughout the year, to talk about progress, questions, and concerns. These network meetings can include the sharing of new research, effective instructional practices, and results. They should be positive and something participants look forward to attending.

YOUR QUESTIONS

How do you plan to keep the school portfolio alive at your school?

What do you need from others in order to keep the school portfolio up-to-date and alive?

ON THE CD RELATED TO MAINTAINING THE MOMENTUM

▼ Frequently Asked Questions about Maintaining the Momentum

▼ School Portfolio Assessment Activity (AKA Treasure Hunt Activity)

▼ Updating the School Portfolio Activity

▼ School Portfolio Update Worksheet

▼ School Portfolio Summary Chart

▼ Evidence to Include when Updating the School Portfolio

▼ School Portfolio Concerns Activity

CHAPTER 12

IMPLEMENTING THE SCHOOL PORTFOLIO:
Case Studies from Around the Country

Chapter Objective: TO PROVIDE REAL EXAMPLES OF HOW SCHOOLS AND DISTRICTS AROUND THE COUNTRY HAVE STARTED AND ARE USING THE SCHOOL PORTFOLIO

Hundreds of schools across the country are using school portfolios for continuous school improvement planning, implementation, and evaluation. Below are examples of what it looks like from different viewpoints. Each of the example organizations entered the process from different places. What follows is at least one example from each of these organization types:

▼ statewide
▼ rural county
▼ large urban district
▼ suburban district
▼ rural district
▼ elementary schools
▼ middle school
▼ high school

A STATEWIDE VIEW:
MISSOURI DEPARTMENT OF ELEMENTARY AND SECONDARY EDUCATION

The Missouri Department of Elementary and Secondary Education's Leadership Academy was looking for an approach to Continuous School Improvement Planning that would engage Missouri schools in data analysis work, while supporting the requirements of the Missouri School Improvement Program (MSIP), and the North Central Association Commission on Accreditation and School Improvement (NCA-CASI).

Judy English, Assistant Director, and Doug Miller, Director, Missouri Leadership Academy, present a plaque of appreciation to Dr. Bernhardt and the SBC Foundation during a 2001 celebration of success.

In 1999, The Leadership Academy established a partnership with Southwestern Bell to support Dr. Victoria Bernhardt's work on her books, *The School Portfolio: A Comprehensive Framework for School Improvement* (1999) and *Data Analysis for Comprehensive School Improvement* (1998). This partnership has also supported the Academy's intent to bring a focus and a framework to leadership development that is research-based, measurable, and aligned to Interstate School Leaders Licensure Consortium (ISLLC) standards.

The Academy has taken a comprehensive approach to implementing these concepts statewide. For two years, the Academy has sponsored awareness sessions for school leaders at all levels to introduce and sustain Dr. Bernhardt's work. Statewide, over 2,000 school leaders have learned from and utilized her books in various professional development and learning community settings. While building statewide capacities of understanding about data and Dr. Bernhardt's school portfolio continuums, intensive partnership implementation work has begun officially in thirty school districts, representing over 300 schools, and over 250,000 students.

Using the school portfolio Continuums for self-assessment to determine a starting point for improvement has changed the way school staffs converse and collaborate with each other. The primary criterion for a district to be considered and supported through The Leadership Academy is an assurance that the work will be supported at the central office level. The aspect of partnership development has been key to the success. During the implementation phase, Leadership Academy staff are partnering with districts to maintain the momentum of continuous improvement. As districts also partner with each other for "lessons learned" and job-embedded staff development, a statewide network is emerging as a significant resource for implementation. Regions are also

Missouri Department of Elementary and Secondary Education Leadership Academy

partnering for ways to expedite data collection and data analysis. Practitioners from the charter partner district, Columbia, and from three other districts, Wentzville and Parkway in surburban St. Louis, as well as the Hickman Mills district in surburban Kansas City, present their school portfolio stories at ongoing sessions for school leaders statewide.

To further encourage schools to develop school portfolios, MSIP, NCA, and ISLLC standards have been cross-referenced to the school portfolio. Schools can create school portfolios to show how state standards and accreditation standards are being met.

Dr. Bernhardt has also conducted ongoing "Train the Trainer" sessions with 48 professional development leaders. Each of the nine Regional Professional Development Centers has at least one trainer qualified to conduct awareness sessions in the local area. Trainers are receiving ongoing follow-up training, as new trainers are added.

Through the nationally recognized Missouri Satellite Academy Program for aspiring and practicing school leaders, awareness sessions have been conducted on *The School Portfolio* (1999) and *Data Analysis for Comprehensive School Improvement* (1998). In addition, The Advanced Leadership Academy participants who have demonstrated expertise in leading school improvement initiatives have developed school portfolios as part of their completion requirements for participation in a two-year advanced leadership development program, based on ISLLC standards. The Leadership Academy encourages experienced Missouri principals to see their school portfolio as evidence of their leadership skills for ongoing continuous improvement—not as a separate document in addition to an individual portfolio. In other words, the principal's portfolio is the school portfolio.

For more information, please contact:

Judy English
Assistant Director
The Leadership Academy
Missouri Department of Elementary and Secondary Education
Jefferson City, MO
JEnglish@mail.dese.state.mo.us
http://www.dese.state.mo.us

A RURAL COUNTY VIEW:
SISKIYOU COUNTY OFFICE OF EDUCATION

Siskiyou County Office of Education is located in the northern most area of rural Northern California, adjacent to the Oregon border, where the county population is approximately seven people per square mile. In one of its capacities, the County Office of Education supports its twenty-eight school districts with their forty-four schools through the Program Quality Review Process (PQR), Focus on Learning Western Association of Schools and Colleges/California Department of Education Joint Process (FOL WASC/CDE) Accreditation, and oversees the Intermediate Underperforming Schools Program (II/USP). In 1999-00 and 2000-01, 20 schools chose to build school portfolios to meet PQR, FOL WASC/CDE, and/or II/USP requirements.  These schools will maintain their school portfolios and dig deeper into the classroom and student level data during their "off" review years. These schools also use the information in their school portfolio to meet coordinated compliance review and schoolwide requirements.

Magnificent Mount Shasta, located in rural Siskiyou County, Northern California.

The schools feel that the comprehensive look at their school is much more valuable than what they have done in the past, meeting just one requirement at a time. They like having all their pertinent program information and student achievement data in one location, and, especially like the information the *Continuous Improvement Continuums* and the Education for the Future student, parent, and staff questionnaires gave them. They will continue to use them annually.

The schools are excited to have documents that describe their schools, that are available to the public, that will live on, and that will not be shelved only to be dusted off in three years for the next state review.

For more information, please contact:

Michael DeRoss
Assistant Superintendent, Curriculum and Instruction
Siskiyou County Office of Education
Yreka, CA
mdeross@sisnet.ssku.k12.ca.us
http://www.sisnet.ssku.k12.ca.us

AN URBAN SCHOOL DISTRICT VIEW: SAN JOSE UNIFIED SCHOOL DISTRICT

San Jose Unified School District

San Jose Unified School District, the twelfth largest urban school district in California, is using the school portfolio in multiple frameworks. With 44 schools and an enrollment of 33,000 students, the considerable cultural and socio-economic diversity of this district has made it a unique implementation ground for Education for the Future's work. Marcy Lauck, Education for the Future's director of the school portfolio process in San Jose, works both to support districtwide capacity for continuous improvement and to find the incentive and timing for the successful implementation of the portfolio process with each school. Marcy's familiarity with the culture of the district has been key to the development of a systematic plan for moving the school portfolio process into the district's organizational structure without mandating it. Marcy leverages the California Distinguished School and the National Blue Ribbon Schools Award Programs, statewide accreditation processes, districtwide Community Conversations, data analysis training, and grant development to successfully initiate and implement the school portfolio process.

National Blue Ribbon Schools of Excellence and the California Distinguished School Awards

When the first Portfolio Pilot Schools used their portfolios as the basis for substantial school improvement funding ($500,000 per school), to join the ranks of the nation's elite National Blue Ribbon Schools, a powerful marriage of intrinsic and extrinsic rewards occurred. The district has found that supporting schools' applications for exemplary program awards such as the California Distinguished Schools and the National Blue Ribbon Schools Program is a powerful incentive for focusing their schools on purposeful continuous school improvement. The research base underlying the school portfolio process and these state and national award programs is highly congruent, and it provides San Jose Unified schools with a strong, yet flexible framework for school improvement (See CD for cross-reference of the school portfolio with the California Distinguished Schools and the National Blue Ribbon Schools Program.) 💿 The scoring rubrics associated with these recognition programs align closely with the *Continuous Improvement Continuums* of the school portfolio process, and together, they provide a compelling self-assessment process for the school community. This strategy, resulting in state and national school recognition, is now written into the district's twelve-year strategic plan. Schools now begin their self assessment several years in advance of their applications, determining where they fall on the Continuums and targeting the improvements they will need to make to have the well-rounded, exemplary program that will earn them recognition, first as a California Distinguished School, and then as a National Blue Ribbon School. These schools gather, analyze, and use data at the school, classroom, teacher, and student levels to continuously improve their performance in order to qualify for these awards. They use their school portfolios to show site visitors what they have been doing and how they get their results. In the past three years, eleven of eleven applying San Jose schools were awarded the California Distinguished School Award. The California School Recognition Program awards this exemplary program designation to the top three to four percent of the 8,600 K-12 public and private schools in the state. Eligible California Distinguished Schools are then invited to enter the rigorous application process to become one of the 49 state nominees to the National Blue Ribbon Schools Award Program. Seven of the ten San Jose Unified schools that applied to represent California in the larger, national pool of 85,000 K-12 schools, were selected. All seven were named National Blue Ribbon Schools of Excellence. The program validation and the public recognition San Jose Unified Schools have received as California Distinguished Schools have boosted school visibility and staff morale, and have strengthened community confidence in the quality of the district's schools.

WASC Accreditation

High schools in California are accredited by the Western Association of Schools and Colleges (WASC). The comprehensive data collection and analysis that are the backbone of the school portfolio's Information and Analysis section become the foundation for each school's self-assessment. San Jose high schools scheduled for review by WASC are able to align the school portfolio/school-recognition program process to tackle WASC requirements. The tools, strategies, and analyses provided by Education for the Future assist San Jose Unified School District high schools to grasp the comprehensive picture they need for accreditation, and to plan for, initiate, and effectively implement their targeted changes throughout the term of their accreditation.

Program Quality Review

California Elementary Schools must be reviewed through the California Department of Education Program Quality Review (PQR) every three years. San Jose uses the school portfolio as an approved alternative to their regular requirements.

Community Conversations

San Jose Unified School District believes that a strong partnership with their community has the power to motivate students to exceptional performance. Their Strategic Communications Plan, distilled from thousands of hours of community conversations and focus groups, is aimed at creating a seamless web of relationships to foster student resiliency and success. Key districtwide activities supporting this plan also flow into the school portfolio process. The first and underlying piece is their annual Climate Survey, adapted from the Education for the Future questionnaires, which is administered to all staff, parents, and students in grades 3–12 in each of their 44 schools. Online student and staff questionnaires (27,000+) put the district's substantial investment in technology to good use. Parent questionnaires (23,000+) are sent home via "backpack mail," and have an 80 percent return rate. Using Education for the Future's *School IQ*, questionnaire data are comprehensively disaggregated and charted to provide each school with valuable information about how students, staff and parents perceive their learning environment. Each school community discusses how they want the perceptions to change in the next year and creates an action plan to support the desired change. Year-to-year comparison data help staffs know if their efforts are succeeding, and are part of the district's annual school evaluation process. The district's Board of Education and all district directors also make effective use of this climate data as part of their results-oriented planning and budgeting process.

For the past four years, the district has sponsored large-scale, annual Community Conversations as part of its Strategic Communication Plan. Teams of student, staff, parent, and community partners from each school participate in thoughtful, structured dialogue around school improvement. Over this same four-year period, the School Portfolio/Award Program process was gathering momentum and becoming a highly effective self-assessment tool for schools. In the second of district-shaping "marriages" supported by Education for the Future, the school portfolio Partnership

Continuum and the scoring guides for partnership development/ community involvement in the Distinguished School and National Blue Ribbon process merged with the Community Conversation format and became the basis for the evening's discussion. Community response has been overwhelmingly positive. Enthusiastic feedback has supported the use of the continuums to help the schools target current practices and future goals. This process has helped them clarify where they are with their community partners, where they want to be, and the progress they have made over time.

Data Analysis Training

With data at the heart of the school portfolio process, Marcy's first years as the Education for the Future/San Jose Unified School District Associate was to initiate a data discovery process to drive data analysis down to the classroom level. As San Jose schools began to understand the importance of data—including individual student, classroom, grade level, subject area, and school data—they championed a district reorganization of the student information and assessment system so that they would have full and timely access to critical student achievement data. Schools knew they not only needed access to digital cumulative files for every student but also to a tool that would let them easily manipulate the data. Marcy brought Education for the Future's data analysis expertise and research into state-of-the-art relational database and reporting software to the district's discovery process. The impact of her data trainings has led to significant changes in the way San Jose Unified School District schools do business and the way they meet individual student needs. Feedback from the schools on what data they need to support schoolwide and action-based classroom research provides the focus for her trainings. The power of this data work has become fundamental to the work of every school. It is unquestionably central to the continuous improvement efforts of the district.

Grant Development

It was because of a grant program that San Jose Unified School District became involved with Education for the Future and in the school portfolio process in the first place. Schools in the San Francisco Bay Area were given the opportunity to apply for Annenberg Dollars through the Bay Area School Reform Collaborative and were asked to submit school portfolios as their proposals.  Several San Jose Unified school representatives attended a School Portfolio Workshop provided by the Santa Clara County Office of Education. They left the workshop with a firm commitment to bringing the portfolio process to their colleagues. They knew that they had no systematic process for determining student or school needs and had no access to the comprehensive student data that would help them support every student's success. Eventually, eight San Jose Unified School District schools submitted portfolios and became Leadership Schools in the Collaborative. The nearly four million dollars in funding they received has vigorously supported their school reform efforts.

What's Next?

Marcy's current focus is on streamlining the existing, annual compulsory plans and reporting requirements each school must fulfill into the school portfolio framework. Her goal is to simplify the merging of these twenty-plus plans into one comprehensive plan.

Marcy is in the process of writing a book on applying for the National Blue Ribbon Award, using *The School Portfolio* (1999).

For more information, please contact:

Marcy Lauck
School Portfolio Director
San Jose Unified School District
San Jose, CA
marcy@imagination-at-work.com
http://www.sjusd.k12.ca.us

Marcy Lauck with a few of the San Jose School Portfolios and Blue Ribbon Award Applications.

A SUBURBAN SCHOOL DISTRICT VIEW: COLUMBIA PUBLIC SCHOOLS

 Columbia, Missouri Public Schools (enrollment: 16,200 plus, with 27 schools) are using school portfolios in all of their elementary schools, in most of their middle schools, and in their Career Center—at the request of the schools. After attending an awareness session offered through the Missouri Leadership Academy, principals started calling Assistant Superintendent for Elementary Education Cheryl Cozette, asking her if they could build school portfolios. Their story follows:

School improvement has been a focus in the Columbia Public Schools for many years. The school portfolio process has helped renew this enthusiasm and has provided a results-based focus on school improvement.

In the spring of 1999, many principals became enthusiastic about the structure the school portfolio provided for school improvement. Other principals whose staff were already invested in particular school improvement model (i.e., Accelerated Schools, Basic Schools, DuFour's Learning Communities, etc.) were interested in the school portfolio as a means of documenting what they were currently doing for school improvement.

The first step we took toward understanding the portfolio was to form a summer study group that met twice to discuss Dr. Bernhardt's book, *The School Portfolio: A Comprehensive Framework for School Improvement* (1999). Enthusiasm for the process, as well as the product, continued to grow. Principals saw the portfolio as a tool that would help them focus on the results. Fifty of Columbia's principals, coordinators, and teachers attended several of Dr. Bernhardt's workshops provided by the Missouri Department of Elementary and Secondary Education's Leadership Academy. A districtwide study group met throughout the winter semester. As more principals enhanced their familiarity with the process, their requests for professional development focused on the need for collaboration and training in data analysis to guide them as leaders of school improvement in their buildings. As a result, administrative staff development was modified to accommodate their requests.

During the 1999-2000 school year, most schools in Columbia began developing school portfolios culminating with a two-day work session. The work session provided quality time with Dr. Bernhardt and her staff for school teams to construct and/or refine their school portfolios. Schools were at various stages of the school improvement process—the portfolios reflected those stages. Schools used various strategies for school improvement—the portfolios reflected those strategies. As staff members analyzed data, a need for additional data became apparent. The school portfolio has been a catalyst for the district to expand examination of multiple measures of assessment at both the building and the district levels. Requests for data, and assistance with analyzing that data, have increased as both teachers and principals have used the portfolio as a tangible method of assessing and developing school improvement goals in their buildings. This work surfaced a need for a consistent student achievement measure at every grade level that can be analyzed over time. The district adopted SAT 9 as that consistent measure to replace the many different norm-referenced tests used at different grade levels. Principals and teachers are now working on action research studies, digging deeper into the data.

Results of the school portfolio process in Columbia are evident. We anticipate an increase in student achievement to be our primary result. In the meantime, teachers are mapping curriculum at the building level; parent, student, and teacher perceptions of education at the building level are being assessed; demographic data is being studied and analyzed as it relates to student achievement; collaboration among teachers has increased; vertical teams have formed to ensure curriculum articulation; and principals are demonstrating a renewed enthusiasm for school improvement and the impact it will have on student achievement.

Our Comprehensive School Improvement Plan (CSIP) is the guiding focus as each building implements their plan to reach building-level and districtwide goals. The school portfolio is a major component of those processes that will allow us to reach our goals for all students in the Columbia Public Schools. As a result of these exciting changes taking place at the school level because of the school portfolio, the district decided it needed to write a district portfolio—currently in progress.

For more information, please contact:

Dr. Cheryl Cozette
Assistant Superintendent
Columbia Public Schools
ccozette@columbia.k12.mo.us
http://www.columbia.k12.mo.us

or

Dr. Mary Anne Graham
Coordinator, Staff Development
Columbia Public Schools
mgraham@columbia.k12.mo.us
http://www.columbia.k12.mo.us

Mabton Public Schools District,
Mabton, Washington

Mabton Public School District in Eastern Washington serves 845 students, grades K-12, in three schools. A large percentage of the student population comes from migrant families and over 31 percent of the community lives below the poverty level. Over 85 percent of students qualify for free and reduced lunch, with 773 students eating both breakfast and lunch at school. Many of the district's students live in Spanish-speaking homes and enter school needing to develop English Language skills. These and other factors make Mabton a somewhat isolated community with limited opportunities for students to gain new experiences. Thus, access to effective instruction and leadership are essential to expanding students' visions of what they can do. This makes Mabton an ideal location to enact districtwide reinvention for all children to reach high levels of achievement.

Mabton Public Schools wanted to apply for a *Bill and Melinda Gates Foundation Grant* to improve student learning through school and district reinvention. While attending a Data Analysis and School Portfolio Workshop given by Victoria Bernhardt and offered through their Educational Service District, Mabton administration and teachers decided that the school portfolio could provide the framework they needed to plan for, implement, and evaluate their approach to technology. The framework would allow for the individual school look, as well as a whole-district look, would be data-driven, and would set them up to meet all other requirements.

Mabton's grant application was successful. Work began by having the entire staff assess where each school and the district were on the *Continuous Improvement Continuums*. It became clear that data needed to be collected and analyzed to understand where they were. It also became clear that a vision for a K-12 continuum of learning that would make sense for all students was needed. A shared vision was developed for the schools and connected for a district vision. Staff committed to implementing specific instructional and assessment strategies and to studying new approaches. During the first school year, a data warehouse was purchased and put into place. Demographic and student achievement data were analyzed. Questionnaires were completed by teachers, students, and parents, and were analyzed to get a picture of where the district and the schools were with respect to student achievement, climate, and technology implementation.

It was during this first year that the plan was to be developed as well. Parts of the plan were developed as enthusiasm waned when the going got hard. To reinspire the troops, the staff took some time to review their history through the History Gram process. What they discovered was that over the years they had started many initiatives for the benefit of their students. They had also stopped the progress on each initiative—not intentionally or even obviously. In reflecting, they determined that when they stopped the other initiatives was exactly at the same spot they were with the school portfolio process—in the planning and implementation stages. It was at this point that staff understood that the work to be done was "huge" and would require a new way of thinking, working, and operating. This time was different, however; this time they had a shared vision based on what they collectively believed in their hearts would improve their students' learning. This time they had to keep going.

Kevin Chase, Superintendent, Mabton Public School District, facilitating a back-to-school planning session with school staffs.

These school's portfolios are a little different from most—they each describe their school and the other two schools, within the context of the district. As the continuum of learning is built with technology as a tool, progress is documented, measured, and celebrated. The portfolio process has been a helpful tool in assisting Mabton to learn how to work differently and to know that what teachers and administrators are doing is making a difference for Mabton students.

For more information, please contact:

Kevin Chase
Superintendent
Mabton Public Schools
Mabton, WA
kchase@mabton.wednet.edu
http://169.204.145.9/msd/index.lasso

VIEWS FROM ELEMENTARY SCHOOLS: NEW HAVEN, FAIRVIEW, AND CALEDONIA

Two of the Columbia Public Schools Elementary Schools, and Caledonia in Grand Rapids, Michigan, had very different reasons and approaches to using the school portfolio. The principals of Fairview, New Haven, and Caledonia Elementary Schools share their stories below.

New Haven Accelerated Elementary School

New Haven Accelerated Elementary School is a small (300 students) rural school in Columbia, Missouri. We are a Title One school with over forty percent of our students on free or reduced lunch. One of our greatest strengths is that we are an accelerated school and work with our parents and our community to make decisions about our building and our educational environment.

Two years ago, after hearing about Victoria Bernhardt's work and becoming part of a district-wide study group, I presented the idea of developing a school portfolio to my building Leadership Team. We studied the idea and decided it would enhance our current school improvement process. As an accelerated school, we had gotten used to looking at data, but it was a rather informal process. The Leadership Team felt that developing a school portfolio would allow us to create a more formalized process of evaluating data. We then presented the idea to our Steering Committee (parent-teacher decision-making body of the school).

We began a two-part process. First, we took stock of where we were by looking at and collecting data. We used multiple measures: student achievement, perceptions, school processes, and demographic data. We began inserting data pieces into the seven sections outlined in *The School Portfolio* (1999), by Dr. Bernhardt.

At the same time, we reviewed the *Continuous Improvement Continuums* found in Appendix A of *The School Portfolio* (1999). We began with the Quality Planning Continuum in order to assess where we were in the planning process. After we identified what needed to be done in order to move forward, we began to formally develop a school improvement plan. Through the development of the plan, we began focusing on the Information and Analysis and

New Haven Staff spend a day working on their school portfolio.

Student Achievement sections of *The School Portfolio*. Each piece kept moving us forward.

At the beginning and end of each year, we use the school portfolio perception surveys. This allows us to keep track of the climate of the building and school community as we make changes. What we have discovered is that the more in-depth we get with our school portfolio process, the more we increase the positive climate of our school and community.

Development of a school portfolio is continuous and ongoing. Our plan for next year is to continue assessing our school progress through the continuums. We realize that we must also continuously assess our data and make adjustments as we go. Through the utilization of our New Haven School Portfolio, we are now making more informed decisions. We are spending less time on trivial matters and even eliminating those events that no longer support the vision of our school. However, our greatest accomplishment is that we have ways of truly assessing our progress and are able to recognize and celebrate our successes.

For more information, please contact:

Dr. Terri L. Martin
Principal
New Haven Accelerated Elementary School
Columbia Public Schools
Columbia, MO
tmartin@columbia.k12.mo.us
http://www.columbia.k12.mo.us/nhe

Fairview Elementary School

Beginning the school portfolio process was like a shot of adrenaline for our school improvement efforts. Prior to the portfolio, we had several different plans for improvement (technology, partnerships, and a variety of grants), but never had a system to bring everything together or a method of evaluating our overall progress. The school portfolio gave us the ability to have one comprehensive plan, which is on going and focused on our mission.

After studying Victoria Bernhardt's work, attending workshops, and participating in a study group, I decided to present the

Fairview Elementary staff sharing their school portfolio.

portfolio to our advisory team. We began the process by evaluating our school using the seven continuums. This was done individually and then discussions were held with the whole faculty to reach consensus. More important than the actual number was the dialog that took place. Our discussions helped us determine areas of strength and areas for further development.

We spent the next year collecting data. This past summer our leadership team actually put our portfolio together. The portfolio is now being used to help develop our long-range plan for improvement.

A Year Later. At the beginning of the next school term, our leadership team developed strategies for maintaining our portfolio and for moving us forward in our improvement plan. Each month at a faculty meeting one of the leadership team members introduced a continuum. They shared what we had in our portfolio and our plan for improvement. This helped to bring new staff members up to speed and allowed us to continue with our growth.

In October, upon receiving a Missouri Gold Star Award, we received information from the state department of education regarding the National Blue Ribbon Recognition Award Program. The administration presented the information to the faculty to see if there was interest in pursuing the application. Immediately after the presentation, a second year teacher stood and shared why we should apply. She referred to the improvement process in place with the school portfolio. The teacher articulated how the information was already together and that we would be missing an opportunity if we did not apply. The staff was astonished to hear that some schools spent two years working on the application. Within a two to three week time period, we were able to submit a quality document using our school portfolio. We just found out that we received the Blue Ribbon Award!

The important thing to always remember is that the school portfolio is a process to help move you toward your vision. It is ongoing and requires continuous assessment of the data. Using this procedure for improvement will enhance student achievement by ensuring that all decisions are made to support the vision of the school. The portfolio is a tool that truly makes a difference in the school improvement process.

For more information, please contact:

Elaine Hassemer
Principal
Fairview Elementary School
Columbia Public Schools, Columbia, MO
ehasseme@columbia.k12.mo.us
http://www.columbia.k12.mo.us/fve

Caledonia Elementary School

For Caledonia Elementary School, the 1998-1999 school year was the year that was. As the oldest elementary school in a rural community quickly becoming suburban, change was happening at a lightning pace. In October of 1998, I was hired as principal, the former principal leaving the building but staying in the district to open a new school. That new school would reduce the size of Caledonia Elementary School by 200 students. Along with the principal and roughly two-fifths of the student population, six teachers, both secretaries, the head custodian, the librarian, the PTO leadership and several paraprofessionals also went to the new building. The result was that those of us who chose to remain at Caledonia Elementary were also left with a bit of an identity crisis.

The circumstances were ripe to look closely at who we are and decide who we wanted to become as a learning community. To help us answer these questions and to focus our attention in this time of transition, we began to create a building portfolio, a picture of who we were as a building. To aid us, our Superintendent gave us a copy of *The School Portfolio* (1999), by Dr. Bernhardt. That same spring we learned of a conference sponsored by our local intermediate school district that featured Dr. Bernhardt. Members of our School Improvement Team went to the conference hoping for some direction on how to disaggregate data. We got more than we bargained for.

**Welcome to
Caledonia Elementary School, Michigan.**

Dr. Bernhardt reviewed our portfolio work and offered her help when she returned to Grand Rapids in the fall. We arranged for all of our teachers to be out of the classroom one day to meet with Dr. Bernhardt and self-assess on the *Continuous Improvement Continuums*. The Continuums offered the opportunity for honest and open dialogue about our strengths and possible areas for growth. Using the Continuums allowed us to avoid becoming hung up on side issues and helped us focus on creating an action plan for improvement.

One of the first things we did was to hold a funeral for our "dead horses." We each chose one thing that we personally needed to let go of in order to move forward as a team. Our personal "dead horse" was written on a piece of paper, enclosed in a small coffin, and buried by a volunteer from our team. This cleared the way to reviewing our mission statement and writing shared value statements.

Another step was to administer the perception surveys. We started with the staff survey, then the parent and student surveys. We were pleasantly surprised by how positive most people felt about our school. We identified our five strongest areas to celebrate and five lowest areas to address both in our school improvement plan and in ad hoc committees created to address specific short-term needs.

So where has this brought us? We have published an Annual Report to Our Stakeholders. Based on our portfolio, the Annual Report was designed to look like the annual report of a business. Having site-based decision-making power, we have undertaken a financial planning process to align our building spending to our values and goals and to shared financial leadership. Our district has made the commitment to achieve Transitions Accreditation through NCA-CASI. The work we have already done on our portfolio has positioned us perfectly for achieving this valuable accreditation.

More important than the extrinsic benefits of our work is the self-confidence that comes from not only knowing who we are but also having the documentation to prove it. We no longer make decisions based on hunches or personal likes and dislikes. We build on identified strengths and on data of what works. In this way, each day we choose to be a true learning community.

For more information, please contact:

Sheryl A. O'Connor
Principal
Caledonia Elementary School
Caledonia, Michigan
oconnors@caledonia.k12.mi.us
http://caledonia.k12.mi.us

A MIDDLE SCHOOL VIEW: CASTILLERO MIDDLE SCHOOL

Castillero Middle School's Vision Team

Castillero Middle School in San Jose, California, is a highly acclaimed Academic, Visual and Performing Arts Magnet School, serving 1,166 students in grades 6-8. Castillero has a record of consistently high academic performance as demonstrated by test scores and the large number of students who receive academic recognition.

In the fall of 1995, the Castillero school improvement team attended a School Portfolio workshop offered at the County Office of Education to prepare attending schools to submit school portfolios to apply for Annenberg dollars through the Bay Area School Reform Collaborative. We left the workshop firmly convinced that, although we still wanted to apply for the grant, our commitment was to the data-based, continuous improvement process at the heart of the school portfolio.

Becoming knowledgeable data users has been central to our reform efforts. Prior to our portfolio work, we had little meaningful or consistent data to help us determine the effectiveness of our program. Using Education for the Future's *Continuous Improvement Continuums*, we began the first of many thorough self-assessments. The rich discussion generated by the continuums underscored that we needed to update our 8-year old vision statement, and further highlighted that we did not have any consistently gathered data to help inform our decision making. We embarked on an ambitious effort to use data as the foundation for a plan of improvement tied to student outcomes. One of the first steps that resulted from our initial self-assessment was a vision retreat to renew a shared direction for the entire community. We also made an initial determination about what data we needed to gather to provide us with a baseline assessment for the school. Using the Education for the Future questionnaires, we surveyed all students, staff, and parents. We also began an unexpectedly arduous process of obtaining digital files of our students' standardized test scores from our district office. We learned that test scores and demographic data were stored in different departments and databases, and that annual tests were not administered at every grade level. Despite these hurdles, we forged ahead, committed to seeking out the tools and expertise to help us develop a comprehensive data analysis of our students' achievement. A representative group of teachers and community partners committed to reporting what data we had, as well as researching and writing the various sections of our portfolio. Success followed each effort and encouraged our continued growth.

Our initial conviction, based on current research regarding the power of arts in education, was that students who were deeply engaged in the arts were more likely to be academically successful. We formed a hypothesis that students fully engaged in Castillero's Visual and Performing Arts, would score higher on standard measures of achievement while evidencing other measures of school success, such as higher GPA and fewer on campus supervision referrals than less-engaged students. To test the hypothesis, we conducted a survey. Three different populations at the eighth grade level—mainstream, special education, and English Language Development—were polled regarding their level of progressive, sustained participation in any one of the Visual and Performing Arts programs. The results of the survey were analyzed, and the data collected indicated that engaged students in each of the three test groups did indeed experience a greater degree of success in what we have labeled the academic areas of the curriculum and also had fewer behavior referrals. We were serving 65 percent of our students with great success both academically and creatively. It was the significant remaining thirty-five percent who inspired our reform efforts. It was our belief that greater integration of the arts and academics would allow all children to experience greater school success. Instead of fragmenting and narrowing a child's learning, Castillero Middle School's vision was that through comprehensive school change, all students would be able to achieve high standards resulting from the best practices of teaching and learning. Our initial plan called for the formation of a Collaborative Action Research Team to design interdisciplinary units that would build on the success of our magnet program by further enhancing the arts/academic integration. However, as our access to more comprehensive, disaggregated data evolved and we were able to explore our data in greater depth, a significant achievement gap between our Caucasian and our Hispanic students in reading/language arts became apparent. Sixty-four percent of our Hispanic students were scoring below the district standard on the Stanford Achievement Test (a rate more than twice that of our Caucasian students), and thirty-one percent of these same students received at least one "D" or "F" on their semester grade report. We readjusted our focus. The arts are still embedded in all that we do, but we have made a commitment to the achievement of high standards in reading by *all* of Castillero's students in *all* content areas. Content area departments have identified essential standards and instructional strategies to support students' mastery of those standards. Teachers are delving more deeply into Hispanic cultures and modifying their practices to accommodate that

Castillero Middle School staff working on their school portfolio.

knowledge. Targeted action research is supporting schoolwide change in teaching practices that is personalized, accessible and varied to fit individual learning needs in order to close the achievement gap. Broad-based action teams focus on data input and timely reporting, explore creative ways to adjust the master schedule to support ongoing reform work and otherwise maximize time and design forums where the voices of traditionally unheard students and parents will be heard. Our work is demanding and fraught with all the ups and downs of any systemic reform. There is no question, however, that it is far-reaching, and deeply meaningful.

Our portfolio efforts have yielded far more than we ever imagined. The tangible rewards have strongly validated our efforts: we were awarded the half million dollar grant as a Bay Area School Reform Collaborative Leadership School, and are recognized as a California Distinguished School and a National Blue Ribbon School of Excellence, with special emphasis recognition for our extensive family and community partnerships. But the intangible rewards continue to resonate even more powerfully through our school and district culture. Our compelling need for meaningful and timely data became the driving impetus for the district's search for a tool to provide its forty-three schools with the capability of mining a comprehensive warehouse of student data. We have become increasingly sophisticated data users. We now have robust, digital cumulative files for every student that can be disaggregated in myriad ways to examine student achievement, and we are able to undertake even the most complex queries with ease. The focus on measurable success for all students will continue to guide our ongoing efforts to meet the needs of an increasingly diverse student population. Our staff members provide school reform leadership throughout the district and beyond. Our strong community partnerships have been recognized as a model throughout the nation. We attract students from all thirty-one elementary schools in the district, and have an annual wait list of 200 students. The school portfolio process provided the positive framework for change that has made all the difference.

For more information, please contact:
    Marcy Lauck
    School Portfolio Director
    San Jose Unified School District
    San Jose, CA
    marcy@imagination-at-work.com
    http://www.sjusd.k12.ca.us/sites/mid/mschools/cast.htm

A HIGH SCHOOL VIEW:
WESTERVILLE SOUTH HIGH SCHOOL

As part of the Ohio Continuous Improvement Plan (CIP) of the Westerville, Ohio, School District—a suburban district with over 13,000 students and twenty schools—each of the schools developed a CIP aligned with the district plan during the 1998-99 school year.

A committee of stakeholders—students, parents, teachers, school support personnel, and community safety personnel—met to develop the Westerville South High School CIP. After we had produced our CIP document, several district personnel attended a data analysis and School Portfolio workshop presented by Dr. Victoria Bernhardt and sponsored by the Regional Professional Development Center (RPDC). It became clear that our CIP—being an evolving document that will be reviewed and revised continually as we stay aligned with the district and state goals—was the beginning of a school portfolio for our learning community.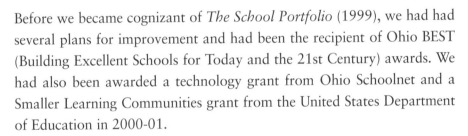

Joy Rose, Principal of Westerville South High School, Ohio.

Before we became cognizant of *The School Portfolio* (1999), we had had several plans for improvement and had been the recipient of Ohio BEST (Building Excellent Schools for Today and the 21st Century) awards. We had also been awarded a technology grant from Ohio Schoolnet and a Smaller Learning Communities grant from the United States Department of Education in 2000-01.

While we had the data required for the application process, the data were not always in a manageable format that the school portfolio provides. Developing the school portfolio is giving us a systematic way to incorporate our data and improvement plans together.

While we are using the data to influence our decision making to support our number one goal of improving student achievement, we still need to make the data more easily available for all teachers to use as they assess where their students are and what strategies can be used to improve the achievement of all students.

The Ohio Department of Education is one of seven states that are part of the Baldrige in Education (BIE) Initiative. Ohio is committed to using the Baldrige model as a valuable tool for school districts to improve. Our district has been chosen as a pilot for the Baldrige Criteria for Performance Excellence in the 2001-02 school year, so the school portfolio data will be even more useful. We expect it to dovetail without improvement processes and assist us as we work toward the highest ranking on our statewide report cards.

Our school portfolio is not in final form yet; however, we are using the data that it will include to make decisions on programs for the 2001-2002 school year, such as improving the academic achievement of incoming freshmen with a different type of class scheduling.

Developing the school portfolio is giving us data so we can make better decisions to improve teaching and learning throughout our building. It is an exciting process for our learning community.

For more information, please contact:

> Joy Rose
> Principal
> Westerville South High School
> Westerville School District, Westerville, OH
> RoseJ@westerville.k12.oh.us
> *http://westerville.k12.oh.us/South/index.html*

SUMMARY

Schools all over the country have found reasons to develop school portfolios. These examples show that each learning organization not only found a reason to develop the school portfolio, they determined how to do this hard work once, use it for many purposes, and then keep it going over time. For more case studies, watch our website, *http://eff.csuchico.edu.* Also, please consider contributing your case study to Dr. Bernhardt at vbernhardt@csuchico.edu.

FREQUENTLY ASKED QUESTIONS ABOUT IMPLEMENTING THE SCHOOL PORTFOLIO

▼ What are the differences in what schools look like before they have a school portfolio and after?

The answers to this question, compiled in the table on the facing page (Figure 12.1), were derived from what schools have told us and from what Education for the Future staff have observed over the past ten years.

FIGURE 12.1

Differences Before and After *The School Portfolio*

Before the school portfolio, we saw, heard and felt:	*After* the school portfolio, we see, hear, and feel:
Schools starting new school improvement strategies every two years	Schools truly implementing their visions for multiple years and assessing for improvement on a continuous basis
Schools without a focus—just doing what they do every day and every year	Schools using a framework for school improvement, focusing on a vision and students
Schools wrestling with multiple plans	Schools building one comprehensive plan to implement the vision
Schools buying stuff	Schools buying only the things that they planned for that will help them implement the vision, and that will lead to improved student learning
Schools doing the same things over and over and expecting different results	Schools knowing if what they are doing is making a difference, and adjusting accordingly to get the results they want
Schools wanting to get away from standardized testing	Schools wanting to use consistent measures at every grade level, at *least* one time every year
A feeling that lots of disparate things are going on in the school	A feeling that something special and consistent is going on throughout the school
Schools working hard and thinking they cannot take on one more thing	Schools working smarter, not harder—dropping things that are not making a difference
School staffs making decisions using hunches	School staffs making decisions using data, with the vision as their target
Schools reacting to many requirements	Schools responding proactively to requests and requirements
Principals doing most of the work of leading school improvement if and when they have time for it	Teachers leading the implementation of the vision in all parts of the school, with regular meeting times
Partners being sought for money	Partners sought to support the implementation of the vision and student learning standards
Professional development activities being politically driven	Professional development focused on helping all staff members understand how to implement the vision in their roles
Conversations in teachers' lounges about everything but the vision	Conversations in the teachers' lounges about the vision, data, and improving student learning
Teachers working independently in their classrooms	Collaborative teams of teachers working together for all students
Teachers working independently in their classrooms	Teachers coaching and supporting each other in the implementation of the vision
Teachers doing what they do, and getting the results they have always gotten	Teachers assessing the impact of their actions on student learning and adjusting to get better results
Teachers focused on their own classrooms and students	Teachers feeling the ownership of every student's learning
Teachers teaching what and how they want to teach	Teachers teaching to a vision and student learning standards and building a continuum of learning that makes sense for students
Teachers resisting data	Teachers asking for more data
Teachers reacting to assessments and to data analyses	Teachers using data proactively to plan for results, and requesting more data to dig deeper

▼ What makes some schools more successful than other schools in really implementing the school portfolio process?

Probably the most obvious difference relates to reading the book, *The School Portfolio* (Bernhardt, 1999). Teachers and administrators who read the book understand the intent of each section of the school portfolio and how the sections work together—in both the process and the product. Those who have the most difficulty with rubric assessments, doing the work, and ultimately placing evidence in the school portfolio usually have not read the book and do not have a good foundation for the work.

As one can read in the case studies above, Columbia Public Schools held study groups on *The School Portfolio*. The actual putting together of their portfolios was done in about two days. We have had other cases where the schools just could not get started with the product in one year. The principals in these schools admitted at the end of the year that they never took the time to read the book.

YOUR QUESTIONS

Do you have a story you would like to share about implementing the school portfolio process in your learning organization? If so, we would like to post it on our website. If possible, please include information about student achievement increases that you can attribute to the school portfolio process. Contact Dr. Bernhardt at vbernhardt@csuchico.edu, and watch for new case studies on our website, *http://eff.csuchico.edu*.

ON THE CD RELATED TO IMPLEMENTING THE SCHOOL PORTFOLIO

▼ Frequently Asked Questions About Implementing the Portfolio

▼ Case Studies

▼ Cross Reference Matrices

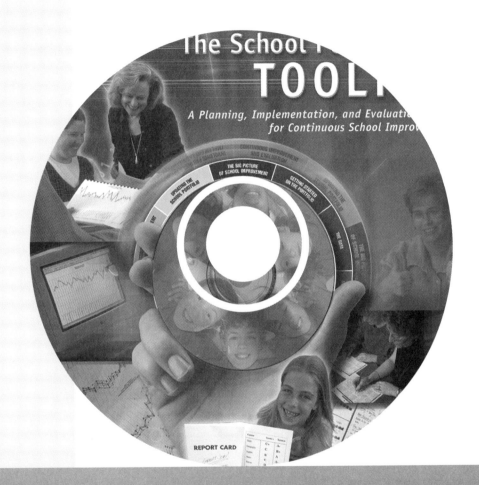

APPENDIX: Overview of the School Portfolio
Toolkit CD Contents

APPENDIX

Overview of the School Portfolio Toolkit CD Contents

The Appendix provides a list of the files as they appear on the accompanying CD. These files are listed by section, along with a description of the file's content and file type. (This list appears as the Index file [Index.pdf] on the CD.)

▼ **THE BIG PICTURE OF SCHOOL IMPROVEMENT** (Chapter 2)
The *Big Picture of Continuous School Improvement* provides an overview of continuous school improvement.

The Big Picture of Continuous School Improvement	BigPictr.pdf	Acrobat Reader

This read only file is a figure of the *Big Picture of Continuous School Improvement,* found in Chapter 2 of *The Toolkit*.

▼ **GETTING STARTED ON THE PORTFOLIO** (Chapter 3)
The files in this section provide an overview of different ways to begin the school portfolio process and product. The files include read only documents, examples, templates, tools, activities, and strategies.

ABCs of the School Portfolio	ABCs.pdf	Acrobat Reader

This read only file describes in ABC fashion how to develop a school portfolio; a useful document for schools starting the school portfolio process and product.

Overview: The School Portfolio	Overview.pdf	Acrobat Reader

This read only file of the *Overview of the School Portfolio* summarizes what the school portfolio is, what it does, and describes the purposes for each of the sections of the school portfolio.

Purposes and Uses of a School Portfolio	Purposes.pdf	Acrobat Reader

This read only file describes the purposes and uses for a school portfolio.

School Portfolio Presentation	SPSlides.ppt	Microsoft PowerPoint

This *PowerPoint* Presentation is the overview to use with your staffs in getting started on the school portfolio. The script of the presentation can be found under "view notes" and by setting the print option to "notes pages." Handouts can be created by setting the print option to "handouts" (three slides to a page).

School Portfolio Summary Chart	SPTable.doc	Microsoft Word

This tabular *Microsoft Word* file lists the categories of the school portfolio along with the major elements of each category in the left-hand column. The middle column is for documenting what your school has for each of these categories. The right-hand column is for listing additional items that your school would like to gather.

School Portfolio Overview Activity	ACTOverv.pdf	Acrobat Reader

This activity is designed to familiarize workshop participants with the school portfolio and its purposes and uses.

ABCs Activity	ACTAbcs.pdf	Acrobat Reader

This activity helps participants to think about the school portfolio in terms of an acronym format.

Frequently Asked Questions About Getting Started on the School Portfolio	FAQsStrt.pdf	Acrobat Reader

This read only file lists the most frequently asked questions, and their answers related to getting started on *The School Portfolio*.

Getting Started with the Product

Documents in this section include everything a school would need to get started on a school portfolio. Templates are provided that have placeholder words for each section of the school portfolio. Activities will help you get your staff actively involved in the work of the school portfolio product.

Getting Started with the School Portfolio Product   GetStartd.pdf   Acrobat Reader

> This read only file provides recommendations on getting started with the school portfolio product. The document references tools, templates, and documents on the CD to help you build your school portfolio.

School Portfolio Indices   SPIndex.doc   Microsoft Word

> This file is a placeholder containing index labels ready to print and place on index dividers for your school portfolio.

School Portfolio Beginning Pages with Header/Footer   BegPages1.pdf   Acrobat Reader

> This read only file contains *The School Portfolio Poem* and beginning pages for the sections of a school portfolio, with *The School Portfolio* header and footer.

School Portfolio Beginning Pages without Header/Footer   BegPages2.pdf   Acrobat Reader

> This read only file has *The School Portfolio Poem* and beginning pages for the sections of a school portfolio, *without* a header and footer. You can print this on your own header and footer pages.

School Portfolio Header Page Example 1   HdrCntr.doc   Microsoft Word

> This changeable file provides an example header page to customize for your school. This example is a centered header.

School Portfolio Header Page Example 2   HdrRt.doc   Microsoft Word

> This changeable file provides an example header page to customize for your school. This example is a right justified header.

School Portfolio Header Page Example 3   HdrRtLft.doc   Microsoft Word

> This changeable file provides an example header page to customize for your school. This example has left and right headers for left and right pages.

The Cover   CoverEx.pdf   Acrobat Reader

> This read only file contains a picture of different covers that schools have used for their school portfolios. It also includes the dimensions of the view binder covers and spines to help you prepare yours.

Group Process Tools and Activities

The files in this section provide an overview of different ways to begin the school portfolio process and can be used in various parts of the continuous school improvement process. The files include read only documents, examples, templates, tools, activities, and strategy recommendations. Many of the group process tools and activities can be used throughout the building of the school portfolio. Some activities will be referenced in other locations of the *Toolkit*.

Getting Started with the School Portfolio Process   SPProces.pdf   Acrobat Reader

> This read only file summarizes the steps to follow to get the school portfolio started through staff processes.

Running Efficient Meetings   Meetings.pdf   Acrobat Reader

> This read only file provides recommendations for running efficient staff meetings.

Ground Rules   GrndRule.pdf   Acrobat Reader

> This read only file provides example ground rules for staff meetings and professional development sessions.

Meeting Etiquette   Etiquete.pdf   Acrobat Reader

> This read only file provides example meeting etiquette agreements.

Norms of Behavior   NormsBhvr.pdf   Acrobat Reader

> This read only file provides recommendations for establishing norms of behavior for reculturing your school.

| Coming to Consensus | Consenss.pdf | Acrobat Reader |

This read only file provides strategies for coming to consensus.

| Guidelines for Brainstorming | Brainstr.pdf | Acrobat Reader |

This read only file provides guidelines for brainstorming.

| Issue Bin/Parking Lot | IssueBin.pdf | Acrobat Reader |

This read only file is an example of an issue bin/parking lot to use during meetings to store issues that need to be addressed at a later time.

| Affinity Diagram Activity | ACTAfnty.pdf | Acrobat Reader |

The affinity diagram encourages honest reflection on the real underlying root causes of a problem and its solutions, and encourages people to agree on the factors. This activity assists teams in discussing and resolving problems, using a nonjudgmental process.

| Cause and Effect Analysis Activity | ACTCause.pdf | Acrobat Reader |

This activity will help teams determine the relationships and complexities between an effect or problem and all the possible causes.

| Fishbowl Activity | ACTFish.pdf | Acrobat Reader |

The *Fishbowl Activity* can be used for dynamic group involvement. The most common configuration is an inner ring, which is the discussion group, surrounded by an outer ring, which is the observation group. Just as people observe the fish in the fishbowl, the outer ring observes the inner ring.

| Forcefield Analysis Activity | ACTForce.pdf | Acrobat Reader |

The *Forcefield Analysis Activity* helps staffs think about the ideal state for the school and the driving and restraining forces regarding that ideal state.

| Placemat Activity | ACTPlace.pdf | Acrobat Reader |

The *Placemat Activity* was developed to invite participants to share their knowledge about the school portfolio, data, a standard, an instructional strategy, a concept, etc.

| T-Chart Activity | ACTTChrt.pdf | Acrobat Reader |

A T-Chart is a simple tool to organize material into two columns. Use a T-Chart to compare and contrast information or to show relationships. Use it to help people see the opposite dimension of an issue.

| "X" Marks the Spot Activity | ACTXSpot.pdf | Acrobat Reader |

This activity helps staff understand levels of expertise or degrees of passion about a topic.

| Quadrant Diagram Activity | ACTQuadr.pdf | Acrobat Reader |

A quadrant diagram is a method to determine which solution best meets two goals at once, such as low cost and high benefit.

Continuous Improvement Continuums

The files in this section include *The School Portfolio Continuous Improvement Continuums* (CICs), the activity for using the CICs for self-assessing, report examples and templates, and graphing templates.

| Continuous Improvement Continuums | Rubrics.pdf | Acrobat Reader |

This read only file contains the seven *School Portfolio Continuous Improvement Continuums*. These can be printed as is, or enlarged to use during staff assessments.

| Continuous Improvement Continuums Self-Assessment Activity | ACTCIC.pdf | Acrobat Reader |

Assessing on the *Continuous Improvement Continuums* will help staffs see where their systems are right now with respect to continuous improvement and ultimately to show they are making progress over time. The discussion begins to write the sections of the school portfolio for staff.

| Continuous Improvement Continuums Report Example | ExReprt1.pdf | Acrobat Reader |

This read only file shows a real school's assessment on the *School Portfolio Continuous Improvement Continuums,* as an example.

Continuous Improvement Continuums Report Example
for Follow-Up Years   ExReprt2.pdf   Acrobat Reader

> This read only file shows a real school's assessment on the *School Portfolio Continuous Improvement Continuums* over time, as an example.

Continuous Improvement Continuums Baseline Report Template   Template.doc   Microsoft Word

> This *Microsoft Word* file provides a template for writing your school's report of its assessment on the *School Portfolio Continuous Improvement Continuums*.

Continuous Improvement Continuums Graphing Templates   CICGraph.xls   Microsoft Excel

> This *Microsoft Excel* file is a template for graphing your assessments on the seven *School Portfolio Continuous Improvement Continuums*.

Cross-Reference Matrices

These read only files cross-reference *The School Portfolio* section requirements to the requirements of specific states and accrediting agencies. The cross-reference shows that any school can meet most of its external requirements through *The School Portfolio*.

SP/Baldrige   Baldrige.pdf   Acrobat Reader

> This read only file cross-references *The School Portfolio* section requirements to the requirements of the *Baldrige Education Criteria for Performance Excellence*.

SP/ISLLC   ISLLC.pdf   Acrobat Reader

> This read only file cross-references *The School Portfolio* section requirements to the requirements of the *Interstate School Leaders Licensure Consortium Standards* (ISLLC).

SP/NSDC   NSDC.pdf   Acrobat Reader

> This read only file cross-references *The School Portfolio* section requirements to the requirements of the *National Staff Development Council* (NSDC) *Standards*.

SP/SACS   SACS.pdf   Acrobat Reader

> This read only file cross-references *The School Portfolio* section requirements to the requirements of the *Southern Association of Colleges and Schools—Middle School Standards*.

SP/California: WASC/PQR/II-USP   Calif.pdf   Acrobat Reader

> This read only file cross-references *The School Portfolio* section requirements to the California state requirements of the *Western Association of Schools and Colleges* (WASC), *California Program Quality Review* (PQR), and *California Immediate Interventions/Underperforming Schools Program* (II/USP).

SP/California Distinguished Schools Award Program   CDSAP.pdf   Acrobat Reader

> This read only file cross-references *The School Portfolio* section requirements to the requirements of the *California Distinguished School Awards Program*.

SP/BASRC   BASRC.pdf   Acrobat Reader

> This read only file cross-references *The School Portfolio* section requirements to the requirements of the *Bay Area School Reform Collaborative* (BASRC) *Criteria*.

SP/CCR/IASA   CCRIASA.pdf   Acrobat Reader

> This read only file cross-references *The School Portfolio* section requirements to the requirements of the *Coordinated Compliance Review* (CCR), and *Improving America's Schools Act* (IASA)—*Schoolwide Programs*.

SP/NCA/Indiana   Indiana.pdf   Acrobat Reader

> This read only file cross-references *The School Portfolio* section requirements to the requirements of the *North Central Association Commission on Accreditation and School Improvement* (NCA-CASI), and the *Indiana Strategic and Continuous School Improvement and Achievement Plan* (ISCSIAP).

SP/NCA/Kansas   Kansas.pdf   Acrobat Reader

> This read only file cross-references *The School Portfolio* section requirements to the requirements of the *North Central Association Commission on Accreditation and School Improvement* (NCA-CASI), and the *Kansas State Board of Education's Quality Performance Accreditation System*.

| SP/NCA/Michigan | Michigan.pdf | Acrobat Reader |

This read only file cross-references *The School Portfolio* section requirements to the requirements of the *North Central Association Commission on Accreditation and School Improvement* (NCA-CASI), and the *Michigan School Improvement Plan*.

| Missouri: SP/NCA/MSIP/ISLLC | MO.pdf | Acrobat Reader |

This read only file cross-references *The School Portfolio* section requirements to the requirements of the *North Central Association Commission on Accreditation and School Improvement* (NCA-CASI), *Missouri School Improvement Program* (MSIP), and the *Interstate School Leaders Licensure Consortium Standards* (ISLLC).

| SP/New York | NewYork.pdf | Acrobat Reader |

This read only file cross-references *The School Portfolio* section requirements to the requirements of the *New York Comprehensive District Education Planning*.

| Ohio: SP/Baldrige/NCA/CIP | Ohio.pdf | Acrobat Reader |

This read only file cross-references *The School Portfolio* section requirements to the requirements of the *Baldrige Education Criteria for Performance*, the *North Central Association Commission on Accreditation and School Improvement* (NCA-CASI), and the *Ohio Continuous Improvement Plan* (CIP).

| SP/Blue Ribbon | BRibbon.pdf | Acrobat Reader |

This read only file cross-references *The School Portfolio* section requirements to the requirements of the *U.S. Department of Education Blue Ribbon Schools Program*.

| SP/NCA/North Dakota | NDakota.pdf | Acrobat Reader |

This read only file cross-references *The School Portfolio* section requirements to the requirements of the *North Central Association Commission on Accreditation and School Improvement* (NCA-CASI), and the *North Dakota Education Improvement Process Standards*.

| SP with Blank Column Template | SPTmpl.doc | Microsoft Word |

This *Microsoft Word* file allows you to cross-reference the requirements of "your" state with *The School Portfolio* sections. Just place your related requirements in the template.

| SP/NCA with Blank Column Template | SPNCA.doc | Microsoft Word |

This *Microsoft Word* file allows you to cross-reference the requirements of "your" state with the *North Central Association Commission on Accreditation and School Improvement* (NCA-CASI), and *The School Portfolio* sections. Just place your related requirements in the template.

| SP/WASC with Blank Column Template | SPWASC.doc | Microsoft Word |

This *Microsoft Word* file allows you to cross-reference the requirements of "your" state with the *Western Association of Schools and Colleges* (WASC), and *The School Portfolio* sections. Just place your related requirements in the template.

Working with a Group of Schools

The files in this section will assist you in working with a group of schools to introduce and implement the school portfolio. The files include agendas, timelines, scope and sequences, activities, templates, and examples.

| Working with a Group of Schools | SchlGrps.pdf | Acrobat Reader |

This read only file provides recommendations to assist you in working with a group of schools to introduce and implement *The School Portfolio*.

| Recommendations for a School Portfolio Overview Workshop Agenda | Recomnd.doc | Microsoft Word |

This *Microsoft Word* file has a recommended agenda for a School Portfolio Overview Workshop.

| Example Agenda School Portfolio Overview | AgendaSP.doc | Microsoft Word |

This *Microsoft Word* file has a recommended agenda for a School Portfolio Overview Workshop, with outcomes.

School Portfolio Scope and Sequence   SPScope.pdf   Acrobat Reader

> This read only file shows the typical scope and sequence for the work of putting together a school portfolio.

Timelines for Working with a Group of Schools   GrpTimes.pdf   Acrobat Reader

> This read only file shows an example timeline for working with a group of schools on building school portfolios.

School Portfolio Implementation Timeline Template   TimeLine.doc   Microsoft Word

> This *Microsoft Word* file provides an example timeline for working with a school or a group of schools on building a school portfolio. You may alter this file completely.

School Portfolio Concerns Activity   ACTConcn.pdf   Acrobat Reader

> This benefits and concerns activity is for the end of a School Portfolio Overview Workshop to give you closure, to know questions and concerns, and to let the participants answer the questions.

▼ WRITING TEMPLATES

The *Microsoft Word* files in this section are templates for jump starting your school portfolio section writing. Change the name of the school and carefully read the text provided to make sure it fits your needs, then add your unique information.

Introduction to the School Portfolio Section Template Files   ReadMe.pdf   Acrobat Reader

> This introductory file describes *The School Portfolio* section templates, their purposes, and how they are to be used.

Introduction Section Template   Intro.doc   Microsoft Word

> This *Microsoft Word* file is a template for the introduction to your school portfolio.

Overview Section Template   Overvw.doc   Microsoft Word

> This *Microsoft Word* file is a template for the overview to your school portfolio. Add your unique information.

Information and Analysis Section Template   InfAnal.doc   Microsoft Word

> This *Microsoft Word* file is a template for jump starting the writing of the Information and Analysis section of your school portfolio. Change the name of the school, add your data, carefully read the text provided to make sure it fits your needs, then add your unique information.

Questionnaire Results Template   QResults.doc   Microsoft Word

> This *Microsoft Word* file is a template guide for interpreting your student, staff, and parent questionnaires, and serves as a template for the narrative for your school portfolio.

Student Achievement Results Template   SAResults.doc   Microsoft Word

> This *Microsoft Word* file is a guide for interpreting your student achievement results and serves as a template for the narrative for your school portfolio.

Student Achievement Section Template   SAchieve.doc   Microsoft Word

> This *Microsoft Word* file is a template for jump starting the writing of the Student Achievement section of your school portfolio. Change the name of the school, add your information, and carefully read the text provided to make sure it fits your needs.

Quality Planning Section Template   QPlang.doc   Microsoft Word

> This *Microsoft Word* file is a template for jump starting the writing of the Quality Planning section of your school portfolio. Change the name of the school, add your information, and carefully read the text provided to make sure it fits your needs.

Professional Development Section Template   ProfDev.doc   Microsoft Word

> This *Microsoft Word* file is a template for jump starting the writing of the Professional Development section of your school portfolio. Change the name of the school, add your information, and carefully read the text provided to make sure it fits your needs.

| Leadership Section Template | Leadshp.doc | Microsoft Word |

This *Microsoft Word* file is a template for jump starting the writing of the Leadership section of your school portfolio. Change the name of the school, add your information, and carefully read the text provided to make sure it fits your needs.

| Partnership Development Section Template | PrtDev.doc | Microsoft Word |

This *Microsoft Word* file is a template for jump starting the writing of the Partnership Development section of your school portfolio. Change the name of the school, add your information, and carefully read the text provided to make sure it fits your needs.

| Continuous Improvement and Evaluation Section Template | CIandE.doc | Microsoft Word |

This *Microsoft Word* file is a template for jump starting the writing of the Continuous Improvement and Evaluation section of your school portfolio. Change the name of the school, add your information, and carefully read the text provided to make sure it fits your needs.

▼ **THE DATA** (Chapter 4)

The files in this section include read only articles related to data analysis, profiles for gathering data, examples, graphing and reporting templates, tools, activities, and strategy recommendations all focused on data analysis.

| Items to Include in the Information and Analysis Section of the School Portfolio | ItemsIA.pdf | Acrobat Reader |

This read only file provides an overview of the items that are typically included in the Information and Analysis section of a school portfolio.

| Information and Analysis Continuous Improvement Continuum | IARubric.pdf | Acrobat Reader |

This read only file is the *Information and Analysis Continuous Improvement Continuum,* one of seven *Education for the Future Continuous Improvement Continuums.* This file can be printed as is or enlarged for the wall to use during staff assessments. (A file containing all seven continuums [Rubrics.pdf] is in the *Getting Started Continuous Improvement Continuums* section of the CD.)

| Frequently Asked Questions About Information and Analysis | FAQsIA.pdf | Acrobat Reader |

This read only file lists the most frequently asked questions, and their answers, related to data.

Articles

This section includes three read only articles, by Victoria L. Bernhardt, that summarize multiple measures, how databases can help with standards implementation, and data intersections. They will be useful in workshops or in getting started on data with staff.

| Multiple Measures | MMeasure.pdf | Acrobat Reader |

This read only article summarizes why and what data are important to continuous school improvement.

| Databases Can Help Teachers with Standards Implementation | Dbases.pdf | Acrobat Reader |

This read only article describes how databases can help with standards implementation.

| Intersections: New Routes Open when One Type of Data Crosses Another | Intersct.pdf | Acrobat Reader |

This read only article, published in the *Journal of Staff Development* (Winter 2000), discusses how much richer your data analyses can be when you intersect multiple data variables.

Demographics

The files in this demographic section include activities and templates for gathering and graphing demographic data for your school portfolio.

| School Profile | ProfilSc.doc | Microsoft Word |

The School Profile is a template for gathering data about your school. Please adjust it to add data elements you feel are important for describing the context of your school. This information is then written into the information and analysis text.

| Community Profile | ProfilCo.doc | Microsoft Word |

The Community Profile is a template for gathering data about your community. Please adjust it to add data elements you feel are important for describing the context of your community. It is important to describe how the community has changed over time, and how it is expected to change in the near future. This information is then written into the information and analysis text.

| Administrator Profile | ProfilAd.doc | Microsoft Word |

The Administrator Profile is a template for gathering data about your school administrators. Please adjust it to fully describe your administrators. This information is then written into the information and analysis and leadership texts.

| Teacher Profile | ProfilTe.doc | Microsoft Word |

The Teacher Profile is a template for gathering data about your school's teachers. Please adjust it to fully describe your teachers. The synthesis of this information will then be written into the information and analysis text.

| Demographic Graphing Templates | Demogr.xls | Microsoft Excel |

These *Microsoft Excel* files are templates for graphing demographic data such as enrollment over time. Simply place your school's numbers in the appropriate locations on the spreadsheet and watch your graph build before your eyes.

| Questions to Guide the Analysis of Demographic Data | QsDemogr.doc | Microsoft Word |

This *Microsoft Word* file provides a guide for interpreting your demographic data. Adjust the questions to better reflect the discussion you would like to have with your staff about the gathered demographic data.

| History Gram Activity | ACTHstry.pdf | Acrobat Reader |

The History Gram is a team-building activity that will "write" the history of the school. It will help everyone see that many initiatives have been started over the years and that most did not last. It is important to get everyone to understand what it will take to keep this current school improvement effort going.

Perceptions

Included as perceptions files are nine standard Education for the Future questionnaires, the *School Improvement Questionnaire Solutions (School IQ)* to analyze results, graphing templates to display results, templates for administering questionnaires online, advice for gathering, analyzing, viewing, and writing the results, and examples.

| Administering the Questionnaires | QAdmin.pdf | Acrobat Reader |

This read only file describes how to administer the Education for the Future questionnaires.

| Questions to Guide the Analysis of Perceptions Data | PerceptQ.doc | Microsoft Word |

This *Microsoft Word* file is a guide for interpreting your perceptions data. You can change the questions if you like or use the file to write in the responses. It will help you write the narrative for your school portfolio.

| Analysis of Questionnaire Data Table | QTable.doc | Microsoft Word |

This *Microsoft Word* file is a tabular guide for interpreting your student, staff, and parent questionnaires, independently and interdependently. It will help you write the narrative for your school portfolio.

| Example Narrative of Student Questionnaire Responses | ExQNarr.doc | Microsoft Word |

This *Microsoft Word* file is an example that can also be used as a template for the writing of your student questionnaire results. Change what is in the file that does not fit your situation and add your information.

| Example Gender Line Graph | Gender.xls | Microsoft Excel |

This questionnaire line graph, disaggregated by gender, is described in the example narrative of student questionnaire responses.

Example Grade-Level Line Graph	Grade.xls	Microsoft Excel

This questionnaire line graph, disaggregated by grade-level, is described in the example narrative of student questionnaire responses.

Example Ethnicity Line Graph	Ethnicty.xls	Microsoft Excel

This questionnaire line graph, disaggregated by ethnicity, is described in the example narrative of student questionnaire responses.

Example Bar Graphs for Questionnaire Items	BarGrphs.xls	Microsoft Excel

These questionnaire bar graphs are described in the example narrative of student questionnaire responses.

School IQ

School IQ: School Improvement Questionnaire Solutions is a powerful tool for analyzing Education for the Future questionnaires. *School IQ* reduces an otherwise technical and complicated process to one that can be navigated with pushbutton ease. There are different versions of *IQ* for each of the nine standard Education for the Future questionnaires.

School IQ and Graphing Templates	School IQ Folder

School Improvement Questionnaire Solutions (School IQ) is a database application for analyzing Education for the Future questionnaires. Custom, preformatted *Microsoft Excel* graph templates are provided in order to create graphic representations of questionnaire results when using *School IQ,* and are provided in the folder with each version of *School IQ*.

Online Templates	Online Folder

The Online Questionnaire Administration Templates are a collection of html files and *FileMaker Pro* databases that allow you to administer Education for the Future questionnaires online from a web server. Files are provided so that Education for the Future student, parent, and staff questionnaires can be administered, and are arranged according to questionnaires that apply to elementary, middle, and high schools.

Questionnaires

The files in this section are example questionnaires for assessing student, parent, and staff perceptions.

Student Grade K-3 Questionnaire	StQKto3.pdf	Acrobat Reader

This read only file is the Education for the Future questionnaire for assessing "young student's" opinions of the learning organization. This questionnaire uses a three-point scale (with happy, neutral, and sad faces).

Student Grade 1-6 Questionnaire	StQ1to6.pdf	Acrobat Reader

This read only file is the Education for the Future questionnaire for assessing students' opinions of the learning organization. This questionnaire uses a five-point scale and is used most often in grades 3 through 6, although some schools have used it additionally at the first and second grade levels.

Student Grade 6-12 Questionnaire	StQ6to12.pdf	Acrobat Reader

This read only file is the Education for the Future questionnaire for assessing students' opinions of the learning organization. This questionnaire uses a five-point scale and is used most often in grades 6 through 12.

High School Student Questionnaire	StQHS.pdf	Acrobat Reader

This read only file is the Education for the Future questionnaire for assessing high school and middle school students' opinions of the learning organization. This questionnaire uses a five-point scale and is used most often in High Schools, although some Middle Schools also prefer this questionnaire over the grades 6 through 12 questionnaire.

Staff Questionnaire	StaffQ.pdf	Acrobat Reader

This read only file is the Education for the Future questionnaire for assessing staff's opinion of the learning organization. The questionnaire uses a five-point scale, with three open-ended questions.

Teachers Predicting Student Grade 1-6 Responses　　　　　　　TchPr1.pdf　　　　Acrobat Reader

> This read only file is the Education for the Future questionnaire for assessing a staff's predictions of what it believes students will say about the learning organization. This questionnaire, related to the Students grades 1 through 6 questionnaire, uses a five-point scale.

Teachers Predicting Student Grade 6-8 Responses　　　　　　　TchPr2.pdf　　　　Acrobat Reader

> This read only file is the Education for the Future questionnaire for assessing a staff's predictions of what it believes students will say about the learning organization. This questionnaire, related to the students grades 6 through 8 questionnaire, uses a five-point scale.

Grade K-12 Parent Questionnaire　　　　　　　　　　　　　　ParntK12.pdf　　　Acrobat Reader

> This read only file is the Education for the Future questionnaire for assessing parents' opinions of the learning organization. This questionnaire uses a five-point scale, with three open-ended questions.

High School Parent Questionnaire　　　　　　　　　　　　　ParntHS.pdf　　　Acrobat Reader

> This read only file is the Education for the Future questionnaire for assessing parents' opinions of the learning organization. This questionnaire uses a five-point scale, with three open-ended questions.

Student Achievement Results

The files in this Student Achievement Results section include activities, examples, and templates for creating student achievement graphs, analyses, and writing the results for your school portfolio.

Questions to Guide the Analysis of Student Achievement Data　　QsStachv.doc　　Microsoft Word

> This *Microsoft Word* file consists of questions to guide the interpretation of your student learning data. You can write your responses into this file.

NCE Scores Graphing Templates　　　　　　　　　　　　　　Scores.xls　　　　Microsoft Excel

> This *Microsoft Excel* file consists of templates for graphing student achievement average NCE standardized test results, over time. Simply place your school's NCE average results, for each subtest, for as many years as you have, in the appropriate locations on the spreadsheets and watch the graph build before your eyes.

NCE Decile Graphing Templates　　　　　　　　　　　　　　Decile.xls　　　　Microsoft Excel

> This *Microsoft Excel* file consists of templates for graphing student achievement deciles on standardized tests. Simply place your school's NCE decile results, for as many years as you have, in the appropriate locations on the spreadsheet and watch the graph build before your eyes.

Quartile Graphing Templates　　　　　　　　　　　　　　　Quartile.xls　　　Microsoft Excel

> This *Microsoft Excel* file consists of templates for graphing the number and the percentage of students scoring in different quartiles on standardized tests. Simply place your school's quartile results, for as many years as you have, in the appropriate locations on the spreadsheet and watch the graphs build before your eyes.

Quartile Table Templates　　　　　　　　　　　　　　　　Quartile.doc　　　Microsoft Word

> This *Microsoft Word* file consists of a table template for charting the number and the percentage of students scoring in different quartiles on standardized tests.

Example Narrative of Student Achievement Graphs　　　　　　SANarrtv.doc　　　Microsoft Word

> This *Microsoft Word* file is an example/template for the writing and interpretation of student achievement results. You can see how the example graphs were interpreted, use the charting templates to build your own graphs, and then write your school's narrative for the Information and Analysis section of your school portfolio.

Example School Multiple Measures Narrative　　　　　　　　MMNarrtv.doc　　　Microsoft Word

> This *Microsoft Word* file is an example/template for the writing and interpretation of student achievement results. You can see how the example graphs were interpreted, use the charting templates to build your own graphs, then write your school's narrative for the Information and Analysis section of your school portfolio.

| Example School Multiple Measures Graphing Template | MMGraph.xls | Microsoft Excel |

This *Microsoft Excel* file consists of templates for graphing the percentage (or number) of students meeting the standard, as measured through multiple sources.

| Teacher Analysis of Test Scores Activity | ACTTestS.pdf | Acrobat Reader |

The Teacher Analysis of Test Scores Activity helps teachers see why their scores are what they are and to determine what to do to get the low scoring students above 50 NCE. This read only file contains a template for listing which students scored in the lowest 50th NCE deciles, by subtests, and who is teaching what with respect to the subtest categories.

| Teacher Analysis of Test Scores Table One | Table1.doc | Microsoft Word |

This *Microsoft Word* file contains templates for listing which students scored in the lowest 50th NCE deciles, by subtests and a listing of who is teaching what with respect to the subtest categories. The result will help teachers see why their scores are what they are and to determine what to do to get the low scoring students above 50 NCE.

| Teacher Analysis of Test Scores Table Two | Table2.doc | Microsoft Word |

This *Microsoft Word* file contains templates for listing which students scored in the lowest 50th NCE deciles, by subtests and a listing of who is teaching what with respect to the subtest categories. The result will help teachers see why their scores are what they are and to determine what to do to get the low scoring students above 50 NCE.

School Processes

The files in this section include activities and templates for looking at your school's processes.

| Charting School Processes Activity | ACTProcs.pdf | Acrobat Reader |

The goal of this activity is to clarify how students are being taught now, so everyone can understand how they are getting current results and determine what needs to change to get different results. A flowchart allows everyone to see the major steps in a process, in sequence, and then evaluate the difference between the theoretical and actual, or actual and desired.

| Top-Down Flowcharting Template | TopDown.doc | Microsoft Word |

The Top Down Flowcharting Template is set up as a *Microsoft Word* file. You can start entering your processes.

All Data

The files in this section include activities and templates for looking at all your data at the same time.

| Gallery Walk Activity and Questions | ACTGalry.pdf | Acrobat Reader |

This activity gives staff an opportunity to look over all school data—independently and interdependently—and to write what they see as strengths and areas for improvement as well as implications for school improvement.

| Fishbowl Activity | ACTFish.pdf | Acrobat Reader |

The Fishbowl Activity can be used for dynamic group involvement. The most common configuration is an inner ring, which is the discussion group, surrounded by an outer ring, which is the observation group. Just as people observe the fish in the fishbowl, the outer ring observes the inner ring.

| Data Discovery Activity | ACTDiscv.pdf | Acrobat Reader |

The purpose of this activity is to look closely at examples of data and to discover specific information and patterns of information, both individually and as a group.

| Intersections Activity | ACTIntrs.pdf | Acrobat Reader |

The purpose of this activity is to motivate school improvement teams to think about the questions they can answer when they cross different data variables. It is also designed to help teams focus their data gathering efforts so they are not collecting everything and anything.

| Creating Intersections Activity | ACTCreat.pdf | Acrobat Reader |

This activity is similar to the *Intersections Activity*. The purpose is to have participants "grow" their intersections.

| Problem-Solving Cycle Activity | ACTCycle.pdf | Acrobat Reader |

The purpose of the *Problem-Solving Cycle Activity* is to get all staff involved in thinking through a problem before jumping to solutions. This activity can also result in a comprehensive data analysis design.

| Root Causes Activity | ACTRoot.pdf | Acrobat Reader |

Root causes are the real causes of our educational problems. We need to find out what they are so we can eliminate the true problem and not just the symptom. This activity asks staff teams to review and analyze data, and ask probing questions to uncover the root cause(s).

| Cause and Effect Analysis Activity | ACTCause.pdf | Acrobat Reader |

This activity will help teams determine the relationships and complexities between an effect or problem and all the possible causes.

| Affinity Diagram Activity | ACTAfnty.pdf | Acrobat Reader |

The affinity diagram encourages honest reflection on the real underlying root causes of a problem and its solutions and encourages people to agree on the factors. This activity assists teams in discussing and resolving problems using a nonjudgmental process.

▼ CREATING THE VISION (Chapter 5)

The files in this section include strategies, tools, activities, and examples focused on helping schools create a shared vision.

| Items to Include in the Student Achievement Section of the School Portfolio | ItemsSA.pdf | Acrobat Reader |

This read only file provides an overview of the items that are typically included in the Student Achievement section of a school portfolio.

| Student Achievement Continuous Improvement Continuum | SARubric.pdf | Acrobat Reader |

This read only file is the *Student Achievement Continuum,* one of seven *Education for the Future Continuous Improvement Continuums*. This file can be printed as is or enlarged for the wall to use during staff assessments. (A file containing all seven continuums [Rubrics.pdf] is in the *Getting Started Continuous Improvement Continuums* section of the CD.)

| Frequently Asked Questions About Student Achievement | FAQsSA.pdf | Acrobat Reader |

This read only file lists the most frequently asked questions, and their answers, related to creating a vision.

| Continuous School Improvement Planning via the School Portfolio | CSIPlang.pdf | Acrobat Reader |

This read only graphic displays the questions that can be answered to create a continuous school improvement plan. The data that can answer the questions, and where the answers would appear in the school portfolio, also appear on the graphic.

| Ground Rules | GrndRule.pdf | Acrobat Reader |

This read only file provides example ground rules for staff meetings and professional development sessions.

| Facilitator's Agenda for Creating a Shared Vision | AgendaFa.pdf | Acrobat Reader |

This read only file provides an annotated agenda for taking staff through a visioning process in one day. Typical time requirements for the different activities are provided.

| Agenda for Creating a Shared Vision | Agenda.doc | Microsoft Word |

This is an example agenda for creating a vision in one day. It accompanies the facilitator's agenda for creating a vision. Add your school's name.

Shared Vision Template   VTemplte.doc   Microsoft Word
> This is a template for staff to use when creating their shared vision. It allows staff to document their
> personal ideas before they are merged into core principles for the whole school.

Vision Notetaking Form   VNotes.doc   Microsoft Word
> This notetaking form is for staff to use when creating a shared vision. It allows staff to write down their
> anecdotal stories, questions, comments, or concerns to share later as opposed to during the process.

Shared Vision Example: *Central City Elementary School*   VExample.pdf   Acrobat Reader
> This read only file provides an example of a real school's guiding principles as created through the
> visioning process.

Vision Quote Posters   VPosters.pdf   Acrobat Reader
> These read only files contain motivating quotes to have enlarged for visioning day. The quotes show
> how to get to the vision, ground rules, and words of wisdom by Peter Senge and Joel Barker.

▼ PLANNING TO ACCOMPLISH THE VISION (Chapter 6)
The files in this section include examples, templates, activities, and strategies for creating an
action plan, and for implementing and evaluating the implementation of the vision.

Items to Include in the Quality Planning Section
of the School Portfolio   ItemsQP.pdf   Acrobat Reader
> This read only file provides an overview of the items that are typically included in the Quality Planning
> section of a school portfolio.

Quality Planning Continuous Improvement Continuum   QPRubric.pdf   Acrobat Reader
> This read only file is the *Quality Planning Continuum,* one of seven *Education for the Future Continuous
> Improvement Continuums.* This file can be printed as is or enlarged for the wall to use during staff
> assessments. (A file containing all seven continuums [Rubrics.pdf] is in the *Getting Started Continuous
> Improvement Continuums* section of the CD.)

Frequently Asked Questions About Quality Planning   FAQsQP.pdf   Acrobat Reader
> This read only file lists the most frequently asked questions, and their answers, related to continuous
> school improvement planning.

Steps in Creating an Action Plan   APSteps.pdf   Acrobat Reader
> This read only file shows the major steps that are important in Creating an Action Plan.

Developing an Action Plan Activity   ACTDevAP.pdf   Acrobat Reader
> The purpose of this activity is to take the shared vision to the action level. The steps in creating an
> action plan are spelled out in this activity.

Gap Analysis and Objectives Activity   ACTGap.pdf   Acrobat Reader
> The purpose of this activity is to look closely at differences between current results and where the
> school wants to be in the future. It is this gap that gets translated into objectives that guide the
> development of the action plan.

Root Cause Analysis Activity   ACTRoot.pdf   Acrobat Reader
> Root causes are the real causes of our educational problems. We need to find out what they are so we
> can eliminate the true problem and not just the symptom. The best way to do this is to have staff
> teams review and analyze data, and ask probing questions to uncover the root cause(s).

Goal Setting Activity   ACTGoals.pdf   Acrobat Reader
> By setting goals, a school can clarify its end targets for the school's vision. This activity will help a
> school set goals for the future.

Action Plan Form   APForm.doc   Microsoft Word
> A quality action plan to implement the vision consists of goals, objectives, strategies, actions, persons
> responsible, resources required, due dates, and timeline. A template with these components is provided
> in *Microsoft Word,* ready to be completed.

Questions to Guide the Refinement of the Continuous
School Improvement Plan   Questns.doc   Microsoft Word

This *Microsoft Word* file consists of questions that will help guide the refinement of the continuous
school improvement plan.

Central City Elementary School Action Plan   APExmple.pdf   Acrobat Reader

Central City Elementary School Action Plan is a real school's action plan to implement the vision. It is
provided here as one example only.

Shared Vision Example: Central City Elementary School   VExmple.pdf   Acrobat Reader

This read only file provides an example of a real school's guiding principles as created through the
visioning process.

Central City Elementary School Evaluation Plan   APEval.pdf   Acrobat Reader

This file shows how Central City Elementary School evaluated its continuous school improvement plan.

Teacher Assessment Tool Related to the Central City School Vision   AssessEx.pdf   Acrobat Reader

Central City developed a tool that would allow teachers to assess where they were with respect to
implementing the vision. The tool clarifies what the teachers are expected to implement. The
assessment helps grade level teams know where everyone is with respect to implementing the vision,
and where they need assistance. It is offered here as an example.

Teacher Assessment Tool Related to Our School Vision   AssessEx.doc   Microsoft Word

This *Microsoft Word* file is a template for the development of a teacher assessment tool for implementing
the shared vision, similar to Central City's example.

Staff-Developed Vision Implementation Rubric Example   StRubric.pdf   Acrobat Reader

This document is an example of one school's assessment tool (*Frank Paul*) for implementing the shared
vision, in rubric form. At the highest level, it is clear to staff what the vision would look like, sound
like, and feel like when implemented.

Our School Shared Vision Implementation Rubric   StRubric.doc   Microsoft Word

This *Microsoft Word* file is a template for the development of a teacher assessment tool for implementing
the shared vision in rubric form. At the highest level, it is clear what the vision would look like, sound
like, and feel like when implemented.

Staff-Developed Rubric Activity   ACTRubric.pdf   Acrobat Reader

This activity will help teachers develop a rubric for assessing the implementation of the vision, similar
to the *Frank Paul* example.

Sharing Progress Activity   ACTShare.pdf   Acrobat Reader

This activity was designed to guide discussion about staff progress in implementing the vision and to
reinforce the implementation of the vision.

▼ PROFESSIONAL DEVELOPMENT TO IMPLEMENT THE VISION (Chapter 7)
The files in this section include examples, templates, activities, and strategies for creating a
professional development plan to implement the vision.

Items to Include in the Professional Development Section
of the School Portfolio   ItemsPrD.pdf   Acrobat Reader

This read only file provides an overview of the items that are typically included in the Professional
Development section of a school portfolio.

Professional Development Continuous Improvement Continuum   ProDRbrc.pdf   Acrobat Reader

This read only file is the *Professional Development Continuum,* one of seven *Education for the Future
Continuous Improvement Continuums.* This file can be printed as is or enlarged for the wall to use during
staff assessments. (A file containing all seven continuums [Rubrics.pdf] is in the *Getting Started
Continuous Improvement Continuums* section of the CD.)

| Frequently Asked Questions About Professional Development | FAQsPrD.pdf | Acrobat Reader |

This read only file lists the most frequently asked questions, and their answers related to professional development within the context of implementing a vision.

| National Partnership for Excellence and Accountablity in Teaching (NPEAT) Report | NPEAT.pdf | Acrobat Reader |

This NPEAT report entitled, *Revisioning professional development: What learner-centered professional development looks like,* defines research-based principles for professional development that will improve student learning.

| National Staff Development Council Standards | NSDCStnd.pdf | Acrobat Reader |

This read only file lists the standards created in 2001 by the *National Staff Development Council.*

| Interstate School Leaders Licensure Consortium (ISLLC) Standards | ISLLCStn.pdf | Acrobat Reader |

This read only file lists the standards created in 2000 by the *Interstate School Leaders Licensure Consortium.*

| Professional Development Planning Example | PDPlan.pdf | Acrobat Reader |

This example documents the framework for pulling a professional development plan out of the action plan that will help staff implement their vision.

| Central City Professional Development Plan Example | CCPlanEx.pdf | Acrobat Reader |

This *Central City Elementary School Professional Development Plan* example documents the next step by grouping common elements and organizing them around an annual calendar.

| Professional Development Planning Template | PlanTmpl.doc | Microsoft Word |

This *Microsoft Word* file is a template for a school's professional development plan that will help staff implement their vision.

Powerful Professional Development Designs

Powerful Professional Development Designs are those that are embedded into the daily operations of a staff. They are ongoing and lead to improvement of instruction and increases in student learning.

| Powerful Professional Development Designs | Designs.pdf | Acrobat Reader |

This read only file describes numerous ways to embed professional development into the learning community.

| Action Research Activity | ACTRsrch.pdf | Acrobat Reader |

Teachers and/or administrators raise questions about the best way to improve teaching and learning, systematically study the literature to answer the questions, implement the best approach, and analyze the results.

| Cadres or Action Teams Activity | ACTCdres.pdf | Acrobat Reader |

Teaming allows for the delegation of responsibilities so teams of educators can study new approaches, plan for the implementation of new strategies or programs, and get work done without every staff member's involvement.

| Case Studies Activity | ACTCases.pdf | Acrobat Reader |

Staff members review case studies of student work, and/or of another teacher's example lessons, which can lead to quality discussions and improved practices.

| Coaching Activity | ACTCoach.pdf | Acrobat Reader |

Teachers form teams of two or three to observe each other, plan together, and to talk and encourage each other in meaningful ways, while reflecting on continuously improving instructional practices.

| Examining Student Data: *Teacher Analysis of Test Scores Table One* | Table1.doc | Microsoft Word |

Examining student data consists of conversations around individual student data results and the processes that created the results. This approach can be a significant form of professional development when skilled team members facilitate the dialogue.

Examining Student Work Activity   ACTSWork.pdf   Acrobat Reader

  Examining student work as professional development ensures that what students learn is aligned to the learning standards. It also shows teachers the impact of their actions.

Example lessons: *Birds of a Feather Unit Example*   UnitEx.pdf   Acrobat Reader

  Some teachers need to see what a lesson that implements all aspects of the school vision would look like. Providing examples for all teachers to see can reward the teacher who is doing a good job of implementing the vision and provide a template for other teachers. It is very effective to store summary examples in a binder for everyone to peruse at any time.

Example lessons: *Unit Template*   UnitTmpl.doc   Microsoft Word

  This template provides the outline for creating instructional units that implement the vision.

Immersion Activity   ACTImrsn.pdf   Acrobat Reader

  Immersion is a method for getting teachers immersed in different content through hands-on experiences as a learner.

Journaling Activity   ACTJourn.pdf   Acrobat Reader

  Journal writing helps teacher constructs meaning for, and reflect on, what they are teaching and learning.

Listening to Students Activity   ACTListn.pdf   Acrobat Reader

  Students' perceptions of the learning environment are very important for continuous improvement. Focus groups, interviews, and questionnaires can be used to discover what students are perceiving.

Needs Assessment: *Professional Development Needs*
  Related to Technology Example   TechnEx.pdf   Acrobat Reader

  Needs assessments help staff understand the professional development needs of staff. At the same time, if done well, a tool can lead to quality staff conversations and sharing of knowledge.

Needs Assessment: *Professional Development Plan*
  Related to Technology Template   TechTmpl.doc   Microsoft Word

  This template provides the outline for doing your own professional development needs assessment.

Networks Activity   ACTNtwrk.pdf   Acrobat Reader

  Purposeful grouping of individuals/schools to further a cause or commitment.

Partnerships: *Creating Partnerships Activity*   ACTParts.pdf   Acrobat Reader

  Teachers partnering with businesses in the community, scientists, and/or university professors can result in real world applications for student learning and deeper understandings of content for the teacher.

Process Mapping: *Charting School Processes Activity*   ACTProcs.pdf   Acrobat Reader

  School processes are instruction, curriculum, and assessment strategies used to ensure the learning of all students. Mapping or flowcharting school processes can help staff objectively look at how students are being taught.

Reflection Log Activity   ACTLog.pdf   Acrobat Reader

  Reflective logs are recordings of key events in the educators work days to reflect for improvement and/or to share learnings with colleagues.

Scheduling Activity   ACTSchdl.pdf   Acrobat Reader

  A real test for whether or not a vision is realistic is to have teacher develop a day's schedule. This would tell them immediately if it is doable, or what needs to change in the vision and plan to make it doable.

School Meetings: *Running Efficient Meetings*   Meetings.pdf   Acrobat Reader

  Staff, department, grade level, cross-grade level meetings can promote learning through study or sharing best practice, while focusing on the implementation of the vision.

Self Assessment: *Teacher Assessment Tool Related*
    to the Central City School Vision   AssessEx.pdf   Acrobat Reader

Staff self-assessments on tools to measure progress toward the vision, such as the *Continuous Improvement Continuums,* will help them see where their school is as a system and what needs to improve for better results.

Self Assessment: *Teacher Assessment Tool Related*
    to Our School Vision   AssessEx.doc   Microsoft Word

Staff self-assessments on tools to measure progress toward the vision, such as the *Continuous Improvement Continuums,* will help them see where their school is as a system and what needs to improve for better results.

Self Assessment: *Our School Shared Vision*
    Implementation Rubric Example   StRubric.pdf   Acrobat Reader

Staff self-assessments on tools to measure progress toward the vision, such as the *Continuous Improvement Continuums,* will help them see where their school is as a system and what needs to improve for better results.

Self Assessment: *Our School Shared Vision*
    Implementation Rubric Template   StRubric.doc   Microsoft Word

Staff self-assessments on tools to measure progress toward the vision, such as the *Continuous Improvement Continuums,* will help them see where their school is as a system and what needs to improve for better results.

Self Assessment: *Staff-Developed Rubric Activity*   ACTRubric.pdf   Acrobat Reader

Staff self-assessments on tools to measure progress toward the vision, such as the *Continuous Improvement Continuums,* will help them see where their school is as a system and what needs to improve for better results.

Shadowing Students Activity   ACTShadw.pdf   Acrobat Reader

Purposefully following students and systematically recording the students' instructional experiences is a wonderful job-embedded approach to understanding what students are experiencing in school.

Storyboarding Activity   ACTStory.pdf   Acrobat Reader

Storyboarding is an activity that will allow participants to share previous knowledge, while reflecting on the topic. It is a structure for facilitating conversations.

Study Groups Activity   ACTStudy.pdf   Acrobat Reader

Groups of educators meet to learn new strategies and programs, to review new publications, or to review student work together.

Teacher Portfolio Activity   ACTTcher.pdf   Acrobat Reader

Teacher portfolios can be built to tell the story of implementing the vision in the classroom, and it's impact on student learning. Portfolios are excellent for reflection, understanding, and showing progress. Portfolios can be used for many things including self-assessment, employment, supervision to replace traditional teacher evaluation, and peer collaboration.

Train the Trainers Activity   ACTTrain.pdf   Acrobat Reader

Train the trainers is an approach to saving time and money. Individuals are trained and return to the school or school district to train others.

Tuning Protocols Activity   ACTTune.pdf   Acrobat Reader

A tuning protocol is a formal process for reviewing, honoring, and fine-tuning colleagues' work through presentation and reflection.

Evaluation of Professional Development Training

The files in this section include examples of different professional development evaluation tools that can be adjusted for your purposes, and activities and examples related to the evaluation of professional development training.

Staff Development Proposal   StaffDev.pdf   Acrobat Reader

This read only file shows an example staff development proposal that one district uses to approve staff development requests.

Evaluation Design: *Implementing Technology*   EvalEx.pdf   Acrobat Reader

This evaluation design provides an example of one staff's thinking through how to study the impact of technology implementation.

Evaluating a Professional Development Program Activity   ACTProD.pdf   Acrobat Reader

The purpose of this activity is to get many people involved in creating a comprehensive evaluation design to determine the impact of a professional development program and to know how to improve the program.

Formative Evaluation Questionnaire One   Eval1.doc   Microsoft Word

This sample formative questionnaire can be adjusted to meet your workshop evaluation needs. It is set up for the evaluation of day one of a two day workshop.

Formative Evaluation Questionnaire Two   Eval2.doc   Microsoft Word

This sample formative questionnaire can be adjusted to meet your workshop evaluation needs. It is set up for the evaluation of day one of a two day workshop.

Summative Evaluation Questionnaire Summary   SumEval1.doc   Microsoft Word

This sample summative questionnaire evaluating a workshop can be adjusted to meet your workshop evaluation needs. Example 1.

Summative Evaluation Questionnaire Form   SumEval2.pdf   Acrobat Reader

This example summative evaluation illustrates another approach to meeting your workshop evaluation needs. Example 2.

Evaluation of Professional Development Training   PrDEval.doc   Microsoft Word

This sample summative evaluation can be adjusted to meet your workshop evaluation needs. Example 3.

NSDC Evaluation Summary   NSDCEval.doc   Microsoft Word

This sample evaluation tool uses the *National Staff Development Council Standards* categories of context, process, and content to assess the quality of a professional development workshop.

Self Assessment of Implementation of NSDC Standards
of Staff Development Questionnaire   NSDCQue.pdf   Acrobat Reader

This read only file lists the standards created in 2001 by the *National Staff Development Council* in a questionnaire format.

Standards Implementation Questionnaire   Implemnt.doc   Microsoft Word

This template is set up to show how you can evaluate the implementation of standards as a part of your professional development evaluation design.

Professional Development Follow-up Questionnaire One   Follow1.doc   Microsoft Word

This sample evaluation provides a follow-up to professional development workshops to determine the degree of implementation and can be adjusted to meet your specific workshop evaluation needs.

Professional Development Follow-up Questionnaire Two   Follow2.doc   Microsoft Word

This sample evaluation provides a follow-up to professional development workshops to determine the degree of implementation and can be adjusted to meet your specific workshop evaluation needs.

Design Questionnaires Activity   ACTDevQ.pdf   Acrobat Reader

This activity was set up to help staffs design their own questionnaires.

The files in this section include strategies, activities, examples, and templates for building a leadership structure to implement the vision.

Items to Include in the Leadership Section
of the School Portfolio | ItemsLead.pdf | Acrobat Reader

This read only file provides an overview of the items that are typically included in the Leadership section of a school portfolio.

Leadership Continuous Improvement Continuum | LeRubric.pdf | Acrobat Reader

This read only file is the *Leadership Continuum,* one of seven *Education for the Future Continuous Improvement Continuums.* This file can be printed as is or enlarged for the wall to use during staff assessments. (A file containing all seven continuums [Rubrics.pdf] is in the *Getting Started Continuous Improvement Continuums* section of the CD.)

Frequently Asked Questions Related to Leadership | FAQsLead.pdf | Acrobat Reader

This read only file lists the most frequently asked questions, and their answers related to leadership within the context of implementing a vision.

Interstate School Leaders Licensure Consortium (ISLLC) Standards | ISLLCStn.pdf | Acrobat Reader

This read only file lists the standards created in 2000 by the *Interstate School Leaders Licensure Consortium.*

Cross-Reference of School Portfolio with ISLLC | ISLLC.pdf | Acrobat Reader

This read only file shows the *Interstate School Leaders Licensure Consortium Standards* compared with the elements of *The School Portfolio.*

Leadership Responsibility Matrix Activity | ACTMtrix.pdf | Acrobat Reader

A matrix diagram shows the relationships between one group of items and another. Because information is laid out in columns and rows, the relationship between two pieces of information can readily be found and compared to the other relationships displayed. Identifying who makes what decisions and when is a good use for this activity.

Central City Elementary School Leadership Structure | CCLeadr.pdf | Acrobat Reader

This read only file shows the leadership structure used by Central City Elementary School.

Running Efficient Meetings | Meetings.pdf | Acrobat Reader

This read only file provides recommendations on running efficient staff meetings.

Issue Bin/Parking Lot | IssueBin.pdf | Acrobat Reader

This read only file is an example of an issue bin/parking lot to use during meetings to store issues that need to be addressed at a later time.

Ground Rules | GrndRules.pdf | Acrobat Reader

This read only file provides example ground rules for staff meetings and professional development sessions.

Meeting Etiquette | Etiquete.pdf | Acrobat Reader

This read only file provides example meeting etiquette agreements.

Norms of Behavior | NormsBhvr.pdf | Acrobat Reader

This read only file provides recommendations for establishing norms of behavior for reculturing your school.

Coming to Consensus | Consenss.pdf | Acrobat Reader

This read only file provides strategies for coming to consensus.

Guidelines for Brainstorming | Brainstr.pdf | Acrobat Reader

This read only file provides guidelines for brainstorming.

The files in this section will assist staffs in building partnerships with parents, community, and businesses.

Items to Include in the Partnership Development Section
of the School Portfolio   ItemsPD.pdf   Acrobat Reader

This read only file provides an overview of the items that are typically included in the Partnership Development section of a school portfolio.

Partnership Development Continuous Improvement Continuum   PartRbrc.pdf   Acrobat Reader

This read only file is the *Partnership Development Continuum,* one of seven *Education for the Future Continuous Improvement Continuums.* This file can be printed as is or enlarged for the wall to use during staff assessments. (A file containing all seven continuums [Rubrics.pdf] is in the *Getting Started Continuous Improvement Continuums* section of the CD.)

Frequently Asked Questions About Partnership Development   FAQsPart.pdf   Acrobat Reader

This read only file lists the most frequently asked questions, and their answers, related to Partnership Development within the context of implementing a vision.

Establishing a Partnership Plan   EstPPlan.pdf   Acrobat Reader

This read only file describes the steps in creating a partnership plan that will become a part of the continuous school improvement plan.

Partnership Team Plan Example   PPlanEx.pdf   Acrobat Reader

This read only file shows an example partnership plan.

Partnership Team Planning Template   PPlanTmp.doc   Microsoft Word

This *Microsoft Word* file is a template for a partnership plan. Change the name of the school, add your information, and carefully read the text provided to make sure it fits your needs.

Creating Partnerships Activity   ACTParts.pdf   Acrobat Reader

This is an activity for brainstorming the types of partnerships that would help students meet learning standards. Adjust it to include your specific standards.

Parent Resource Questionnaire   Resource.pdf   Acrobat Reader

This example questionnaire is used in San Jose, CA, to assess what parents want to do to support the schools.

Partnership Evaluation Questionnaire   PartnrQ.doc   Microsoft Word

This example questionnaire is a start on a questionnaire you might want to develop for evaluating your partnership efforts.

▼ CONTINUOUS IMPROVEMENT AND EVALUATION (Chapter 10)
The files in this section provide support for the continuous improvement of all parts of the system.

Items to Include in the Continuous Improvement and Evaluation
Section of the School Portfolio   ItemsCI.pdf   Acrobat Reader

This read only file provides an overview of the items that are typically included in the Continuous Improvement and Evaluation section of a school portfolio.

Continuous Improvement Continuous Improvement Continuum   CIRubric.pdf   Acrobat Reader

This read only file is the *Continuous Improvement and Evaluation Continuum,* one of seven *Education for the Future Continuous Improvement Continuums.* This file can be printed as is or enlarged for the wall to use during staff assessments. (A file containing all seven continuums [Rubrics.pdf] is in the *Getting Started Continuous Improvement Continuums* section of the CD.)

Evaluation Questions Outline Example   EvalExmp.pdf   Acrobat Reader

This read only file describes the most common and logical questions that are asked in the continuous school improvement process.

| Evaluation Questions Outline Template | EvalExmp.doc | Microsoft Word |

This *Microsoft Word* file is a placeholder/ template for building your own continuous improvement evaluation plan.

| Frequently Asked Questions Related to Continuous Improvement | FAQsCI.pdf | Acrobat Reader |

This read only file lists the most frequently asked questions, and their answers, related to continuous improvement and evaluation within the context of implementing a vision.

| Troubleshooting Your Continuous Improvement Efforts | Trblsht.pdf | Acrobat Reader |

This read only file describes the most common problems that occur during the school improvement process, suggests what most often is the reason for the problem, and then offers recommendations to alleviate the problem. The file is offered as a trouble-shooting, continuous improvement guide.

| What Would It Be Like *If*... | WhatIf.pdf | Acrobat Reader |

This read only file describes "what it would be like if . . . " a school had a shared vision, and other such occurrences. The file is offered as a continuous improvement thinking piece.

| Continuous Improvement Continuums | Rubrics.pdf | Acrobat Reader |

This read only file is of the seven *School Portfolio Continuous Improvement Continuums.* These can be printed out as is or enlarged for the wall to use during staff assessments.

| Continuous Improvement Continuums Assessment Activity | ACTCIC.pdf | Acrobat Reader |

Assessing on the *Continuous Improvement Continuums* will help staffs see where their systems are right now with respect to continuous improvement and ultimately to show they are making progress over time.

| Continuous Improvement Continuums Report Example | ExReprt1.pdf | Acrobat Reader |

This read only file shows a real school's assessment on the *School Portfolio Continuous Improvement Continuums*, as an example.

| Continuous Improvement Continuums Report Example for Follow-Up Years | ExReprt2.pdf | Acrobat Reader |

This read only file shows a real school's assessment on the *School Portfolio Continuous Improvement Continuums* over time, as an example.

| Continuous Improvement Continuums Baseline Report Template | Template.doc | Microsoft Word |

This *Microsoft Word* file provides a template for writing your school's report of its assessment on the *School Portfolio Continuous Improvement Continuums.*

| Continuous Improvement Continuums Graphing Templates | CICGraph.xls | Microsoft Excel |

This *Microsoft Excel* file is a template for graphing your assessments on the seven *School Portfolio Continuous Improvement Continuums.*

▼ UPDATING THE SCHOOL PORTFOLIO (Chapter 11)

The files in this section will help keep the school portfolio updated and the school assessing its continuous improvement efforts.

| Frequently Asked Questions About Maintaining the Momentum | FAQsMntm.pdf | Acrobat Reader |

This read only file lists the most frequently asked questions, and their answers, related to maintaining the momentum for the school portfolio.

| The School Portfolio Assessment and Updating Activity (AKA The Treasure Hunt) | ACTTreas.pdf | Acrobat Reader |

This activity is to help staff in evidence gathering, reflecting, and maintaining the school portfolio. This is a variation of the *Updating the School Portfolio Activity.*

| Updating the School Portfolio Activity | ACTUpdte.pdf | Acrobat Reader |

The purpose of this activity is to update the staff assessments on the *Continuous Improvement Continuums* and the school portfolio at the same time. This is a variation of the *School Portfolio Assessment and Updating Activity (AKA The Treasure Hunt).*

| School Portfolio Update Worksheet | SPUpdate.doc | Microsoft Word |

This *Microsoft Word* file is a guide for updating your school portfolio.

| School Portfolio Summary Chart | SPTable.doc | Microsoft Word |

This tabular *Microsoft Word* file has the categories of the school portfolio along with the major elements of each category in the left-hand column. The middle column is for documenting what your school has for each of these categories. The right-hand column is for listing additional items that your school would like to gather.

| Evidence to Include when Updating Your School Portfolio | Evidence.pdf | Acrobat Reader |

This read only file discusses the evidence to include when updating the school portfolio.

| School Portfolio Concerns Activity | ACTConcn.pdf | Acrobat Reader |

This benefits and concerns activity is for the end of a School Portfolio Overview Workshop for closure, to know questions and concerns, and to let the participants answer the questions.

▼ CASE STUDIES (Chapter 12)

The read only files in this section are case studies of schools using school portfolios.

| A Statewide View: The Leadership Academy of the Missouri Department of Elementary and Secondary Education | Missouri.pdf | Acrobat Reader |

This read only file is the case study of *The Leadership Academy of the Missouri Department of Elementary and Secondary Education.*

| A Rural County View: Siskiyou County, CA | Siskiyou.pdf | Acrobat Reader |

This read only file is the case study of *Siskiyou County Office of Education.*

| An Urban School District View: San Jose Unified School District, CA | SanJose.pdf | Acrobat Reader |

This read only file is the case study of *San Jose Unified School District.*

| A Suburban School District View: Columbia Public Schools, MO | Columbia.pdf | Acrobat Reader |

This read only file is the case study of *Columbia Public Schools.*

| A Rural School District View: Mabton Public Schools, WA | Mabton.pdf | Acrobat Reader |

This read only file is the case study of *Mabton Public Schools.*

| An Elementary School View: New Haven, Columbia, MO | NHaven.pdf | Acrobat Reader |

This read only file is the case study of *New Haven Elementary School.*

| An Elementary School View: Fairview, Columbia, MO | Fairview.pdf | Acrobat Reader |

This read only file is the case study of *Fairview Elementary School.*

| An Elementary School View: Caledonia, Grand Rapids, MI | Caledona.pdf | Acrobat Reader |

This read only file is the case study of *Caledonia Elementary School.*

| A Middle School View: Castillero, San Jose, CA | Castlero.pdf | Acrobat Reader |

This read only file is the case study of *Castillero Middle School.*

| A High School View: Westerville South High School, Westerville, OH | Westvlle.pdf | Acrobat Reader |

This read only file is the case study of *Westerville South High School.*

| Frequently Asked Questions About Implementing the School Portfolio | FAQsImpl.pdf | Acrobat Reader |

This read only file lists the most frequently asked questions, and their answers, related to implementing the school portfolio.

GLOSSARY OF TERMS

The Glossary provides brief definitions of terms used throughout *The School Portfolio Toolkit*.

▼ **Accountability**
Being accountable is the act of being responsible to somebody else or to others. It also means capable of being explained.

▼ **Action**
Specific steps, tasks, or activity used to implement a strategy.

▼ **Action Plan**
The part of continuous school improvement planning that describes the tasks that must be performed, when they will be performed, who is responsible, and how much it will cost to implement.

▼ **Action Research**
Teachers and/or administrators raise questions about the best way to improve teaching and learning, systematically study the literature to answer the questions, implement the best approach(es), and analyze the results.

▼ **Activities**
Activities on *The School Portfolio Toolkit* CD are tools and strategies designed to get staff engaged in continuous improvement that leads to increased student learning.

▼ **Affinity Diagram**
The affinity diagram gives a visual picture of reflective thinking. The result is that more participants are likely to deal with problems that emerge.

▼ **Aggregate**
Combining the results of all groups that make up the sample or population.

▼ **Alignment**
Alignment is an arrangement of groups or forces in relation to one another. In continuous school improvement planning, we align all parts of the system to the vision. With curriculum, we align instruction and materials to student learning standards.

▼ **Assessment**
Assessment refers to the act of determining a value or degree.

▼ **Authentic Assessments**
Refer to a variety of ways to assess a student's demonstration of knowledge and skills, but does not include traditional testing. Authentic assessments may include performances, projects, exhibitions, and portfolios.

▼ **Benchmarks**
A standard against which something can be measured or assessed.

▼ **Brainstorming**
Brainstorming is the act of listing ideas without judgment. Brainstorming generates creative ideas spontaneously.

▼ Cadres or Action Teams

Teaming allows for the delegation of responsibilities so teams of educators can study new approaches, plan for the implementation of new strategies or programs, and get work done without every staff member's involvement.

▼ Case Studies

Staff members review student's work, and/or another teacher's example lessons, which can lead to quality discussions and improved practices.

▼ Cause and Effect

The cause and effect activity will show you the relationship and the complexities between an effect or problems and the possible causes.

▼ Coaching

Teachers form teams of two or three to observe each other, plan together, to talk and encourage each other in meaningful ways while reflecting on continuously improving instructional practices.

▼ Cohort

Refers to a group of individuals sharing a particular statistical or demographic characteristic, such as the year they were in a specific school grade level. Following cohorts over time helps teachers understand the effects particular circumstances may have on results. Matched cohort studies follow the same individuals over time and unmatched cohort studies follow the same group over time.

▼ Collaborative

Refers to working jointly with others or together especially in an intellectual endeavor.

▼ Comprehensive Action Plan

A comprehensive action plan defines the specific actions needed to implement the vision, sets forth when the actions will take place, designates who is responsible for accomplishing the action, how much it will cost, and where the funds are coming from.

▼ Consensus

Consensus is decision-making where a group finds a proposal acceptable enough that all members can support it; no member opposes it.

▼ Continuous

Continuous in the context of continuous school improvement planning means not stopping, progressing on an on-going basis.

▼ Continuous Improvement

Continuous improvement means to keep the process of planning, implementing, evaluating, and improving alive over time.

▼ Continuous Improvement and Evaluation

The continuous improvement and evaluation section of the school portfolio assists schools in further understanding where they are and what they need to do to move forward in the big picture of continuous school improvement.

▼ **Continuous Improvement Continuums**

The *Education for the Future Initiative Continuous Improvement Continuums* are seven rubrics that represent the theoretical flow of systemic school improvement. The *Continuous Improvement Continuums* take the theory and spirit of continuous school improvement, interweave educational research, and offer practical meaning to the components that must change simultaneously and systematically.

▼ **Continuous School Improvement Plan**

Continuous School Improvement Planning is the process of answering the following questions: Who are we? How do we do business? What are our strengths and areas for improvement? Why do we exist? Where do we want to be? What are the gaps? How can we get to where we want to be? How will we implement? How will we evaluate our efforts?

▼ **Criterion-Referenced Tests**

Tests that judge how well a test taker does on an explicit objective relative to a pre-determined performance level. There is no comparison to any other test takers.

▼ **Culture**

Attitudes, values, beliefs, goals, and practices that characterize a group.

▼ **Curriculum Development**

Curriculum is the way content is designed and delivered. Teachers must think deeply about the content, student learning standards, and how it must be managed and delivered.

▼ **Curriculum Implementation**

Curriculum implementation is putting curriculum into practice.

▼ **Curriculum Mapping**

Curriculum mapping and webbing are approaches that require teachers to align the curriculum and student learning standards and look across grade levels to ensure a continuum of learning that makes sense for all students.

▼ **Database**

A system of complete, retrievable and organized information that is accessible electronically and that can be easily manipulated.

▼ **Deciles**

The values of a variable that divide the frequency distribution into ten equal frequency groups. The ninth decile is the value below which 90 percent of the norming group lie.

▼ **Demographics**

Statistical characteristics of a population, such as average age, number of students in a school, percentages of ethnicities, etc. Dissaggregation with demographic data allows us to isolate variations among different subgroups.

▼ **Demonstration Lessons**

Teachers demonstrate lessons for other teachers wishing to see what a quality lesson in a particular area would look like, sound like, and feel like. The lesson can be demonstrated to colleagues in the classroom with students, or outside of the classroom to illustrate what it would look like to teach to the vision and standards.

▼ **Disaggregate**

Separating the results of different groups that make up the sample or population.

▼ **Ends**

The goals of continuous school improvement planning. The targets.

▼ **Enroll**

Enrolling staff into the continuous school improvement planning process is making sure they will own the process and ultimately implement the vision.

▼ **Evaluation**

Evaluation is the understanding of the interrelationships of the components of continuous improvement and the impact of the components together and separately.

▼ **Examining Student Data**

Examining student data consists of conversations around individual student data results and the processes that created the results. This approach can be a significant form of professional development when skilled team members facilitate the dialogue.

▼ **Examining Student Work**

Examining student work as professional development ensures that what students learn is aligned to the learning standards. It also shows teachers the impact of their actions.

▼ **Example Lessons**

Some teachers need to see what a lesson that implements all aspects of the school vision would look like. Providing examples for all teachers to see can reward the teacher who is doing a good job of implementing the vision and provide a template for other teachers. It is very effective to store summary examples in a binder for everyone to peruse at any time.

▼ **Fishbowl**

Fishbowl is used for dynamic group involvement. The setting is a common configuration of an *inner* and an *outer* ring. The inner ring is the discussion group, while the outer ring is the observation group.

▼ **Forcefield Analysis**

Forcefield analysis is another way to think through all aspects of a situation so that solutions can be easily considered. This analysis forces people to think together about problems and desired changes.

▼ **Frequency Distribution**

A frequency distribution describes how often observations fall within designated categories. It can be expressed in either numbers or percent.

▼ **Gain Score**

Gain scores are the change of difference between two administrations of the same test. Gain scores are calculated by subtracting the previous score from the most recent score.

▼ **Gaps**

A gap refers to the difference between where the school is now and where the school wants to be in the future. It is this gap that gets translated into goals, objectives, strategies, and actions in the action plan.

▼ Goals

Goals are achievements or end results. Goal statements describe the intended outcome of the vision and are stated in terms that are broad, general, abstract, and non-measurable.

▼ Ground Rules

Ground rules are a list of etiquette for all involved in a group or discussion.

▼ Group Processes

Group processes are strategies or actions that encourage individuals to work together with peers whom they may not know well or normally do not have the opportunity to work with.

▼ Immersion

Immersion is a method for getting teachers immersed in different content through hands-on experiences as a learner.

▼ Information and Analysis

Establishes systematic and rigorous reliance on data for decision making in all parts of the organization. This is the section of the school portfolio that sets the context of the learning organization.

▼ Journaling

Journal writing helps teachers construct meaning for, and reflect on, what they are teaching and learning.

▼ Leadership

The leadership section of the school portfolio assists schools in thinking through their vision, shared decision making, and leadership structures that will work with their specific population, culture, and climate.

▼ Listening to Students

Students' perceptions of the learning environment are very important for continuous improvement. Focus groups, interviews, and questionnaires can be used to discover what students are perceiving.

▼ Mean

Average score in a set of scores. Calculate by summing all the scores and dividing by the total number of scores.

▼ Means

Methods, strategies, actions, and processes by which a school plans to improve student achievement.

▼ Measures

A way of evaluating something, how we know we have achieved the objective.

▼ Median

The score that splits a distribution in half: 50 percent of the scores lie above and 50 percent of the scores lie below the median. If the number of scores is odd, the median is the middle score. If the number of scores is even, one must add the two middle scores and divide by two to calculate the median.

▼ **Meeting Etiquette**

Meeting etiquette is the rules that are set to give respect to the ideas and participation of others.

▼ **Mentoring**

Mentoring typically pairs an experienced teacher with a teacher with less experience to assist the novice.

▼ **Mission**

The mission is a brief, clear and compelling goal that serves to unify an organization's efforts. A mission has a finish line for its achievement and is proactive. A mission should walk the boundary between the possible and impossible.

▼ **Needs Assessment**

Needs assessment help staff understand the professional development needs of staff. At the same time, if done well, a tool can lead to quality staff conversations and sharing of knowledge.

▼ **Networks**

Purposeful grouping of individuals/schools to further a cause or commitment.

▼ **Normal Curve**

The normal curve is the bell-shaped curve of the normal distribution.

▼ **Normal Curve Equivalent (NCE)**

Equivalent scores are standard scores with a mean of 50 and a standard deviation of 21.06 and a range of 1 to 99.

▼ **Normal Distribution**

A distribution of scores or other measures that in graphic form has a distinctive bell-shaped appearance. In a normal distribution, the measures are distributed symmetrically about the mean. Cases are concentrated near the mean and decrease in frequency, according to a precise mathematical equation, the farther one departs from the mean.

▼ **Norm-Referenced Test**

Any test in which the score acquires additional meaning by comparing it to the scores of people in an identified norming group. A test can be both norm- and criterion-referenced. Most standardized achievement tests are referred to as norm-referenced.

▼ **Norms**

The distribution of test scores of some specified group called the norm group. For example, this may be a national sample of all fourth graders, a national sample of all fourth-grade males, or perhaps all fourth graders in some local district.

▼ **Norms of Behavior**

A list of guidelines to help individuals work together to behave in a manner that will increase teachers' abilities to meet the needs of students.

▼ **Norms vs. Standards**

Norms are not standards. Norms are indicators of what students of similar characteristics did when confronted with the same test items as those taken by students in the norming group. Standards, on the other hand, are arbitrary judgments of what students should be able to do, given a set of test items.

▼ **Objectives**

Objectives are goals that are redrafted in terms that are clearly tangible. Objective statements are narrow, specific, concrete, and measurable. When writing the objectives, it is important to describe the intended results, rather than the process or means to accomplish them and state the time frame.

▼ **Observation**

Teacher and observer agree on what is being observed, the type of information to be recorded, when the observation will take place, and how the information will be analyzed. The observee is someone implementing strategies and actions that others want to know about. Observer might be a colleague, a supervisor, or a visitor from another location.

▼ **Partnership Development**

This section of the school portfolio assists schools in understanding the purposes of, approaches to, and planning for educational partnerships with business and community groups, parents, other educational professionals, and students.

▼ **Partnerships**

Teachers partnering with businesses in the community, scientists, and/or university professors can result in real world applications for student learning and deeper understandings of content for the teacher.

▼ **Percent Correct**

A calculated score implying the percentage of students meeting and exceeding some number, usually a cut score, or a standard. Percent passing equals the number passing the test divided by the number taking the test.

▼ **Percent Proficient**

Represents the percentage of students who passed a particular test at a *proficient* level, as defined by the test creators, or the test interpreters.

▼ **Percentile or Percentile Rank**

A point on the norms distribution below which a certain percentage of the scores fall. For example, if 70 percent of the scores fall below a raw score of 56, then the score of 56 is at the 70th percentile. The term *local percentile* indicates that the norm group is obtained locally. The term *national percentile* indicates that the norm group represents a national group.

▼ **Perceptions Data**

Information that reflects opinions and views of questionnaire responses.

▼ **Powerful Professional Development Designs**

Powerful professional development designs are those that are embedded into the daily operations of a staff. They are ongoing and lead to improvement of instruction and increases in student learning.

▼ **Process Mapping**

School processes are instruction, curriculum, and assessment strategies used to ensure the learning of all students. Mapping or flowcharting school processes can help staff objectively look at how students are being taught.

▼ **Processes**

Processes describe what is being done to get results, such as programs, strategies, and practices.

▼ **Professional Development**

Professional development helps staff members, teachers, and administrators change the manner in which they work, i.e., how they make decisions; gather, analyze, and utilize data; plan, teach, and monitor achievement; evaluate personnel; and assess the impact of new approaches to instruction and assessment on students.

▼ **Program Evaluation**

Program evaluation is the examination of a program to understand its quality and impact.

▼ **Purpose**

Purpose is the aim of the organization: The reason for existence.

▼ **Quality Planning**

Quality planning assists schools in developing the elements of a strategic plan including a vision, mission, goals, action plan, outcome measures, and strategies for continuous improvement and evaluation. Quality planning is a section of the school portfolio.

▼ **Quartiles**

One of three points that divided the scores in a distribution into four groups of equal size. The first quartile, or 25th percentile, separates the lowest fourth of the group; the middle quartile, the 50th percentile or median, divides the second fourth of the cases from the third; and the third quartile, the 75th percentile, separates the top quarter.

▼ **Reflective Logs**

Reflective logs are recordings of key events in the educators work days to reflect for improvement and/or to share learnings with colleagues.

▼ **Research**

The act of methodically collecting information about a particular subject to discover facts or to develop a plan of action based on the facts discovered.

▼ **Resources**

Identification of resources which support the continuous school improvement plan is required in a comprehensive action plan. Resources may include: dollars, time, staff, physical space, professional development activities, equipment, staffing, collaborations, and/or partnerships.

▼ **Responsibility**

As used in the continuous school improvement plan, responsibility refers to the individual, who is identified as being the person for seeing an action or strategy of school improvement through to its full implementation and/or completion.

▼ **Root Cause**

Root cause, as used in the continuous school improvement plan, refers to the deep underlying reason for a specific situation. While a symptom may be made evident from a needs assessment or gap analysis—the symptom (low student scores) is not the cause. To find a root cause one often has to ask *Why?* at least five levels down to uncover the root reason for the symptom.

▼ **Rubric**

A scoring tool that rates performance according to clearly stated levels of criteria. The scales can be numeric or descriptive. For instance, school process rubrics are used to give schools an idea of where they started, where they want to be with respect to implementation, and where they are right now.

▼ **Scheduling: What a Day Would Look Like**

A real test for whether or not a vision is realistic is to have teachers develop a day's schedule. This would tell them immediately if it is doable, or what needs to change in the vision and plan to make it doable.

▼ **School Improvement Planning**

Planning to implement the vision requires studying the research, determining strategies that will work with the students, and determining what the vision would look like, sound like, and feel like when the vision is implemented, and how to get all staff members implementing the vision.

▼ **School Meetings**

Staff, department, grade level, cross-grade level meetings can promote learning through study or sharing best practice, while focusing on the implementation of the vision.

▼ **School Portfolio**

The school portfolio is a professional development tool that gathers evidence about the way work is done in the school and a self-assessment tool to ensure the alignment of all parts to the vision. A school portfolio can also serve as a principal portfolio.

▼ **School Processes**

School processes are instruction, curriculum, and assessment strategies used to ensure the learning of all students.

▼ **Self-Assessments**

Staff self-assessments on tools to measure progress toward the vision, such as the Continuous Improvement Continuums, will help them see where their school is as a system and what needs to improve for better results.

▼ **Shadowing Students**

Purposefully following students and systematically recording the students' instructional experiences is a wonderful job-embedded approach to understanding what students are experiencing in school.

▼ **Specialty Area Leaders**

When implementing a vision requiring teachers to implement strategies they have never used before, teachers or specialists who understand and use these processes regularly can provide support for those trying strategies for the first time. Subject focused teams can be a part of the leadership team.

▼ **Staff Development**

Staff development is learning for staff that improves the learning of all students.

▼ **Standard**

Something that is considered as a basis of comparison or a guideline that is used for judgment.

▼ **Standardized Tests**

Tests that are uniform in content, administration, and scoring. They can be used for comparing results across classrooms, schools, school districts, and states.

▼ **Stanines**

A nine-point normalized standard score scale. It divides the normal curve distribution of scores into nine equal points: one to nine. The mean of a stanine distribution is five and the standard deviation is approximately two.

▼ **Storyboarding**

Storyboarding is an activity that will allow participants to share previous knowledge, while reflecting on the topic. It is a structure for facilitating conversations.

▼ **Strategies**

Strategies are procedures, methods, or techniques to accomplish an objective.

▼ **Student Achievement**

The section in the school portfolio that focuses on how the school teaches and results they are getting.

▼ **Student Achievement Data**

Information that reflects a level of knowledge, skill, or accomplishment, usually in something that has been explicitly taught.

▼ **Student-Led Conferences**

Student-teacher-parent conferences led by the student can give the student an opportunity to describe and take ownership of what she/he is learning. The teacher and students would have to prepare for the conference together, allowing the teacher to gain more intimate knowledge of what the student is thinking and learning.

▼ **Study Groups**

Groups of educators meet to learn new strategies and programs, to review new publications, or to review student work together.

▼ **Supervision and Evaluation**

Both of these strategies include pre-conferences, observations, and post conferences for feedback and dialogue that can determine needs and lead to improved instruction and continuous school improvement.

▼ **Symptom**

A symptom is the outward (most visible) indicator of a deeper root cause.

▼ **T-Chart**

A T-Chart is used to compare and contrast information or to show relationships. It is used to help people see the opposite dimension of an issue.

▼ **Teacher Portfolios**

Teacher portfolios document a teacher as learner, reflections, observations, and evidence. Portfolios can be used for many things including self-assessment, employment, supervision to replace traditional teacher evaluation, and for peer collaboration.

▼ **Team Development**

Team development builds collegiality, and can change the school culture. Norms of behavior, team meeting protocols, teambuilding training, and structures to work together develop teams. Many of the tools on the *Toolkit* CD support team development.

▼ **Team Planning and Teaching**

Actual planning, teaching, and sharing plans and results with colleagues can lead to rich discussions of practices and possibilities.

▼ **Tools**

The tools of *The School Portfolio Toolkit* include strategies, activities, examples, and templates used to organize and develop the school portfolio product and process.

▼ **Train the Trainers**

Train the trainers is an approach to saving time and money. Individuals are trained and return to the school or school district to train others.

▼ **Training**

Training as professional development is common. Training assists with the understanding of theory, and is most effective when modeling, demonstrations, and/or practice are included.

▼ **Triangulation**

Triangulation is the term used for combining three or more measures to get a more complete picture of student achievement.

▼ **Tuning Protocols**

A tuning protocol is a formal process for reviewing, honoring, and fine-tuning colleagues' work through presentation and reflection.

▼ **Values and Beliefs**

Values and beliefs are at the core of who we are, what we do, and how we think and feel. Values and beliefs reflect what is important to us; they describe what we think about work and how we think it should operate. Core values and beliefs are the first step in reaching a shared vision.

▼ **Vision**

A vision is a specific description of what it will be like when the mission is achieved. A vision is a mental image. It must be written in practical, concrete terms that everyone can understand and see in the same way.

▼ **Workshops**

Workshops as professional development are a common approach for gaining new knowledge of content areas. It is a way to learn from experts or others with more expertise.

REFERENCES AND RESOURCES

The references used in this book, along with other resources that will assist busy school administrators and teachers in continuously improving, appear below.

Adobe® Acrobat® Reader®. (2001). Available: http://www.adobe.com.

Adobe® PageMaker®. (2001). Available: http://www.adobe.com.

Allen, D. (1995). The tuning protocol: A process for reflection. *Studies on Exhibitions No. 15*. Providence, RI: Coalition of Essential Schools.

Allen, D., & McDonald, J. (1993). Keeping student performance central: The New York assessment collection. *Studies on Exhibitions No. 14*. Providence, RI: Coalition of Essential Schools.

Ardovino, J., Hollingsworth, J., & Ybarra, S. (2000). *Multiple measures: Accurate ways to assess student achievement*. Thousand Oaks, CA: Corwin Press, Inc.

Baldrige National Quality Program. (2001). *Education criteria for performance excellence*. Gaithersburg, MD: National Institute of Standards and Technology.

Ball, D.L., & Cohen, D.K. (1996). Reform by the book: What is—or might be—the role of curriculum materials in teacher learning and instructional reform? *Educational Research, 25*(9), 6-8 & 14.

Ban, J.R. (1993). *Parents assuring student success (PASS): Achievement made easy by learning together*. Bloomington, IN: National Educational Service.

Barkely, S. (1999). Time: It's made, not found. *Journal of Staff Development, 20*(4).

Barnett, C. (1999). Cases. *Journal of Staff Development, 20*(3), 26-27.

Barnett, C. (1998). Mathematics teaching cases as a catalyst for informed strategic inquiry. *Teaching and Teacher Education, 14*(1), 81-93.

BASRC. (1998). *Scoring rubric for BASRC support provider membership (Long form criteria)*. San Francisco, CA: Bay Area School Reform Collaborative.

Bean, W.C. (1993). *Strategic planning that makes things happen: Getting from where you are to where you want to be*. Amherst, MA: Human Resource Development Press, Inc.

Bernhardt, V.L. (1998). *Data analysis for comprehensive schoolwide improvement*. Larchmont, NY: Eye on Education, Inc.

Bernhardt, V.L. (1999, June). *Databases can help teachers with standards implementation*. Monograph No. 5. California Association for Supervision and Curriculum Development (CASCD).

Bernhardt, V.L. (2000). *Designing and using databases for school improvement*. Larchmont, NY: Eye on Education, Inc.

Bernhardt, V.L. (2000). Intersections: New routes open when one type of data crosses another. *Journal of Staff Development, 21*(1), 33-36.

Bernhardt, V.L. (1998, March). *Multiple Measures.* Monograph No. 4. California Association for Supervision and Curriculum Development (CASCD).

Bernhardt, V.L. (1994). *The school portfolio: A comprehensive framework for school improvement.* Larchmont, NY: Eye on Education, Inc.

Bernhardt, V.L. (1999). *The school portfolio: A comprehensive framework for school improvement.* (2nd ed.). Larchmont, NY: Eye on Education, Inc.

Bernhardt, V.L., von Blanckensee, L., Lauck, M., Rebello, F., Bonilla, G., and Tribbey, M. (2000). *The example school portfolio, A companion to the school portfolio: A comprehensive framework for school improvement.* Larchmont, NY: Eye on Education, Inc.

Brassard, M. (1998). *The memory jogger: A pocket guide of tools for continuous improvement.* (2nd ed.). Methuen, MA: Goal/QPC.

Byrnes, M.A., Cornesky, R.A., & Byrnes, L.W. (1992). *The quality teacher: Implementing total quality management in the classroom.* Bunnell, FL: Cornesky & Associates Press.

Calabrese, R., Short, G., & Zepeda, S. (1996). *Hands-on leadership tools for principals.* Princeton, NJ: Eye on Education, Inc.

Calhoun, E.F. (1993). Action research: Three approaches. *Educational Research, 51*(2), 62-65.

Calhoun, E.F. (1994). *How to use action research in self-renewing school.* Alexandria, VA: Association for Supervision and Curriculum Development.

California Department of Education. (2001). *Transitional PQR resource guide: An optional K-12 resource guide for program quality review.* Sacramento, CA: Author.

California Distinguished Schools Award Program. (2001). [online]. Available: http://www.cde.ca.gov/ope/csrp.

California Immediate Interventions/Underperforming Schools Program II/USP. (2001). [online]. Available: http://www.cde.ca.gov/iiusp.

California Program Quality Review (PQR). (2001). [online]. Available: http://goldmine.cde.ca.gov/ccpdiv/index.htm.

Carr, J.F., & Harris, D.E. (2001). *Succeeding with standards: Linking curriculum, assessment, and action planning.* Alexandria, VA: Association of Supervision and Curriculum Development.

Carver, J. (1997). *Creating a mission that makes a difference.* San Francisco, CA: Jossey-Bass, Inc.

Clark, T.A., & Lacey, R.A. (1997). *Learning by doing: Panasonic partnerships and systemic school reform.* Delray Beach, FL: St. Lucie Press.

Colbert, J.A., Desberg, P., & Trimble, K. (Eds.). (1996). *The case for education: Contemporary approaches for using case methods.* Needham Heights, MA: Allyn & Bacon.

Collins, D. (1997). *Achieving your vision of professional development: How to assess your needs and get what you want.* Greensboro, NC: The Regional Educational Laboratory at SouthEastern Regional Vision for Education (SERVE).

Collins, D. (1999). Common design principals. *Achieving your vision of professional development: How to assess your needs and get what you want.* (2nd ed.). Greensboro, NC: SouthEastern Regional Vision for Education (SERVE).

Coordinated Compliance Review (CCR). (2001). [online]. Available: http://goldmine.cde.ca.gov/ccpdiv/index.htm.

Costa, A., & Garmston, R. (1994). *Cognitive coaching: Approaching renaissance schools.* Norwood, MA: Christopher-Gordon.

Costa, A., & Garmston, R. (1994). *Cognitive coaching: A foundation for renaissance schools.* Norwood, MA: Christopher-Gordon.

Cowley, M., & Domb, E. (1997). *Beyond strategic vision: Effective corporate action with hoshin planning.* Newton, MA: Butterworth-Heinemann.

Cushman, K. (1995, March). Making the good school better: The essential question of rigor. *Horace, 11*(4). Providence, RI: Coalition of Essential Schools.

Danielson, C. (1996). *Enhancing professional practice: A framework for teaching.* Alexandria, VA: Association for Supervision and Curriculum Development.

Danielson, C., & McGreal, T.L. (2000). *Teacher evaluation: To enhance professional practice.* Alexandria, VA: Association for Supervision and Curriculum Development.

Deal, T., & Peterson, K. (1999). *Shaping school culture: The heart of leadership.* San Francisco, CA: Jossey-Bass, Inc.

Deal, T., & Peterson, K. (1994). *The leadership paradox.* San Francisco, CA: Jossey-Bass, Inc.

Deming, W.E. (1993). *Out of crisis.* Cambridge, MA: Massachusetts Institute of Technology Center for Advanced Engineering Study.

Deming, W.E. (1993). *The new economics for industry, government, education.* Cambridge, MA: Massachusetts Institute of Technology Center for Advanced Engineering Study.

Dietz, M.E. (1995). Using portfolios as a framework for professional development. *Journal of Staff Development, 16*(2), 40-43.

Dietz, M.E. (1999). Portfolios. *Journal of Staff Development, 20*(3), 45-46.

Doyle, M., & Straus, D. (1993, September). *How to make meetings work: The new interaction method.* New York, NY: Berkley Publishing Group.

DuFour, R., Eaker, R., & Ranells, M. (1992). School improvement and the art of visioning. *Tennessee Educational Leadership, XXIV*(1), 6-12.

DuFour, R., & Eaker, R. (1998). *Professional learning communities at work: Best practices for enhancing student achievement.* Bloomington, IN: National Educational Services.

DuFour, R.P. (1991). *The principal as staff developer.* Bloomington, IN: National Educational Services.

Easton, L. (1999). Tuning protocols. *Journal of Staff Development, 20*(3), 54-55.

Education for the Future Webpage. (2001). Available: http://eff.csuchico.edu.

Elmore, R.F. (2000). *Building a new structure for school leadership.* Washington, DC: Albert Shanker Institute.

English, F. (2000). *Deciding what to teach and test.* Thousand Oaks, CA: Corwin Press, Inc.

Epstein, J.L. (1995, May). School/family/community partnerships: Caring for children we share. *Phi Delta Kappan 76*(9), 701-712.

Evans, R. (2001). *The human side of school change: Reform, resistance, and the life problems of innovation.* San Francisco, CA: Jossey-Bass, Inc.

©FastTrack Schedule. (1998-2001). AEC Software, Inc. Available: http://www.aecsoft.com.

FileMaker Pro, ©FileMaker, Inc. (1994-2001). Available: http://www.filemakerpro.com.

Fitzharris, L. (1999). Curriculum development. *Journal of Staff Development, 20*(3), 30-31.

Foshay, A.W. (1994). Action research: An early history in the United States. *Journal of Curriculum and Supervision, 9*(4), 317-325.

Frank, M. (1989). *How to run a successful meeting in half the time.* New York, NY: Simon & Schuster, Inc.

Fullan, M.G. (1991). *The new meaning of educational change.* New York, NY: Teachers College Press.

Fullan, M. (1993). *Changing forces: Probing the depths of educational reform.* Bristol, PA: Falmer Press.

Fullan, M. (1997). *What's worth fighting for in the principalship?* New York, NY: Teachers College Press.

Fullan, M., & Hargreaves, A. (1996). *What's worth fighting for in your school?* New York, NY: Teachers College Press.

Garmston, R., & Wellman, B. (1996). *The adaptive school: Developing and facilitating collaborative groups.* El Dorado Hills, CA: Four Hats Press.

Garmston, R.J., & Wellman, B.M. (1999). *The adaptive school: A sourcebook for developing collaborative groups.* Norwood, MA: Christopher-Gordon Publishers, Inc.

Glanz, J. (1998). *Action research: An educational leader's guide to school improvement.* Norwood, MA: Christopher-Gordon Publishers, Inc.

Glasser, W. (1985). *Control theory: A new explanation of how we control our lives.* New York, NY: HarperCollins Publishers, Inc.

Glasser, W. (1992). *The quality school: Managing students without coercion.* New York, NY: HarperCollins Publishers, Inc.

Glasser, W. (1993). *The quality school teacher.* New York, NY: HarperCollins Publishers, Inc.

Green, J.E., & Smyser, S.O. (1996). *The teacher portfolio: A strategy for professional development and evaluation.* Lancaster, PA: Technomic Publishing Company, Inc.

Greenbaum, T.L. (1998). *The handbook for focus group research.* (2nd ed.). Thousand Oaks, CA: Sage Publications, Inc.

Griffin, M.L. (1999). Training of trainers. *Journal of Staff Development, 20*(3), 52-53.

Guskey, T.R. (1986). Staff development and the process of teacher change. *Educational Researcher, 15*(5), 5-12.

Guskey, T.R. (2000). *Evaluating professional development.* Thousand Oaks, CA: Corwin Press, Inc.

Guskey, T.R. (1996). Staff development and the process of teacher change. *Educational Researcher, 15*(5), 5-12.

Guskey, T.R., & Huberman, M. (Eds.). (1995). *Professional development in education: New paradigms & practices.* New York: Teachers College Press.

Hargreaves, A., & Fullan, M.G. (1992). *Understanding teacher development.* New York, NY: Teachers College Press.

Hargreaves, A., & Fullan, M. (1998). *What's worth fighting for out there?* New York, NY: Teachers College Press.

Harwell-Kee, K. (1999). Coaching. *Journal of Staff Development, 20*(3), 28-29.

Haycock, K. (1999, March). *Results: Good teaching matters.* Oxford, OH: National Staff Development Council.

Hawley, W.D., & Valli, L. (2000, August). Learner-centered professional development. *Research Bulletin, 27,* 4. Bloomington, IN: Phi Delta Kappa International.

Hirsh, S., Delehant, A., & Sparks, S. (1994). *Key to successful meetings.* Oxford, OH: National Staff Development Council.

Hord, S. (1997). *Professional learning communities: Communities of continuous inquiry and improvement.* (Rev. ed.). Austin, TX: Southwest Educational Development Laboratory.

Hord, S., & Robertson, H. (1999). Listening to students. *Journal of Staff Development, 20*(3), 38-39.

Hurst, B., & Reding, G. (1999). *Keeping the light in your eyes: A guide to helping teachers discover, remember, relive, and rediscover the joy of teaching.* Scottsdale, AZ: Holcomb Hathaway, Inc.

Improving America's Schools Act (IASA). (2001). Available: http://www.ed.gov/legislation/ESEA/toc.html.

Indiana Strategic and Continuous School Improvement and Achievement Plan. (2001). [online]. Available: http://www.state.in.us/legislative/ic/code/title20/ar10.2/ch3.html.

Inspiration® Software, Inc. (2000). Available: http://www.inspiration.com.

Interstate School Leaders Licensure Consortium. (2000). *Proposition for quality professional development of school leaders.* [online]. Available: http://www.ccsso.org/isllc.html. (March 6, 2001)

Interstate School Leaders Licensure Consortium. (2000). *Collaborative professional development process for school leaders.* Washington, DC: Council of Chief State School Officers in partnership with The National Policy Board for Educational Administration.

Interstate School Leaders Licensure Consortium. (1996, November). *Standards for school leaders.* Washington, DC: Council of Chief State School Officers.

Jacobs, H.H. (1997). *Mapping the big picture: Integrating curriculum and assessment K-12.* Alexandria, VA: Association for Supervision and Curriculum Development.

Joyce, B., & Showers, B. (1988). *Student Achievement through staff development.* New York, NY: Longman, Inc.

Joyce, B., Calhoun, E., & Hopkins, D. (1999). *The new structure of school improvement: Inquiring schools and achieving students.* Buckingham, MK: Open University Press.

Kaner, S., Lind, L., Toldi, C., Fisk, S., & Berger, D. (1996). *Facilitator's guide to participatory decision-making.* Gabriola Island, BC: New Society Publishers.

Kansas State Board of Education's Quality Performance Accreditation System. (2001). [online]. Available: http://www.ksbe.state.ks.us/Welcome.html.

Kaplan, R., & Norton, D. (1996). *The balanced scorecard: Translating strategy into action.* Boston, MA: Harvard Business School Press.

Killion, J.P. (1993). Staff development and curriculum development: Two sides of the same coin. *Journal of Staff Development, 14*(1), 38-41.

Killion, J. (1999). Journaling. *Journal of Staff Development, 20*(3), 36-37.

Killion, J. (1999). *What works in the middle: Results-based staff development.* Oxford, OH: National Staff Development Council.

Killion, J., & Harrison, C. (1997). The multiple roles of staff developers. *Journal of Staff Development, 18*(3), 34-44.

Killion, J., & Todnem, G. (1991). Reflection-for-action: A process for personal reflection. *Educational Leadership, 48,* 14-17.

King, M.B., & Newmann, F. (2000, April). Will teacher learning advance student goals? *Phi Delta Kappan, 81*(8), 576-580.

Kohn, A. (1999). *The schools our children deserve.* New York, NY: Houghton Mifflin Company.

Kouzes, J.M., & Posner, B.Z. (1995). *The leadership challenge: How to keep getting extraordinary things done in organizations.* San Francisco, CA: Jossey-Bass Inc.

Kushman, J.W. (1997). *Look who's talking now: Student views of learning in restructuring schools.* Portland, OR: School Improvement Program, Northwest Regional Educational Laboratory.

Lambert, L. (1998). *Building leadership capacity in schools.* Alexandria, VA: Association of Supervision and Curriculum Development.

Lambert, L., Walker, D., Zimmerman, D.P., Cooper, J.E., Lambert, M.D., Gardner, M.E., & Slack, P.J.F. (1995). *The constructivist leader.* New York, NY: Teachers College Press.

Lappan, G. (1999). Immersion. *Journal of Staff Development, 20*(3), 34-35.

Lezotte, L. (1997). *Learning for all.* Okemos, MI: Effective Schools Products, Ltd.

Lieberman, A. (1986). Collaborative research: Working with, not working on. *Education Leadership, 43*(5), 28-32.

Lieberman, A. (1999). Networks. *Journal of Staff Development, 20*(3), 43-44.

Lieberman, A., & Grolnick, M. (1996). Networks and Reform in American Education. *Teachers College Record, 98*(1), 7-45.

Lipton, L., & Wellman, B. (1999). *Pathways to understanding: Patterns and practices in the learning-focused classroom.* Guilford, VT: Pathways Publishing.

Loucks-Horsley, S., Hewson, P.W., Love, N., & Stiles, K.E. (1998). *Designing professional development for teachers of science and mathematics.* Thousand Oaks, CA: Corwin Press, Inc.

Loucks-Horsley, S. (1998). *Ideas that work: Mathematics professional development.* Columbus, OH: Eisenhower National Clearinghouse for Mathematics and Science Education. Available: http://www.enc.org.

Loucks-Horsley, S., Harding, C.K., Arbuckle, M.A., Murray, L.B., Dubea, C., & Williams, M.K. (1987). *Continuing to learn: A guidebook for teacher development.* Andover, MA: The Regional Laboratory for Educational Improvement of the Northeast and Islands and Oxford, OH: National Staff Development Council.

Love, N. (2000). *Using data-getting results: Collaborative inquiry for school based mathematics and science reform.* Columbia, MA: The Regional TERC Alliance for Mathematics and Science Education Reform.

Ludin, S. C. Ph.D., Paul, H., & Christensen, J. (2000). *Fish! A remarkable way to boost morale and improve results.* Hyperion Press.

Martin-Kniep, G.O., Sussman, E.S., & Meltzer, E. (1995). The north shore collaborative inquiry project: A reflective study of assessment and learning. *Journal of Staff Development, 16*(4), 46-51.

Martinello, M.L., & Cook, G.E. (1994). *Interdisciplinary inquiry in teaching and learning.* New York: Merrill.

MacSchedule. (2001). ©Mainstay software. Available: http://www.mstay.com.

Marzano, R.J., Pickering, D.J., & Pollock, J.E. (2001). *Classroom instruction that works: Research-based strategies for increasing student achievement.* Alexandria, VA: Association for Supervision and Curriculum Development.

McQuarrie, F., & Wood, F.H. (1999). On-the-job learning. *Journal of Staff Development, 20*(3), 47-48.

Melaville, A.I., Blank, M.J., & Asayesh, G. (1993). *Together we can: A guide to crafting a profamily system of education and human services.* Washington, DC: United States Printing Office.

Melum, M.M., & Collett, C. (1995). *Breakthrough leadership: Achieving organizational alignment through hoshin planning.* Chicago, IL: American Hospital Publishing, Inc.

Merseth, K. (1996). *Cases and case methods in teacher education.* In J. Sikula (Ed.). Handbook of research on teacher education. (pp. 722-744). New York, NY: Macmillan.

Michigan School Improvement Plan. (2001). [online]. Available: http://www.state.mi.us/mde/money/grants/g2000/mischimprove.html.

Microsoft Excel. (2001). Available: http://www.microsoft.com.

Microsoft Project. (2001). Available: http://www.microsoft.com.

Microsoft Visio. (2001). Available: http://www.microsoft.com.

Microsoft Word. (2001). Available: http://www.microsoft.com.

Missouri School Improvement Plan. (2001). [online]. Available: http://services.dese.state.mo.us/divimprove/sia/msip.

Mitchell, R. (1999). Examining student work. *Journal of Staff Development, 20*(3), 32-33.

Morton, J., & Cohn, A. (1998). *Kids on the 'net: Conducting internet research in K-5 classrooms.* Westport, CT: Heinemann.

Mundry, Susan, et al. (2000). *Designing successful professional meetings and conferences in education: Planning, implementing, and evaluating.* Thousand Oaks, CA: Corwin Press, Inc.

Murphy, C. (1995). Whole-faculty study groups. *Journal of Staff Development, 16*(3), 37-44.

Murphy, C. (1997). Finding time for faculties to study together. *Journal of Staff Development, 18*(3), 29-32.

Murphy, C. (1999). Use time for faculty study. *Journal of Staff Development, 20*(2), 20-25.

Murphy, C.U. (1999). Study groups. *Journal of Staff Development, 20*(3), 49-51.

Murphy, C., & Lick, D. (1998). *Whole-faculty study groups: A powerful way to change schools and enhance learning.* Thousand Oaks, CA: Corwin Press.

Murphy, C.U., & Lick, D.W. (2001). The principal as study group leader: Clear thoughtful guidance allows the process to thrive. *Journal of Staff Development, 22*(1), 37-38.

National Association Secondary School Principals (NASSP). (2001). *Leader 1, 2, 3: A development program for instructional leaders.* [online]. Available: http://www.nassp.org/training/04-03-02-02.html#programs. (June 5, 2001).

National Partnership for Excellence and Accountability in Teaching (NPEAT). (1999). Revisioning professional development: What learner-centered professional development looks like. *Journal of Staff Development, 21*(3), 19.

National Staff Development Council (2000, December). *Learning to lead, leading to learn.* Oxford, OH: Author.

National Staff Development Council (NSDC). (2001). *Standards for staff development.* [online]. Available: http://www.nsdc.org/standards.htm. (June 1, 2001)National Staff Development Council (NSDC). (2001). *Self-assessment of implementation of NSDC standards.* Oxford, OH: Author.

National Staff Development Council (NSDC). (2001). Self-assessment of implementation of NSDC standards. *Tools for growing the NSDC standards.* 23-29.

New York Comprehensive District Education Planning. *The Journey,* 2000-2001. [online]. Available: http://www.emsc.nysed.gov:80/rscs/Innovative/CDEP/revised guidance2000.doc. (July 5, 2001).

Newman, F., & King, B. (2000, Spring). Professional Development to Improve Schools. *WCER Highlights, 12,* 1. Madison, WI: Wisconsin Center for Education Research, UW—Madison School of Education.

North Central Association Commission on Schools. (1996). *NCA's school improvement endorsement: A handbook for schools.* Tempe, AZ: Author.

North Central Association Commission on Accreditation and School Improvement. (2001). [online]. Available: http://www.ncacasi.org.

North Central Regional Educational Laboratory. (2000). *A practical toolkit for designing and facilitating professional development: A product of the Eisenhower Regional Consortia for Mathematics and Science Education and the Eisenhower National Clearinghouse.* [CD-ROM]. Oak Brook, IL: Author.

North Dakota Department of Public Instruction. (2000). *North Dakota Education Improvement Process Standards.* Bismark, ND: North Dakota Department of Public Instruction. Available: http://www.dpi.state.nd.us.

Northwest Association of Schools and Colleges Commission on Schools. (1997, September). *School improvement: Focusing on desired learner results.* (2nd ed.). Boise, ID: Author.

Ohio Department of Education. (2000). *Reference guide to continuous improvement planning.* Columbus, OH: Author.Peters, T. (1987). *Thriving on chaos: A handbook for a management revolution.* New York, NY: HarperPerrenial.

Putz, G.B. (1998). *Facilitation skills: Helping groups make decisions.* Bountiful, UT: Deep Space Technology Company.

Quark XPress™ . (2001). Available: http://www.quark.com.

Ramsey, R. (1999). *Lead, follow, or get out of the way: How to be a more effective leader in today's schools.* Thousand Oaks, CA: Corwin Press.

Rees, F. (1998). *The facilitator excellence handbook: Helping people work creatively and productively together.* San Francisco, CA: Jossey-Bass/Pfeiffer.

Rees, F. (1998). *Facilitator excellence instructor's guide: Helping people work creatively and productively together.* San Francisco, CA: Jossey-Bass/Pfeiffer.

Reeves, D.B. (2001). *101 questions & answers about standards, assessment, and accountability.* Denver, CO: Advanced Learning Press.

Reeves, D.B. (2000). *Accountability in action: A blueprint for learning organizations.* Denver, CO: Advanced Learning Centers, Inc.

Richardson, J. (2000). Focus principal development on student learning. *Results, September.* (pp. 1 & 6).

Rigden, D.W. (1989). *Business and the schools: A guide to effective programs.* New York, NY: Council for Aid to Education, Inc.

Rigden, D.W. (1992). *Business and the schools: A guide to effective programs.* (2nd ed.). New York, NY: Council for Aid to Education, Inc.

Robbins, P. (1999). Mentoring. *Journal of Staff Development, 20*(3), 40-43.

Sagor, R. (2000). *Guiding school improvement with action research.* Alexandria, VA: Association for Supervision and Curriculum Development.

Sagor, R. (1992). *How to conduct collaborative action research.* Alexandria, VA: Association for Supervision and Curriculum Development.

Schlechty, P. (1997). *Inventing better schools: An action plan for educational reform.* San Francisco, CA: Jossey-Bass, Inc.

Schlechty, P.C. (2000). *Shaking up the schoolhouse: How to support and sustain educational innovation.* San Francisco, CA: Jossey-Bass, Inc.

Schlechty, P. (2000). *Shaking up the schoolhouse.* San Francisco, CA: Jossey-Bass, Inc.

Schmoker, M. (1996). *Results: The key to continuous school improvement.* Alexandria, VA: Association for Supervision and Curriculum Development.

Schmoker, M. (1999). *Results: The key to continuous school improvement.* (2nd ed.). Alexandria, VA: Association for Supervision and Curriculum Development.

Scholtes, P.R., & Others. (1988). *The team handbook: How to use teams to improve quality.* Madison, WI: Joiner Associates, Inc.

Scott, C.D., Jaffe, D.T., & Tobe, G.R. (1993). *Organizational vision, values and mission.* Menlo Park, CA: Crisp Publications, Inc.

Senge, P., Cambron-McCabe, N., Lucas, T., Smith, B., Dutton, J., & Kleiner, A. (2000). *Schools that learn: A fifth discipline fieldbook for educators, parents, and everyone who cares about education.* New York, NY: Doubleday Dell Publishing Group, Inc.

Senge, P.M., Kleiner, A., Roberts, C., Ross, R.B., & Smith, B.J. (1994). *The fifth discipline field book: Strategies and tools for building a learning organization.* New York, NY: Doubleday Dell Publishing Group, Inc.

Senge, P., Kleiner, A., Roberts, C., Ross, R., Roth, G., & Smith, B. (1999). *The dance of change: The challenges to sustaining momentum in learning organizations.* New York, NY: Doubleday Dell Publishing Group, Inc.

Senge, P.M. (1990). *The fifth discipline: The art and practice of the learning organization field book.* New York, NY: Doubleday Dell Publishing Group, Inc.

Sergiovanni, T. (2000). *The lifeworld of leadership.* San Francisco, CA: Jossey-Bass, Inc.

Sergiovanni, T. (1994). *Building community in schools.* San Francisco, CA: Jossey-Bass, Inc.

Shipley, J., & Collins, C. (1997). *Going to scale with TQM: The Pinellas County Schools' journey toward quality.* Greensboro, NC: The Regional Educational Laboratory at SouthEastern Regional Vision for Education (SERVE); Associated With the School of Education, University of North Carolina at Greensboro.

Showers, B., & Joyce, B. (1996). The evolution of peer coaching. *Educational Leadership, 53*(6), 6-12.

Shulman, J. (1992). *Case methods in teacher education.* New York, NY: Teachers College Press.

Shulman, J.H., & Colbert, J.A. (Eds.). (1987). *The mentor teacher casebook.* Eugene, OR: ERIC Clearinghouse on Educational Management, University of Oregon and San Francisco, CA: Far West Laboratory.

Southern Association of Colleges and Schools. (2001). *Elementary standards for accreditation 2001-2002.* Available: http://www.sacs.org.

Southern Association of Colleges and Schools. (2001). *Middle school standards 2001-2002.* Available: http://www.sacs.org.

Sparks, D. (1990, Spring). Cognitive coaching: An interview with Robert Garmston. *Journal of Staff Development, 11*(2), 12-15.

Sparks, D. (2000). Six ways to immediately improve professional development. *Results.* [online]. Available: http://www.nsdc.org/library/results/res9-00spar.html. (May 31, 2001).

Sparks, D., & Hirsch, S. (1999). *A national plan for improving professional development.* [online]. Available: http://www.nsdc.org/library/NSDCPlan.html. (June 1, 2001).

Sparks, D., & Hirsch, S. (1997). *A new vision for staff development.* Alexandria, VA: Association for Supervision and Curriculum Development.

Stiggins, R.J. (1999). Teams. *Journal of Staff Development, 20*(3), 17-21.

Stringer, E.T. (1996). *Action research: A handbook for practitioners.* Thousand Oaks, CA: Sage Publications.

Tomlinson, C.A., & Allan, S.D. (2000). *Leadership for differentiating schools and classrooms.* Alexandria, VA: Association for Supervision and Curriculum Development.

United States Department of Education. (2001). 2000-2001 Blue Ribbon Schools Program Elementary School Nomination Requirements. Washington, DC: Author.

Wasserman, S. (1993). *Getting down to cases: Learning to teach with case studies.* New York, NY: Teachers College Press.

Western Association of Schools and Colleges/California Department of Education. *Focus on learning.* (2001). [online]. Available: http://www.wascweb.org/default.htm. (July 5, 2001)

Wheatley, M.J. (1992). *Leadership and the new science: Learning about organization from an orderly universe.* San Francisco, CA: Berrett-Koehler Publishers, Inc.

Whitaker, T. (1999). *Dealing with difficult teachers.* Larchmont, NY: Eye On Education, Inc.

Wiggins, G. (1990). *Finding Time.* Washington, DC: Council for Basic Education.

Wiggins, G., & McTighe, J. (1998). *Understanding by design.* Alexandria, VA: Association for Supervision and Curriculum Development.

Wilson, B., & Corbett, H. (1999). Shadowing students. *Journal of Staff Development, 20*(3), 47-48.

Wood, F., & Killion, J. (1998). Job-embedded learning matters to school improvement. *Journal of Staff Development, 19*(1), 52-54.

Wood, F., & McQuarrie, F. (1999). On-the-job learning. *Journal of Staff Development, 20*(3), 10-13.

INDEX

Vision

Y

Your Questions Related to

EYE ON EDUCATION and EDUCATION FOR THE FUTURE INITIATIVE
END-USER LICENSE AGREEMENT

READ THIS

You should carefully read these terms and conditions before opening the software packet (s) included with this book ("Book"). This is a license agreement ("Agreement") between you and EYE ON EDUCATION. By opening the accompanying software packet(s), you acknowledge that you have read and accept the following terms and conditions. If you do not agree and do not want to be bound by such terms and conditions, promptly return the Book and the unopened software packet (s) to the place you obtained them for a full refund.

1. License Grant

EYE ON EDUCATION grants to you (either an individual or entity) a nonexclusive license to use the software and files (collectively, the "Software") solely for your own personal or business purposes on a single computer (whether a standard computer or a workstation component of a multiuser network). The Software is in use on a computer when it is loaded into temporary memory (RAM) or installed into permanent memory (hard disk, CD-ROM, or other storage device). EYE ON EDUCATION reserves all rights not expressly granted herein.

2. Ownership

EYE ON EDUCATION is the owner of all rights, title, and interests, including copyright, in and to the compilation of the Software recorded on the CD-ROM ("Software Media"). Copyright to the individual programs recorded on the Software Media is owned by the author or other authorized copyright owner of each program. Ownership of the Software and all proprietary rights relating thereto remain with EYE ON EDUCATION and its licensers.

3. Restrictions On Use and Transfer

(a) You may only (i) make one copy of the Software for backup or archival purposes, or (ii) transfer the Software to a single hard disk, provided that you keep the original for backup or archival purposes. You may not (i) rent or lease the Software, (ii) copy or reproduce the Software through a LAN or other network system or through any computer subscriber system or bulletin-board system, or (iii) adapt or create derivative works based on the Software.

(b) You may not reverse engineer, decompile, or disassemble the Software. You may transfer the Software and user documentation on a permanent basis, provided that the transferee agrees to accept the terms and conditions of this Agreement and you retain no copies. If the Software is an update or has been updated, any transfer must include the most recent update and all prior versions.

4. Restrictions On Use of Individual Programs

You must follow the individual requirements and restrictions detailed for each individual program on the Software Media. These limitations are contained in the individual license agreements recorded on the Software Media. By opening the Software packet, you will be agreeing to abide by the licenses and restrictions for these individual programs that are detailed on the Software Media. None of the material on this Software Media or listed in this Book may ever be redistributed, in original or modified form, for commercial purposes.

5. Limited Warranty

(a) EDUCATION FOR THE FUTURE INITIATIVE warrants that the Software and Software Media are free from defects in materials and workmanship under normal use for a period of thirty

(30) days from the date of purchase of this Book. If EDUCATION FOR THE FUTURE INITIATIVE receives notification within the warranty period of defects in materials or workmanship, EDUCATION FOR THE FUTURE INITIATIVE will replace the defective Software Media.

(b) EYE ON EDUCATION, EDUCATION FOR THE FUTURE INITIATIVE, AND THE AUTHOR OF THIS BOOK DISCLAIM OTHER WARRANTIES, EXPRESSED OR IMPLIED, INCLUDING WITHOUT LIMITATION IMPLIED WARRANTIES OF MERCHANTABILITY AND FITNESS FOR A PARTICULAR PURPOSE WITH RESPECT TO THE SOFTWARE AND FILES, AND/OR THE TECHNIQUES DESCRIBED IN THIS BOOK. EYE ON EDUCATION DOES NOT WARRANT THAT THE FUNCTIONS CONTAINED IN THE SOFTWARE WILL MEET YOUR REQUIREMENTS OR THAT THE OPERATION OF THE SOFTWARE WILL BE ERROR FREE.

(c) This limited warranty gives you specific legal rights, and you may have other rights that vary from jurisdiction to jurisdiction.

6. Remedies

(a) EYE ON EDUCATION's entire liability and your exclusive remedy for defects in materials and workmanship shall be limited to replacement of the Software Media, which may be returned to EDUCATION FOR THE FUTURE INITIATIVE with a copy of your receipt at the following address: EDUCATION FOR THE FUTURE INITIATIVE, ATTN: Brad Geise, 400 West 1st. St., Chico, CA 95929-0230, or call 1-530-898-4482. Please allow three to four weeks for delivery. This Limited Warranty is void if failure of the Software Media has resulted from accident, abuse, or misapplication. Any replacement Software Media will be warranted for thirty (30) days.

(b) In no event shall EYE ON EDUCATION, EDUCATION FOR THE FUTURE INITIATIVE, or the author be liable for any damages whatsoever (including without limitation damages for loss of business profits, business interruption, loss of business information, or any other pecuniary loss) arising from the use of or inability to use the Book or the Software, even if EYE ON EDUCATION, EDUCATION FOR THE FUTURE INITIATIVE, or the author has been advised of the possibility of damages.

(c) Because some jurisdictions do not allow the exclusion or limitation of liability for consequential or incidental damages, the above limitation or exclusion may not apply to you.

7. U.S. Government Restriction Rights

Use, duplication, or disclosure of the Software by the U.S. Government is subject to restrictions stated in paragraph (c) (1)(ii) of the Rights in Technical Data and Computer Software clause of DFARS 252.227-7013, and in subparagraphs (a) through (d) of the Commercial Computer— Restricted Rights clause at FAR 52. 227–19, and in similar clauses in the NASA FAR supplement, when applicable.

8. General

This Agreement constitutes the entire understanding of the parties and revokes and supersedes all prior agreements, oral or written, between them and may not be modified or amended except in writing signed by both parties hereto that specifically refers to this Agreement. This Agreement shall take precedence over any other documents that may be in conflict herewith. If any one or more provisions contained in this Agreement are held by any court or tribunal to be invalid, illegal, or otherwise unenforceable, each and every other provision shall remain in full force and effect.